Race and British electoral politics

# Race and British electoral politics

### Edited by

### Shamit Saggar

First published in 1998 by UCL Press

UCL Press Limited
1 Gunpowder Square
London
EC4A 3DE

and

1900 Frost Road, Suite 101
Bristol
Pennsylvania 19007-1598
USA

The name of University College London (UCL) is a registered
trade mark used by UCL Press with the consent of the owner.


**British Library Cataloguing in Publication Data**
A catalogue record for this book is available from the British Library.


ISBN: 1-85728-829-7    HB
   1-85728-830-0    PB

Typeset in Sabon and Gill Sans by Santype International Ltd,
Salisbury, U.K.
Printed by T. J. International Ltd, Padstow, U.K.

# Contents

# CONTENTS

# List of Tables

# Foreword

## *Zerbanoo Gifford*

This book is a timely contribution to the literature on ethnic minority representation in British politics. At each general election, the issue of underrepresentation is examined as the main political parties compete for the votes and money of the ethnic minorities. An unwritten rule of British politics seems to be that, unless there is a race riot, elections are the only time the political parties take an interest and the media rediscover the issue of fair representation and social justice.

Yet the issue of race in British politics is not just a "pigment of the imagination". The issue has been around for almost as long as there have been black and Asian candidates in Britain. In 1885 the distinguished Bengali, Lal Mohun Ghose, first stood as a Liberal candidate, unsuccessfully fighting Deptford. He was followed a year later by Dadabhai Naoroji who stood as a Liberal for the London seat of Holborn, losing to the Conservative candidate, Colonel Duncan. When Duncan retired as an MP two years later in 1888, both the Liberal and Conservative parties picked new candidates for the subsequent by-election which the Conservatives won, but with a much reduced majority. In a speech, the Conservative Prime Minister of the day, Lord Salisbury, gave the following excuse for his party's poor result:

> It was undoubtedly a smaller majority than Colonel Duncan obtained, but Colonel Duncan was opposed by a blackman. However far we have advanced in overcoming prejudice, I doubt if we have yet got to that point of view where a British constituency would elect a blackman.

Salisbury, who had been Secretary of State for India, was soon proved wrong. At the next General Election in 1892, Naoroji became Britain's first non-white MP, representing Finsbury Central until 1895. Although Salisbury's comments had won approval from his audience, the storm of protest that followed helped Naoroji's victory by making him a household name. Salisbury had unwittingly contributed to the transformation of Naoroji into "Mr Narrow Majority" as the magazine *Punch* nicknamed him, referring to his majority of just five votes.

Naoroji was followed by a Conservative, Sir Mancherjee Bhownagree who sat for Bethnal Green from 1895 to 1905, and then Shapurji Saklatvala, who represented Battersea North from 1922 to 1923 as a Labour MP and from 1924 to 1929 as a Communist. After Saklatvala's defeat, the nearest any non-white candidate came to being elected was when Dr David Pitt defended the Labour seat of Clapham in a 1970 by-election. He lost a controversial campaign and was not selected to fight the seat again in the General Election later that year. He finally reached Parliament when the Labour Party sent him as a life peer to the House of Lords in 1975.

It took until 1987 for the election of four ethnic minority MPs, Diane Abbott, Paul Boateng, Bernie Grant and Keith Vaz, all Labour members. It was a watershed in many ways. Unlike most previous General Elections, the media interest in the possibility of ethnic minority MPs being elected was very high because, for the first time, several non-whites had been selected for winnable seats. Consequently, the ethnic minority communities placed an impossible burden of expectation on them. It hoped they could and would change the status quo, not realising that there is a limit to what any back-bench MP can realistically do, especially in opposition. It is probable that the election of this cohort of MPs without any visible benefit to the wider ethnic minority communities indirectly added to the alienation which dissuades many ethnic minority young people from participating in the system themselves.

## THE MOST IMPORTANT ELECTION IS SELECTION

Despite the limited electoral progress made over the past century, Lord Salisbury's views are still held by many in the political system and non-white candidates are frequently seen as risky to select. "The electorate wouldn't vote for them," is the convenient response described as vicarious or displaced racism.

It is true that canvassers discover racist attitudes on some doorsteps, but this occurs whether or not the candidate is a member of an ethnic minority. Some canvassers come back shocked at being told that "it's all the fault of the blacks". Yet it is the rarity of such responses that makes them stick in the mind of party workers. If the electorate really were overwhelmingly racist, then no-one would be surprised at encountering it on the doorstep and ethnic minority candidates would not do as well as they do in "white" areas. Comparing canvass sheets with the published lists of people who voted makes it clear that openly racist voters typically either do not turn out at elections or vote for fringe candidates.

In any case, most politicians delight in taking risks, although they prefer to call it "taking a lead". Under the last administration, Conservative politicians were almost proud about how unpopular their policies had been before, they assert, the positive results were seen. Yet curiously, lack of ethnic minority representation is one issue on which few are prepared to take a lead.

The fact that the current electoral system guarantees hundreds of safe seats to both Conservative and Labour means, in effect, that it is the selection of candidates which determines the make-up of up to two-thirds of the House of Commons at any election. Local choices are therefore crucial, and any party that is serious about increasing the number of its ethnic minority MPs has to ensure that it selects ethnic minority candidates for its *safe* seats. Revealingly, women and ethnic minority candidates typically end up in a hopeless fight for the other parties' safe seats. This enables these parties to claim they have numerous women and ethnic minority candidates, secure in the knowledge that few of them will actually get elected.

Today, selection panels are almost united in believing that there should be more women and ethnic minorities in Parliament, provided they contest a seat somewhere else. "You're not representative," is the cry of local panels, even in areas with a substantial ethnic minority population, before suggesting Southall to Asian candidates or Brixton to Afro-Caribbeans. The fact that professional middle-aged white men are a minority everywhere except in Parliament and at the core of national decision-making is conveniently ignored.

One presumably unintended side-effect of the televising of Parliament is visibly to demonstrate the shortage of women and ethnic minority MPs, showing those few who have made it there lost amongst the ranks of grey men in grey suits. It is visible proof of the outdated attitudes of all parties. Attempts to overcome such prejudice are not welcome. Witness the problems over black-only and women-only short lists in the Labour Party. Neither the Conservatives or Liberal Democrats have even reached this far although, before the 1992 general election, the Conservatives did present the selection panel in Cheltenham with a short list of one, the black barrister, John Taylor. The resulting row, with some local Tories complaining about the "bloody nigger", led to nation-wide fame just as it had for Naoroji a

xi

hundred years earlier, but Taylor went on to lose the previously Conservative-held seat. To be sure, the same "mistake" was not repeated by any other Tory constituency selectors in 1997.

All party leaders have the opportunity to nominate people to become life peers and join the House of Lords without ever troubling selection panels and the electorate. A succession of failed ministers and defeated MPs have been allowed to swap the green leather seats of the Commons for the red leather of the Lords. Yet there have been just five post-war party appointments from the ethnic minorities: Lords Pitt, Desai and Paul for Labour and Baroness Flather and Lord Bagri for the Tories. Significantly, only the former ever stood for the House of Commons before being sent to the Lords. Until 1997, the absence of a Liberal Democrat peer from the ethnic minorities was particularly noticeable, given the party's professed desire to involve the ethnic minorities in decision-making.[1]

## "THERE TO PRETTY UP THE STAGE, LIKE POTTED PLANTS"

While the views of the ethnic minorities are not courted, their money and votes certainly are. Substantial donations have been received by all parties, particularly from the wealthy sections of the British Indian communities. Yet, acting like a cashpoint machine and producing large sums of money if the right buttons are pushed, is not necessarily the way to influence politicians and policy. Cashpoints are not thanked or asked for their opinions.

We have seen how, within all parties, most ethnic minority activists either marginalize themselves or are marginalized by the party machine. Interestingly, each party has sought to replace a trouble-some, internal, ethnic minority pressure group with something more controllable. In the Labour Party, for instance, the influence of the unofficial Black Sections in several constituencies led indirectly to the all-black short lists which produced the four ethnic minority Labour MPs in 1987. The saga of how the Black Sections were considered too radical by the leadership, and replaced by an official Black Socialist Society, is well documented by Kalbir in this volume. The Society has representation on many party bodies, but not the critical National Executive Committee which has, however, reserved places for women amongst others. The Anglo-Asian and Anglo-West Indian Conserva-tive Societies were closed down in the late 1980s after the former was deemed to have been taken over by people with, of all things, a poli-tical agenda. In this case it was the issue of support for an indepen-dent Sikh state, and the Society was soon replaced by a new, bland, fund-raising body, the One Nation Forum, of the sort the AACS had once been. Within the Liberal Democrats, the initial hopes for the Asian Liberal Democrats, which raised substantial funds for the leadership in the run-up to the 1992 election campaign but had no official status, led to disillusionment and internal arguments. Problems continued when it was succeeded by the official Ethnic Minority Liberal Democrats, yet the leadership seems unwilling to take action over a demonstrable lack of democracy and the exclusion of all but a small clique from membership.

All of these bodies were set up to increase ethnic minority involvement in their respective parties. Each party would like to be able to point to having a proportion of ethnic minority members roughly equal to that in the UK population, around 5 per cent. Yet this task is not made a priority, as is shown by the fact that none of the parties seriously monitors the ethnic make-up of its membership and officials. It has even been suggested that a proportion much higher than 5 per cent would be unwelcome for fear of a party's being seen as "black-dominated".

What influence does membership bring? In all parties, membership means a stream of direct-mail begging letters asking for money to fight this or that election. Withholding such money could be an effective weapon for change, but no boycott has ever been organized. Apart from that, the power of individual members varies from party to party.

Despite the efforts of an internal pressure group, the Conservative party is renowned for its lack of internal democracy, and is legally the personal property of the party leader. For individual members influence is minimal, unless they manage to rise through the system to become constituency officials or members of selection panels. This may prove easier in the future, because the number of Tory activists is falling, while their average age is increasing. A well-organised group might be able to take over the running of several constituency parties.

Meanwhile, the Labour Party is in the process of moving in the direction of more power for individual members, with the use of the one member one vote principle. Ironically, because ethnic minority issues have typically had the backing of certain major trades unions, this may weaken the influence of ethnic minorities in the party. This is a problem to which the "modernizers" have yet to respond in any meaningful way. A recent progressive experiment with women-only short lists in winnable seats was abandoned because of "not in my constituency" opposition in many areas, to say nothing of the legal wrangles associated with the device. Black-only short lists only occurred in the past in seats with a strong Black Sections presence and are unlikely to return.

The Liberal Democrats were formed from the merger of the Liberals and SDP, both with good records of giving power to members. Unfortunately, when drawing up the constitution for the new party, they picked some of the worst aspects of both old parties, with the SDP's preoccupation with central control of policy joined to the Liberal down to the local ward level autonomy for candidates and campaigning. Constituency parties have a very strong preference for "local" candidates, which makes it very difficult for anyone not already living in one of the few winnable seats to be elected. The centre is left with a perfect excuse for not doing anything, namely, the need to ensure a balance of candidates in winnable seats.

Three important issues arise with the unofficial aim of 5 per cent, ethnic minority membership. First, in the parties that have some internal democracy, 5 per cent is too small to have much effect, except on issues where the voting is already close. Secondly, the ethnic minority population is not evenly spread across the UK. A number of Labour safe seats in particular have substantial black or Asian electorates. Many of these seats have typically had white MPs approaching retirement. Especially in the areas of high Asian settlement, a variety of potential successors from the Asian community have sought to enrol as many new members from their community as possible. When asked by the typically white constituency officials why they want to join, their reply is clear: to have an Asian MP. A more historically-based reading of the charge of "entryism" is suggested by Geddes in his analysis of political opportunity in this volume. The result has been the suspension of whole constituency selection procedures, as accusations of membership irregularities fly around. The third issue is the atypical character of people from all communities who join political parties in the first place.

## BOWING AND AGREEING

To be accepted into the system, many ethnic minority candidates have had to be even more middle-class than their white counterparts. The result is that those with backgrounds as lawyers, Christians, or with a public school and Oxbridge education make up a higher proportion of the ethnic minority MPs than the rest of the Commons. This is nothing new. The first three Asian MPs, Naoroji, Bhownagree and Saklatvala, were all professionals from India's tiny Parsi Zoroastrian community. Despite this, both Naoroji, "the Grand Old Man of India", and Saklatvala, "Comrade Saks", were respected and held in great affection by both the people of India and their constituents, thanks to their tireless work on their behalf. Both supported a wide range of other liberation campaigns, particularly female emancipation.

In contrast, Bhownagree is remembered most for his derisory nickname of "bow and agree", given by the Indian National Congress for his attitude towards the British rulers of India. Once Naoroji had been elected, the Conservatives saw they had to have an Indian MP to, so Bhownagree was promoted as "truly British" to the people of Bethnal Green who elected him from 1895 to 1906. He was knighted on the request of the same Lord Salisbury who had earlier made the infamous "blackman" speech against Naroji.

It is perhaps the best example of parties going out of their way to find the "right" ethnic minority activists, no matter how unrepresentative. The criticism is that equal opportunities within parties has been extended more for people willing to act as placemen and *apparatchiks* than for those interested in genuinely changing the status quo. The extent to which ethnic minority political elites are expected to speak on behalf of ethnic minorities and notionally "represent" their concerns is a question that has dogged the post-1987 wave of non-white parliamentarians and is examined in great detail in Nixon's essay in this volume. It has become a pressing issue since the 1997 election in which nine MPs from the ethnic minorities were returned.

Yet, regardless of what small recognition is handed to them by the established "gatekeepers", people willing to act as "tokens" have little influence, because they win no-one's respect. In the Asian community they are known as *chumchars* (literally "teaspoons" – Indians who used to spoonfeed their British sahibs with sugar). Invariably they are discarded by the establishment without having changed anything for the better or helped anyone. For as long as there are so few ethnic minorities representatives in high positions who have real authority, the minority communities will continue to be misunderstood.

The danger, then, arises of a mismatch developing between, on the one hand, the political parties' perception of what issues and concerns are of importance to the ethnic minorities and, on the other, the reality of grassroots, non-white, political attitudes. A certain degree of caution is perhaps advisable when drawing general conclusions about ethnic minorities, their social and economic structures and, inevitably, their attachment to identifiable strands of opinion. This is the central message found in Saggar's chapter [in this volume] devoted to conceptual and methodological themes. There are two obvious results arising from this mismatch. First, the underrepresentation of ethnic minority opinion, which is shown, for example, by the response to the rising number of racial attacks. It is the highest political priority for ethnic minorities, but one of the lowest for the political parties. Secondly, misrepresentation, which can be even more damaging in the longer run.

Indeed, one of the most noticeable features of the past twenty years has been the way in which political parties have understood that class-based politics as a whole is in decline, and have joined with advertising interests in dividing the population into socio-economic groups (such as the famous C2s – skilled manual workers) and further smaller subdivisions. These groups are then sent "targeted" political messages, in the hope, backed up with some evidence, that everyone within one grouping has broadly the same aspirations and interests. While all these subdivisions of the white population are identified and courted, it is striking that the ethnic minority population is still seen as an homogeneous group, with perhaps some recognition of the difference between Asian and Afro-Caribbean communities. The fine distinctions within both groups are overlooked, while the Chinese and South-east Asian communities are almost entirely ignored.

## RHETORIC AND REALITY

All political parties have shown themselves willing to use the so-called "race card" in order to try to win an election, an observation made most convincingly by Messina in his contribution to this volume. At one end of the scale is the subtle approach: when an ethnic minority opponent has lived in the area for over twenty years, voters know only too well what another party means when it says in its election leaflets that their white candidate is the only one who is "local". At the other end of the scale is, perhaps, the campaign in Tower Hamlets where parties were more willing to exploit racist votes. It culminated in 1993 with a successful British National Party by-election candidate accusing local Liberal Democrats of stealing his "islander" policies.

No party came well out of that by-election. The Tories, the party of government for over a half a generation, were seen as irrelevant in an area of London which had once returned Conservative MPs. A group within Labour had deliberately exaggerated the support for the BNP campaign and so given it crucial credibility. Finally, the Liberal Democrats were forced into a messy public investigation into their local populist campaigning. For years, Asian party members had been complaining about the perceived willingness to exploit racism in Tower Hamlets, without response from the leadership.

Such complaints were not made public earlier because of the immense pressure within all parties to be "loyal" and not create trouble. The threat, explicit or implied, is that people who criticize their party on racial grounds will not be selected as candidates. The fate of Sharon Atkin, who was dropped as a Labour candidate in

Nottingham – days after making a comment about "the racist Labour party" – in the run-up to the 1987 General Election, is a powerful reminder of the high stakes involved. If you try to rock the boat, you may be made to walk the plank.

Yet, whenever two or more black politicians are gathered together, the talk is of the prejudice they have suffered from within their own party, as well as from outside. In fact, overt racism is rare, but unconscious racism is an ever-present and ugly reality within all parties.

Anyone who survives this far in the political scene can hope to be given the chance to fight an unwinnable council seat. (The winnable ones are often already taken, though Le Lohé's analysis in this volume suggests that this pattern has begun a rapid change in several areas of local government.) Sometimes sheer hard work results in winning a seat – to the amazement of everyone else. More often, it is merely a chance to come up against the double standards of performance assessment: when white candidates fail, it is because the seat was unwinnable; when ethnic minority candidates fail, it is because they are non-white.

Candidates who win at the first attempt, or who survive to win later, can face two other hurdles. If the area has a high proportion of ethnic minority voters, they can be marginalized by being perceived as in some sense less of an MP or councillor than if they were elected for a "white" area. If you are not white, people would respect you more if you had a white electorate. This is a particularly difficult, even impossible, constraint upon ethnic minority political ambition.

With all this, it is not surprising that there is such a high drop-out rate amongst the ethnic minorities candidates who don't hit the jackpot and get elected straightaway. The uncertainties and unpleasantness of politics combined with the financial cost of political involvement can be daunting.

## QUO VADIS?

Those who control access to, and influence policy within, the political parties appear to be running out of excuses for their failure to deal effectively with discrimination and underrepresentation. The extent and causes are known, so too are most of the remedies. What is lacking is the will to apply the remedies within a timescale that makes sense to those who suffer from the lack of them.

The solution is simple to set out, although probably not so simple to implement. First, the main political parties must commit themselves to serious action against racism and its myriad effects, and unambiguously condemn it in their communications to the whole population, not just to the ethnic minorities. In some cases, this will mean deselecting MPs notorious for their xenophobic views. The likelihood of this policy being implemented must however be remote, as a reading of Rich's essay on the post-Thatcher Conservatives makes all too plain. Furthermore, the essay by the Runnymede Trust team indicates that ethnic minorities themselves have a key stake in shaping future discussions about diversity in an advanced liberal democracy.

Secondly, the views of the ethnic minorities must be represented when it comes to policy formation. The parties must recognise that this means polling the whole range of black, Asian, Chinese and South-east Asian communities rather than just listening to the "acceptable activists", who are often forced by the present system to be unrepresentative – even occasionally misrepresentative – of the wider population. Nanton's chapter in this volume shows just how difficult this task can be in even one specific area of public policy.

Following the almost unprecedented exposure given to "race politics" in the 1997 contest, this book serves as a valuable and pertinent contribution to the debate over the future of race and ethnicity in British elections. A first-rate team of scholars has been gathered to shed light on this debate. Moreover, it is a debate that is long overdue and one which, through academic research of this kind, aims to synthesize analysis of "race politics" with that of electoral engagement. This is a vital connection, which this book succeeds in making.

## NOTE

1. Lord Chitnis, Liberal agent at the Orpington by-election and former national organiser for the Liberal Party, was made a life peer in 1977 at the request of the Queen rather than the Liberals, and sits as a cross-bencher. More recently, in 1997, three new life peerages were granted to ethnic minorities: Baroness Amos, Baroness Scotland and Lord Dholakia.

# Preface

This book has been in gestation for a number of years, during which time the debates it addresses have grown in relevance in academic electoral analysis. It is hoped that it meets a clear void in our understanding of the politics of race and ethnicity in Britain. The literature devoted to this topic in general has mushroomed considerably and, in the last decade, these works have emerged as an identifiable theme within research and scholarship on political participation and political integration. This was not always so and the origins of this book can be traced from that point.

## REVISITING ELECTORAL ANALYSIS

Several years ago I was asked to write a review essay that drew on several studies that had been publised in the late 1980s concerned with the politics of race.[1] One of the arguments that I stressed in my piece was that the literature – and hence our understanding of "race politics" – had become skewed by the heavy attention placed on electoral participation. Indeed, starting with Deakin's landmark study of the 1964 election, *Colour and the British electorate*,[2] it was quite striking to note that political studies of ethnic pluralism had got so bogged down as to be lost in, the stuff of electoral behaviour. This type of work was no bad thing in itself, since it provided at least one ready indicator of broader social integration among non-white immigrants in relation to their white counterparts. The electoral behaviour approach, significantly, had been the subject of my own first research in this field.[3] The electoral studies slant was also understandable as it reflected the significance of electoral analysis within the discipline and, additionally, served to attract considerable interest among senior politicians, pollsters, parties, journalists, and ethnic minority political leaders. In other words, at about the time that Crewe published his timely essay entitled "The black, brown and green votes",[4] the business of assessing minority political participation had developed into a considerable industry in itself.

The task that I set myself in compiling this book was, first, to ask what had been the fruits of that industry, and secondly, to map out the intellectual debates that had arisen in relation to the electoral politics of race in a way that was helpful to students of both race and ethnic relations and modern British politics. If the finished product successfully hits these buttons in a way that influences views of racial themes in British political life, then I will consider the project worthwhile and rewarding.

The attention given electoral concerns in the research literature contained more than a few shortcomings, however. The most disturbing of these was that electoral-led analyses tended to overshadow pertinent questions regarding ethnic minority involvement in, and relationships to, policy-making processes. Additionally, there was a danger of focusing too heavily on voting divisions and partisanship without fully understanding the socialisation and mobilisation forces at play beneath. Yet another difficulty lay in the glaring inadequacy in much of the electoral literature in dealing with the notion of "exclusion" from policy and decision-making that was widely thought to have afflicted immigrant communities' experience in postwar Britain.

The upshot of these and other problems was that in my original review I found myself arguing for important improvements in research and/or a widening of research agendas working on race/politics themes. If this suggestion was a valid one, it also, sadly, remained unanswered, despite obvious extensions in the literature. It may be, of course, that this critique was too subtle in nature or possibly even poorly synchronised with developments in academic research at the time. In any case, the case had been made for doing what I perceived could be a rather better job.

Fortunately, elements of a more interesting research agenda could, be detected in part in the work of a small handful of established scholars, notably Le Lohé, Messina and Rich. However, helpful though their earlier contributions had been, it remained the case that fresh work was needed, coupled with a degree of rethinking of familiar assumptions about ethnic minority political engagement. It was quite clear that colleagues had begun to make some important steps in this direction and the job then became one of trying to harness and synthesise these efforts. This, then, was the point of departure in commissioning the papers that comprise this book.

## UNDERSTANDING DATA, PROMOTING DEBATE

Quite apart from trying to address the core weaknesses, the idea of editing a new volume was spurred on by three important, though second-order, reasons. The first and most significant was the realisation that some key schools of thought had begun to emerge on ethnic minority participation and, secondly, the impact of race on the mainstream political landscape. As the early chapters in this book illustrate, the latter debate has taken on something of an identity of its own. The differences and the agreements between writers are well illustrated in this volume. Moreover, they matter because they show that the debate remains wide open as to how well existing strategies have served ethnic minorities.

Secondly, the book goes a long way towards facing up to the implications of the Labour Party's overwhelming success in attracting non-white votes. Of course there are positive and negative messages associated with this allegiance. However, the book has brought together in several chapters an attempt to go beyond this familiar understanding. Clearly there are implications that can be seen in areas such as the role of parties in articulation and aggregation processes, the conceptualisation of racial or ethnic issues, the tensions that have been felt within the major parties over race and the spectacle of autonomous organisations. It was the task of this book to engage these and other implications. The contributions on such debates appear to measure up well against current literature.

Finally, the book hoped to stimulate a more thorough examination of the data on electoral participation. This would involve not merely re-examining what the limited number of data sets had previously reported, but also assessing whether these empirical exercises had asked the right sort of questions. Three important messages seem to have been thrown up in response. The first was that much of the data was unusually shallow in its coverage of non-white participation. Little, for instance, has been discovered through survey work about non-white party identification patterns and processes. Secondly, the data were characterized by the poor or non-existent sense of comparison with the electoral participation of non-ethnic minorities. Better strategies for dealing with this flaw could easily be pointed to, not least the possibility of administering large scale post-election questionnaires to booster samples of ethnic minorities. Thirdly, and most worrying of all, it was apparent that so much of what was debated was in fact based on a remarkably small number of reliable data sets. The call for fresh empirical data of a substantial, deeper and comparative nature, was a conclusion that this book could certainly reiterate, if not remedy.[5]

## THE COLLABORATING AND SYNTHESISING PROCESS

Having launched the exercise, I was fortunate in working with a first-rate set of contributors. All readily engaged the core objectives of the book, whilst at the same time showing sensitivity to the need to put their work into a manageable and intellectually useful framework. The results published here are the outcome of these partnerships. Given the various levels at which collaboration has operated, the exercise has worked well from an editor's point of view. I have tried to exercise a light editorial hand in bringing together diverse contributions, though on occasion I have had to be on the interventionist side in order to facilitate debate between authors. By and large, the sense of chapters that address one another has been a rewarding feature of the book.

By design, the contributory team contained both established figures as well as new researchers. It was one of my original aims to put together a book that genuinely brought in the perspectives of a new generation of scholars working in this specialist field. With a number of promising new writers to choose from, they were not hard to find. It is interesting to note that, in my view at least, the analysis of younger researchers is accommodated well alongside that of their older colleagues. Many have done a good job of probing more deeply into the evidence and reasoning of established generalisations, most notably in relation to the nature of political opportunity, leadership at sub-national level, and Labour's dilemmas and difficulties.

In bringing together these contributors the idea was to produce a book that contained a good spread of concerns. Political participation, as all contributors agreed, contained a number of elements that went beyond electoral politics. Community politics and informal patterns of mobilization could not afford to be ignored and it is heartening to see that this perspective was evident, directly or indirectly, throughout the book. The contributors in that sense recognised with little prompting that their job was to go beyond their respective patches. Indeed, the task was to add value to a larger project on race and electoral politics, and my own job as an editor was lightened by this collective recognition. The outcome of a single-theme, multi-authored volume will be judged as much as anything in terms of its overall coherence. As an editor, one could not have wished for a more integrated and co-operative team.

## NOTES

1. Saggar, S. 1990 Discovering and rediscovering race. *Parliamentary Affairs* 43, 392–94.
2. Deakin, N. 1965. *Colour and the British electorate*, London. Pall Mall.
3. Saggar, S. 1984. Ethnic minority political participation in the 1983 general election. Unpublished paper, Department of Government, University of Essex.
4. Crewe, I. 1979. The black, brown and green votes. *New Society* 12 April.
5. A pioneering booster sample of ethnic minorities (designed by the author in collaboration with Anthony Heath and the Centre for Research into Social Trends) formed a part of the 1997 British Election Study. The findings of this research will become available in 1998.

# Acknowledgements

The book naturally would not have become a reality without the input of its ten contributors, and I must thank them for living up to, and sometimes even exceeding, my expectations. In addition, my own thinking on the broad theme of the book has been assisted through discussions with the following: John Crowley, Andrew Geddes, Anthony Heath, Marco Martiniello, Tony Messina, Pippa Norris, and David Sanders. I am indebted to them for the time and thought they have given to my work.

In my home department, my work has benefited from the support given by colleagues and students. The ideas that have developed into this book have received a number of helpful nudges from, among others, Wayne Parsons, Anne Kershen, Tolis Malakos, and Ken Young. The latter, as ever, provided his usual steady encouragement to my work, an important and rare commodity in the academic trade nowadays.

I should also like to thank Caroline Wintersgill and Kevin Young at UCL Press.

The book is also a part of my record of achievement in academic life. It is therefore a product of a wider family effort. The encouragement provided by my father, Krishan D. Saggar, has been a great asset. Likewise, I have always valued the support shown by my uncle, Devinder K. Saggar, despite the physical distance of many thousands of miles between us. But the deepest inspiration for my work has always come from another uncle, the late Braham D. Saggar. It is to him, and the memory of my mother, that this book is dedicated.

Finally, back at base where so much of the book has been constructed, I am grateful to my wife, Rita Alfred, for the warm and fun-filled home she has created. On the question of fun, the assignment has been more-or-less taken over by my daughter, Shelley, whose first and last contribution has been to fill our house with laughter. The two of them, usually partners in distracting me from the laptop, have been a tonic beyond description and this project has been made a great deal easier with their presence.

The rest, as the saying goes, is my own industry and thought. Any errors that remain are also mine and are probably accounted for by the large volume of papers sitting in my "in" tray. I shall endeavour to balance things up now this book has been completed. With the 1997 general election over with, I look forward to the emergence of fresh debates and assessments of racial and ethnic politics in our country's political life. If this book can play a small part in these developments, I will be immensely pleased.

SHAMIT SAGGAR
*London, 1997*

# Notes on contributors

**Zerbanoo Gifford** became a Liberal councillor in the London Borough of Harrow in 1982. She chaired the party's Community Relations panel and the 1986 'Commission into Ethnic Involvement in British Life'. Three times a parliamentary candidate, she was twice elected to the Liberal Democrat's Federal Executive. Zerbanoo is founder and Honorary Director of the ASHA Foundation, which aims to bridge religions, cultures and communities by harnessing support for charitable projects internationally. She is also the author of five books including *Dadabhai Naoroji* on Britain's first Indian MP and is currently completing a book on Asian philanthropy.

**Shamit Saggar** is Senior Lecturer in Government at Queen Mary and Westfield College, University of London. He has held visiting appointments at UCLA and ANU, and in 1993 was a Harkness Fellow of the Commonwealth Fund of New York. He has previously published *Race and public policy* (1991) and *Race and politics in Britain* (1992). He is currently working on a book-length study of ethnic minority electoral participation based on data from the 1997 British Election Study. A further book is underway that is concerned with Anglo-American racial dilemmas. Dr Saggar's principal research interests are in the politics of race and ethnicity, urban economic development, "think-tanks" and policy advocacy groups, and comparative immigration policies.

**Anthony M. Messina** is Associate Professor of Political Science at Tufts University. He has published numerous journal articles on the politics of race and immigration in Britain and Western Europe and he is the author of *Race and party competition in Britain* (Clarendon Press, 1989) and the co-editor of *Ethnic and racial minorities in* *advanced industrial societies* (Greenwood, 1992). He is currently developing two projects: a book-length manuscript on post-war migration to Western Europe and a study of party competition in post-war Britain and Germany. The latter project has spawned an overview of the dynamics of party competition during the period of West Germany's Grand Coalition government (1966–69) which was published in the journal *German politics and society*.

**Michel Le Lohé** recently retired as Senior Lecturer in Politics after over 30 years service at the University of Bradford. He has had a particular interest in ethnic minority participation in British politics since observing the first contest by Asian candidates in council elections at Bradford in 1963. Subsequently he has written several pieces in this field and was the author of the "Political Issues" section in *New community* between 1988 and 1994. He was once a city councillor in Bradford where he developed an interest in housing – an interest which has since led to the chair of the largest housing association in England. He has appeared, as commentator and analyst, covering local and national elections for Yorkshire Television, regularly since 1968.

**Paul Rich** is currently Principal Lecturer in the Department of Politics and Public Policy at the University of Luton. He has previously taught at the universities of Bristol and Melbourne and has published extensively on Southern Africa as well as on the politics of race in Britain. His recent publications include *State power and black politics* (1996), *Reaction and renewal in South Africa* (1996) as editor and *The counter insurgent state* (1997) as co-editor. He is now working on a comparative study of politics in Algeria and South Africa.

**Kalbir Shukra** is Lecturer in Community and Youth Work-in the Department of Applied Human Sciences at Goldsmiths College, University of London. She is currently writing a book on black politics in Britain.

**Andrew Geddes** is Lecturer in the School of Politics and Communication Studies at the University of Liverpool. During 1997–98 he is a Jean Monnet fellow at the European University Institute in Florence researching EU immigration policy. He is the author of *Britain in the European Community* (1993) and *The politics of race and immigration* (1996).

**Jessica R. Adolino** is Assistant Professor of Political Science and International Affairs at James Madison University in Harrisonburg, Virginia. She received a BA in Politics from Fairfield University, Fairfield, Connecticut in 1984 and the PhD in Political Science in 1993 from The Ohio State University, Columbus, Ohio. She has conducted field research in the area of ethnic minority politics in Britain and is presently writing about the experiences of ethnic minority elected officials within British local governmental institutions. She is also working on an undergraduate reader on the topic of the changing role of European governments.

**Jaqi Nixon** is Head of Department of Health and Social Studies, Bradford and Ilkley College. Her previous publications have been concerned with the implementation of race relations policy and the role of Parliamentary Select Committees in policy-making.

**Philip Nanton** is a Lecturer in the Institute of Local Government Studies (INLOGOV), part of the School of Public Policy at the University of Birmingham. He has published widely in local government studies, equal opportunities, community development and urban regeneration. His work has appeared in journals such as *Policy and politics*, *Local government studies* and *New community*.

**Kaushika Amin** has worked since 1988 as an information and research officer for the Runnymede Trust, and as an editor of *The Runnymede bulletin*. She previously worked for the Newham Monitoring Project. With Carey Oppenheim, she is the author of *Politics in black and white: deprivation and ethnic minorities* (Child Poverty Action Group, 1992) and, with Robin Richardson, of *Politics for all: culture, equality and the general election 1992* (Runneymede Trust, 1992).

**Robin Richardson** was Director of the Runnymede Trust between 1990–96. Previously he worked as adviser for multicultural education in Berkshire, 1979–1985, and as chief inspector for Brent Education Authority, 1985–1990. He is the author of many books and articles on education, including, most recently, *Fortunes and fables: education for hope in troubled times* (Trentham Books, 1996).

# PART ONE

# Examining race and ethnicity in the British electoral context

# CHAPTER ONE

# Introductory remarks

## *Shamit Saggar*

### RACE, ELECTORAL CHOICE AND POLITICAL RESEARCH

The electoral presence of ethnic minority voters in British politics has been noted, scrutinized and debated for more than two decades. The stuff of "black and brown votes", as one commentator once put it, has never been far from academic discussion of race and political participation. Indeed, with the swelling of non-white numbers following post-war immigration and high levels of residential concentration, the theme of ethnic minority voting quickly emerged as a specialist area of psephological inquiry. There is little doubt that in recent years it has grown into a significant cottage industry in its own right.

Yet, the substantive content and product of this work have yielded a mixed picture of empirical findings. These data have not always been well understood at a theoretical or conceptual level, and there have been a number of problems associated with linking voting studies to related research on non-white political mobilization. In sum, an ever growing volume of quantitative evidence has not necessarily added to the understanding of the electoral process, nor has it contributed much to what is known about the political choices facing ethnic minorities.

The two essays in Part 1 of the book are devoted to re-examining and rethinking this imbalance from a conceptual, methodological and empirical perspective. The approaches taken by, and within, each of these perspectives are not only underpinned by theoretical understandings of the politics of race but, crucially, themselves drive theoretical debate and controversy. Whatever is known or surmised about participation, representation and party strategy can be disputed, but only to the extent that contrasting theoretical schools of thought are identifiable and engagable. This degree of transparency has not always been obvious in the research and debate conducted on race and electoral politics. It is a void that this volume aims to address and, specialist colleagues willing, to develop in future research efforts.

A further set of problems has arisen in the research work done on political parties. These are taken up in the contributions making up Part 2. Here two approaches have been taken, one dealing with ethnic minority political elites and activists within the mainstream parties, and the other concerned with party strategies on questions of race and ethnicity. The two approaches share an interest in themes of representation, noting that racial questions have been mirrored in growing party sensitivities over "who represents whom?" in contemporary British politics. To be sure, no-one seriously argues any more that representative democracy in British politics can be measured by the yardsticks of party loyalty and Burkean thought alone. That is not to say that ethnic group membership has become the new yardstick, because even fewer would or could credibly claim that it has. Rather, the old orthodoxies about the essence of political representation have been rendered less certain. The new political discourse of representation at the very least recognizes racial and ethnic identity as one factor among many in the equation.

Extant work on party members, activists and representatives has tended to highlight the glaring fact of low or modest participation. Shortcomings have been identified in party structures, internal policies and attitudes, which have contributed to this picture. At the same time, different priorities, orientations and participation styles amongst ethnic minority activists have also influenced the roles and relationships they have played in the political parties. However, very little has been understood about how party-structure-specific factors have interacted with non-white, activist-specific factors in shaping these relationships. The chapters by Geddes and Shukra both tackle these points and represent important extensions to our understanding of parties and non-white activists, both in terms of access to elective office and ideological controversies over black autonomy.

Of course the central focus of writing on parties and ethnic minorities has tended to be on questions concerning party competition, strategy and campaigning. This is the most familiar face of the politics of race as a specialist area of scholarship. Its presence in this volume has been deliberately restricted to the core coverage provided in two chapters: by Messina and by Rich (excepting Chapters 2 and 12 where discussion by myself of these themes is advanced at a macro level). The parties, according to these writers, have continued to pursue an interest in courting the votes – and money! – of ethnic minorities, continuing a twenty-year pattern first initiated on the back of a largely mythological "ethnic marginals" thesis from the 1970s. These efforts, whilst colourful and sometimes sensitive, have, however, tended to miss the point, namely that the Labour Party has held on to and even consolidated its overwhelming lead in capturing this electorate. Labour has undoubtedly benefited from this electoral fact, though it is easy, perhaps, to exaggerate the importance of this asset. As Messina reminds us, seepage of support away from Labour has been minimal and can at least partly be explained by the continuing legacy of hostility to immigrants and ethnic minorities in the ranks of the Conservative Party. Rich's essay on the Conservatives, meanwhile, focuses on post-Thatcher developments and suggests that the fault-line on racial attitudes persists, although frequently manifested in altered and unfamiliar terms.

Away from direct discussion of parties and voters, there is a need for specialist research to examine variances between national and subnational levels of participation more rigorously, as well as non-party mobilization and influences upon the policy process. Part 3 of the book takes on these tasks with contributions on Westminster, local politics, community-based politics, and a normative argument on the policy agenda. Interestingly, the pictures sketched of ethnic minority elites in national and local politics reveal few dramatic breakthroughs (perhaps as expected), but at the same time fail to support arguments for ethnic minority non-participation or anti-democratic channels of activity. The prospects for these elected (and would-be elected) elites may be bleak, but clear alternatives to ballot-box-style politics are hard to see from the evidence. Where traditional participatory politics based on parties can be, and often is, supplemented, it is through community-based organizations and initiatives that may work alongside parties and sometimes even rely on them for patronage, influence and informal access to decision-making. These efforts can not only deliver benefits and influence for their non-white constituency, but they may tell us a great deal about the limits of party politics in mobilizing large segments of the ethnic minority population. All told, it is important to remember that electoral participation, however welltuned and focused, amounts to only one aspect of policy influence in an ethnically-plural society. It is, I would argue, important for any book devoted to race and electoral politics to recognize this point.

## TWO-PARTYISM AND ETHNIC MINORITIES

The electoral behaviour of ethnic minorities is a remarkable phenomenon in modern British politics. To begin with, it is true that voters with a recent Afro-Caribbean or South Asian ethnic ancestry support the Labour Party in overwhelming numbers. In 1992, around four in every five non-white electors backed Labour. More recently, in 1997, there was barely any reduction in this proportion. Additionally, this picture of impressive loyalty has remained much the same over more than twenty years, encompassing half a dozen elections. These voters, in other words, have stuck with the embattled Labour Party throughout the period for which reliable data are available (1974 onwards) and, in particular, they remained largely unaffected by the corrosion in Labour's electoral performance between 1979 and 1997. Moreover, Asian voters, especially, have exhibited remarkably high registration and turnout rates, factors which have counted for quite a lot, given the long winter of Labour's Opposition. Finally, as if this were not enough, it should be remembered that ethnic minorities have been a geographically-concentrated population and their voting muscle – such as it is – has been largely confined to the urban areas of the electoral map. It is these areas in which much of the Labour Party's electoral strength is to be found. One consequence has been that, whilst Labour has been indebted to non-white supporters, it has tended to attract their votes in constituencies where it is already well placed to win. Though many may be unhappy with the suggestion, it is not hard to see how the opportunity for neglect has arisen.

All of the above features of ethnic minority electoral behaviour (EMEB) demonstrate that the relationship between non-white voters and the Labour Party has been both novel and the subject of intense debate. Not even the traditional British working class (a group which, incidently, overlaps significantly with ethnic minorities) has remained loyal to anything like the same degree. The relationship has tended to foster both positive and negative by-products. On the plus side, the Labour Party has been quite clearly the most active of the major parties in shaping its policies toward the (perceived) needs of ethnic minorities. The party has justifiably earned a reputation for periodic warmth and sensitivity on race relations questions, particularly when compared with the Conservatives' lingering anti-immigrant posture. However, on the debit side, some non-white Labour activists have begun to doubt the depth of their party's commitment. Specifically, these critics have made the charge that the interests of ethnic minorities are widely thought by party managers to be vote losers. This kind of prejudice, they feel, lies behind: a) a neglect of racial injustice and disadvantage in the development of party policy, and b) the poor progress made by non-white Labour candidates, especially in parliamentary elections.

Consequently, the link with Labour can seem to many observers rather puzzling. The Labour Party succeeds like no other party in capturing non-white votes, but its *de facto* "ownership" of this vote has been dogged with difficulties. For example, as Shukra's essay in this volume observes, the attempt, first begun in the mid-1980s, to establish a Black Section in the party revealed just how tense relations had become. Even in the late 1990s fairly substantial pressure is exerted on the Labour Party – both from within and beyond its ranks – to, in some way, "speak" for Britain's ethnic minorities. Students of the British party system will sense that this is an enormous task for Labour, and one in which it is almost bound to fail or, at the least, cause offence. But it is not necessarily failure that counts, in the sense that the party is likely to lose its voters' support. As Messina's essay stresses, if not to Labour, where are these voters to go? Moreover, the challenge may also be rather meaningless if ethnic minority voters are shown to be influenced by factors other than their ethnic origin or identity.

Meanwhile, the past two decades have been alive with speculation about Conservative strategies to lure ethnic minorities into their ranks. These voters' Labour moorings, argued Tory tacticians, were beginning to loosen and some groups, such as middle-class Asian voters, were thought to be ideal recruitment material. As several of the following chapters note, by and large the defection from Labour has been overplayed by the other parties and the media, but this has barely dented the enthusiasm of both Conservative and centre party attempts to go after the so-called "ethnic vote".

One notable upshot of all of this has been that the factors underpinning EMEB have come under scrutiny. It is clear to (almost) everyone that relatively little is known about: a) why ethnic minorities behave as they do at the ballot box; b) what they think about political issues; c) whether they are motivated by the same forces as their white counterparts; and d) to what extent influences common to all ethnic groups take on a different and distinctive meaning for ethnic minorities alone. The challenge that this presents to academic research is important because so many of the answers to these questions depend upon the interpretation of empirical evidence. For that reason, it is of the utmost importance that we first understand and try to map out explanations for patterns of EMEB. This task is the central one in my own extended contribution in Chapter 2.

## RACE POLITICS AND BRITISH POLITICS

As has already been suggested, the specialist literature on the politics of race has been dominated for many years by electoral and party matters. The insights and limitations of this body of work have been partially rehearsed here, but the rationale of this volume has not merely been built on filling gaps in a specialist literature. Many of the chapters in this book certainly take on this task and provide a number of fresh insights into racial and electoral themes. There is an additional reason for the book which has to do with: a) synthesizing knowledge and understanding of specialist race/politics and broader political participation questions, and b) bringing the consideration of ethnic minority electoral behaviour into greater focus within established psephological inquiry.

Despite a number of empirical studies on ethnic minority political participation over twenty years, it is quite striking how little of this work has left any residue in the mainstream research literature on political participation in general and electoral choice in particular. No doubt one could debate endlessly the causes behind this fact, but in a sense it is of little importance. What is clear is that political-science research activity on citizen participation has, in general, either overlooked the ethnic minority electorate or else relegated it to a minor descriptive footnote. This body of knowledge, with only a tiny handful of exceptions, has certainly not been informed by ethnic minority behaviour, except to note its heavily-skewed, pro-Labour character. Equally, the bulk of specialist publications on EMEB have made little effort either to utilize existing psephological work or draw upon recent debates over multiple political identities, motives and messages. The specialist volume on the politics of race and ethnicity has, in the view of this commentator, been thinner and less rigorous as a consequence.

In essence, therefore, and despite extensive empirical effort, the volume of research on EMEB remains immature and lacking in analytical depth. This is not an easy criticism to make, nor is it advanced lightly, since the collective work cited naturally contains elements of strength and incisiveness. That said, the work has generally avoided or failed to grapple satisfactorily with several central points of dispute, whether conceptual, methodological, theoretical or empirical. Let us take an example of each to make the point. All are reflected in contributions to this volume and without doubt are well tackled by the authors in question.

First, starting with the empirical, it has frequently been claimed that ethnic minority elected politicians at local level have been the product of an electoral landscape in which there have been few political spoils. Additionally, Westminster held few promises for non-white representation owing to the difficulties in competing for scarce single-member vacancies. As several chapters on local politics and participation have demonstrated, it is clear that the scale and dynamics of elected representation have come to be driven by a new set of factors. Ethnic minorities have organized, or been organized, to press for candidates, policies and commitments, particularly in Labour's ranks, in enough places to show that the local election option has amounted to more than just a consolation prize. It may still be premature to draw grand general conclusions from this point, but fresh empirical research in this volume shows that the picture is changing. This amounts, at the least, to a very good case for further empirical work in the future.

Secondly, in the past most theoretical questions have stemmed from arguments over class, race or ethnic-based strategies for political participation. These disputes continue to be pertinent, but have not been advanced significantly in their own terms. This has resulted in a staleness, since they have not made any headway in linking non-white strategies to party strategies. This kind of linkage, one might suggest, is the very stuff of political-science theorizing about group-institution relations. As a distinctive contribution to the specialist literature, exploration of the linkage has been fairly scant and arguably would have remained so without the input of specifically-political, institutional approaches. Two notable examples of this approach and theoretical contribution are to be found in this volume – the chapters by Messina and myself – although readers will observe the contrasting interpretations of the group-institution relationship.

Thirdly, conceptual and methodological concerns have only featured modestly in research on the politics of race, but have nevertheless raised some interesting points. One of these has been the perceived need to flesh out the widespread assumption that non-white voters are interested in a specific group or cluster of issues. These are sometimes referred to as "race issues" or, more loosely, as "racial concerns" but without adequate regard being given to what, if anything, they consist of. Several chapters in the book address themselves to this point, reinforcing the argument that certain conceptual assumptions have led to the analysis of certain types of political phenomena being given precedence over others. Another disputed question relates to non-party, non-mainstream political participation. The complication has arisen not so much because of differences over whether these forms of activity mattered – most agree that they do – but more because of uncertainties over how to measure and evaluate them empirically. Various researchers have ploughed on and developed a range of partial solutions to these problems, but the overall results have been far from conclusive. This difficulty has, in turn, been compounded by trying to integrate the understanding of electoral participation with that of public policy processes. At least two chapters in this volume have concerned themselves with this task and have confirmed that this is a priority area for future research.

This book has set out to address what may be termed an intellectual maturity deficit. It has done this partly by recognizing this deficiency in the extant literature, but has also actively looked for ways to promote the mutual understanding of the politics of race and British politics. This is a devil of a task to set for a single volume, and if it has been even partially realized I would consider the job done well. The point to stress is that for too long the specialist literature has remained isolated and weakened. The reasons given for this can no longer be easily defended and, equally, understanding and appreciation of EMEB has been viewed, unreasonably, as a fringe concern among students of the British political tradition. Ultimately, that is the interface to which this book has been directed. If it has hit its target, it is hoped that the deficit will have been closed a little.

# CHAPTER TWO

# Analyzing race and elections in British politics: some conceptual and theoretical concerns

## *Shamit Saggar*

"I am a professional businessman, not a professional Pakistani you fool. I make money, not gestures".

(*My Beautiful Launderette*, 1985)

## INTRODUCTION

In the late 1990s it is commonplace to hear suggestions that ethnic minority[1] political participation, whatever the advances of recent years, still lags behind the standards expected of a mature industrial democracy. In everyday terms this suggestion is illustrated by a broad, cross-party willingness to encourage enhanced, ethnic minority, voter participation and occupation of elective office. It is further encouraged by a range of party and extra-party efforts to build democratic institutions that are social microcosms of British society. Against this backdrop, it is also common to witness sharply-contrasting claims made by political activists and party managers alike concerning the nature and behaviour of ethnic minorities in the democratic process. Some twenty years after the first party-based attempts to capture the so-called "ethnic vote", conceptual understanding of that term remains as wide

11

open as ever. The search is on for the essence of ethnic minority political identity.

This chapter explores some of the ways in which the British political tradition has conceptualised ethnic minority political participation. It is primarily interested in the central race/voting nexus and sets the discussion within a wider conceptual framework. The chapter begins by highlighting the kinds of conceptual and conceptually-related difficulties that are thrown up in the study of race and ethnicity as variables in electoral behaviour. It then considers a major recurring controversy in both academic research and practical politics – namely the existence and inherent character of a distinctive ethnic minority political agenda. Moving away from minority voters, the chapter then assesses the ways in which party strategy has developed to take account of ethnicity and ethnic minorities. Lastly, there is a discussion of the need for greater conceptual clarity, in order to offset, at least partly, loose speculation about the motives and interests of ethnic minorities as citizen-participants in British electoral politics.

## Conceptual uncertainties

The importance attached to race and ethnicity in shaping voting choice has been the subject of considerable academic – and indeed journalistic – interest. It has however been a topic associated with muddled thinking. A large element of this fascination has been both predictable and, to an extent, understandable. For one thing, significance may be afforded to ethnicity as a variable in the sense that it is associated with, and may even yield, a powerful influence upon party choice. That is to say, ethnicity amounts to an amalgam of contributory factors shaping voting, selectively symbolizing and uniting aspects of shared experience and common outlook. Few theorists of electoral behaviour have made much headway in explaining what it is about (or what is embodied within), the concept of ethnicity that counts in shaping political outlook and action (although notable exceptions to this generalization might include the work of Verba and Nie (1972: ch. 10) and Nie et al. (1976: 104–5). This central job of mapping out the terms and scope of such an *ethnically-related form of political thinking and political action* is something that is considered more fully later in this chapter.

In itself, however, ethnicity does not count for very much in the task of predicting voting other than to measure group membership sizes and proportions. Moreover, confusion sets in once ethnicity is described as a scientific variable when, in fact, empirical studies seldom attempt to treat it as something that actually varies. Academic studies usually go no further than to treat it as a nominal variable, typically distinguishing patterns of non-white and white political behaviour. The only variance that does show up in such studies is that which distinguishes membership from one group from another. The familiar argument that a variable must vary is thus especially pertinent here. Furthermore, no appreciable attempt is made in empirical research to link either "lower" or "higher" forms of ethnicity or ethnic identity with political behaviour. It is not in that sense a particularly useful or adaptable variable, let alone one that counts greatly or can be measured meaningfully. One reason for this may be that ethnicity tends to work well enough as a scientific variable for the narrow purposes of survey research, but lacks sufficient coherence in content to be useful as an analytical concept. This approach to identifying its meaning and use, whilst radically different from what has been described previously, nevertheless draws attention to the task of interpreting correctly the relatively limited "hard" data that exists on race/ethnicity and voting in Britain. Both approaches then arrive at the same kinds of question.

These questions aside, ethnicity remains a concept that clearly matters for the purposes of moulding electoral choice. What is less clear is whether it is a metaphor for underlying causal relationships or indeed something that has a direct bearing on political orientation and activity.

If ethnicity is to be treated as an analytical category – as, arguably, it should – it is usually thought of as an explanatory factor that applies to only a small segment of the electorate (Heath et al. 1991: 99). As such, it is the *ethnicity of ethnic minorities* that analysts are concerned with, something which in Britain is incapable of having a large impact across the electorate as a whole. For that reason, we have become used to thinking that ethnic minorities do not influence overall election outcomes. These voters are too few in number and too concentrated away from the seats that matter, so the argument goes, for them to be significant across the wider political landscape (Crewe 1983). Yet, despite this stark message, there have been numerous claims regarding their great potential in delivering electoral victory (e.g. the much embellished "ethnic bloc" voting argument), or in avoiding electoral oblivion (e.g. the Labour Party's reliance on "ethnic safe seats" in its rout during the 1980s).

The complicating twist has been that commentators and researchers alike have been driven by the assumption that, for ethnic minority voters, ethnicity *alone* counts. In what sense does it count? Is it something of a coincidental feature of their ethnic identity, or is it the product of a distinctive agenda of issue and policy concerns? This problem seems to lie at the heart of most of the conceptual muddle in the literature, and is explored in the following section.

# A DISTINCTIVE AGENDA?

Over the past twenty years the volume of research on ethnic minority political behaviour in Britain has grown at a tremendous pace (Saggar 1992). However, a feature of this explosion of research interest has been an underlying confusion over the distinctiveness of non-white political outlook and action alike. At one end of the spectrum there have been strong cases made in favour of the idea that ethnic minorities are united under a common banner of shared political interests and persuasions (Werbner 1991). A theoretical variant of this line has been an insistence that an *ethnically-related* way of thinking and behaving politically is at work. The body of this, arguably, strong assertion is examined below. At the other end of the spectrum, harsh denials of such claims have been advanced, concluding that the basis of common behaviour has been a response to shared class and racial experiences, *without* any real sense of collective consciousness (FitzGerald 1987, and Studlar 1993).

In considering the empirical evidence of ethnic minority political behaviour, a number of different approaches have emerged in the academic and non-academic literature. It is important to emphasize that these approaches themselves are reflections of wider disagreements, usually, though not exclusively, linked to normative discussions about non-white political advancement. To that extent, the task of mapping the political behaviour of ethnic minorities is as much about interpreting the evidence at the heart of disputed conceptual territory as it is about describing positivist models of voting behaviour.

It is perhaps useful to think of relevant behaviour as comprising *four* interrelated faces. Furthermore, it will probably advance our understanding if we think of ethnic minority political attitudes and behaviour as several overlapping and interrelated phenomena.

## A separate "race agenda"

First, *ethnic minorities collectively may vote in line with a fully separate and discrete set of issues not shared by their white counterparts.* For instance, ethnic minority voters may base their discrete agenda on a sense that racial discrimination and exclusion is both widespread and endemic in British society. Constructing a political view of the world that is centred on racialization as a fundamental feature of society is probably what is meant by the term "race dimension". There is considerable reason to think, for example, that this kind of dimension has been at the heart of radical black political activists' efforts to promote Black Sections in the Labour Party (Shukra 1990). By the same token, the common experience of racism in British politics – and society generally – has undoubtedly contributed to the development of something of a "race dimension" for ethnic minority voters and political elites across all parties (FitzGerald 1990: 21–6).

What is important for the analyst to assess, however, is the degree to which ethnic minorities' political outlook is based *exclusively* on racial divisions. Only if the evidence suggests a strong degree of such exclusivity, may this be dubbed a "race agenda" in the sense that race and race-related issues are the prism through which the world is perceived politically.

For the most part empirical evidence tends not to affirm such a position. In a 1991 NOP survey, for instance, four in every five Afro-Caribbeans agreed with the proposition that Britain was a "very or fairly racist society" (Kellner and Cohen 1991). (The comparable figures for Whites and Asians in the survey were 67 and 56 per cent respectively.) This kind and level of feeling might be described as the building blocks of a wider "race agenda" world view. In some instances a strong sense of counter-hostility toward "white society", combined with reactive ethnic pride, has been highlighted by researchers interested in the so-called "culture of resistance" of black youth (Miles 1978, Troyna 1979). That said, the NOP survey data – in common with other similar survey findings – had little to say about the *depth* of feeling over race. These data may indeed conceal another hidden face – one which would show the relevant ethnic minority's views highly skewed in one direction but not held terribly strongly. Indeed, numerous commentators, observing the broad canvas of race relations in Britain, make the common assumption that these groups of voters are intensely motivated by racial considerations and that shared assessments about racism in society are the strongest motivators of all.

The disappointingly limited evidence that is available on this point may, in fact, hint at the reverse being closer to the truth. In another 1991 survey, carried out by Harris, of Asian voters, 37 per cent reported that the question of racial attacks was the most important issue they faced (BBC/Harris 1991). For this group at least, race and racism were not political issues in any general sense, however much they may have felt themselves to be the victims of racial hostility, either individually or collectively. Race and racism for them were priorities in the sense that their ethnic group membership left them especially vulnerable to a particular form of violence and intimidation. It would certainly be safe to infer that this concern amounted to a racialized dimension of issues relating to crime and law and order; it may be less safe to claim that their perception of the violence directed at them on the basis of visible appearance necessarily led them to interpret race and racism in broad political terms. At another, related level, one might ask: does survey data showing that over a third of a specific group are anxious about "racial attacks" tell us something about the racial significance of their concerns, or something about perceptions of individual and collective security? Table 2.1 below tells the story.

Another common presumption is that ethnic minorities themselves necessarily hold liberal or progressive views on race relations issues. Again, the limited evidence on this point usually ends by clouding the issue and seldom gives conclusive reasons to support such a claim. A 1991 NOP survey revealed that 12 and 15 per cent of Asians and blacks, respectively, *disagreed* with the suggestion that immigration had enriched the quality of life in Britain; furthermore, 5 and 7 per cent of each respective group felt that British laws against racial discrimination were in fact *too* tough (Kellner and Cohen 1991). A 1997 MORI survey reinforced the idea that many Asians held fairly illiberal views on immigration (MORI 1997). These figures, whilst fairly modest, would presumably come as a shock to many commentators and would be treated with a large dose of politically-correct scepticism.

A similar pattern is seen when considering the old chestnut of ethnic minority support for the principle of ethnic minority political representatives. Only a small fraction of Asian voters in 1991 said that they were more likely to vote for a candidate of the same ethnic origin as themselves (BBC/Harris 1991). Just 27 per cent of Asians in 1997 thought they were either certain, very or quite likely to change their vote to a candidate of their own ethnic group (MORI 1997). The same note of ambivalence, possibly even scepticism, is arguably at play when it comes to political leaders taking up fixed positions on issues in order to influence votes along ethnic lines. However, the ethnic background of certain leaders, rather than simplifying putative "ethnic issues", may turn out to undermine and blur claims made by such leaders: for example, in the early 1990s both Keith Vaz's and Max

TABLE 2.1  Most significant issue among Asian voters, 1991 (per cent)

| Issue | Per cent |
| --- | --- |
| Education | 41 |
| Racial attacks | 37 |
| Health service | 29 |
| Housing | 25 |
| Immigration | 17 |
| Poll tax | 11 |
| Mother tongue teaching | 10 |
| Separate schools | 4 |

Source: BBC/Harris (1991).

Madden's similar responses to the Rushdie affair were heavily motivated by their perceived constituency interests and seemed unaffected by the fact that one of them was an Asian MP and other a white one.

More typically perhaps, suggestions that a race agenda characterizes the political orientation of ethnic minorities are commonly expressed by those activists who have a stake in such a claim and also hold a normative commitment to such an agenda. Partial support amongst the ethnic minority electorate for a race agenda will usually mean that these voters at least are undecided as to whether political participation can be understood in exclusively racial terms. More typically, such voters would not particularly want to rule out the existence of, and subscription to, a race agenda but, at one and the same time, would fail to give much more than nominal support to race agenda political activists. In a sense, then, critics might argue that these voters want to have things both ways. To be fair, this criticism has some weight, since the normally racially-subdued texture of everyday British politics ensures that such starkly opposed choices are seldom forced upon minority voters.

The account of the race agenda presented above may be merely to put forward a caricature of ethnic minority voters who are motivated on racial grounds alone. This would be simplistic to the point of naiveté. What may be taking place is an unusual and specific way of looking at politics. A hardline perspective based on racial divisions is, of course, one, rather crude, illustration of this phenomenon, but it may not be particularly representative of ethnic minority voters in general. An alternative to this might be to suggest that ethnic minority cultures themselves create a sufficiently distinct approach to politics and political activity (Field 1984). At first glance, the cultural link displayed by many Asian and Caribbean voters seem to provide plentiful evidence for such an agenda, though it would be only fair to describe this as a *cultural* rather than *racial* approach to politics. In any case, however attractive this line of argument may seem (and it is regularly exploited by the media and politicians alike), the question remains whether this agenda shapes ethnic minority political participation in any exclusive or near-exclusive sense. Whatever the strength of the cultural basis of, say, Asians' political outlook may be, the argument is undermined if this factor is only one of *several* shaping political behaviour. We will return to the theme of culture in modelling non-white electoral behaviour in the discussion at the end of the chapter.

The key point that counts about "race agenda"-type claims is that, whilst there is much that ethnic minorities have in common with one another, researchers are hard put to say with confidence that this kind of commonality forms a *sufficient* basis for a unique and exclusive political outlook. The distinct cultural heritage of South Asians, for example, provides a rich seam for researchers interested in this topic, but few have been able to provide generalizable interpretations of the impact of their ethnicity upon politics. The most that can be said with confidence is that ethnicity undoubtedly does have an impact at the collective, group level. The evidence for this assessment stems largely from studies of the involvement of ethnic minorities in local politics and focuses on the mobilization of ethnicity for various tangible spoils. The ethnicity of ethnic minorities even here tends to serve as an additional influence on their political behaviour, alongside a range of familiar non-ethnic factors (Rath and Saggar 1992).

## Similar agendas, different priorities

Secondly, *the political outlook and behaviour of ethnic minorities and their white counterparts may be based on the same range of issues and policy concerns but reordered in priority and emphasis.* In very simple terms, what we are interested in is the likelihood of overlap between black and white political agendas, allowing additionally for differences of emphasis across ethnic boundaries. A fairly typical illustration can be seen in survey data from the 1987 general election which showed wide variations in the importance white, Asian and Afro-Caribbean voters attached to issues such as housing and defence (see Table 2.2 below). Broadly speaking, for white voters the latter held greater significance than among black voters; meanwhile, the former issue resonated strongly among one group of ethnic minority voters and not at all among the other. Recent data in the run-up to the 1997 election showed quite significant reordering of priorities across different issues among Asians and Afro-Caribbeans (MORI 1996, 1997).

TABLE 2.2 Most important issues (of two) by ethnic group, 1987 general election (per cent)

| Issues | Asian | Afro-Caribbean | White |
| --- | --- | --- | --- |
| Unemployment | 65 | 70 | 45 |
| Health | 34 | 25 | 32 |
| Education | 17 | 13 | 19 |
| Defence | 32 | 18 | 37 |
| Law and order | 11 | 4 | 6 |
| Pensions | 6 | 7 | 9 |
| Housing | 0 | 21 | 5 |
| Prices | 10 | 15 | 7 |
| Race | 1 | 0 | 1 |

Source: BBC/Gallup (1987).

The crucial point is that black and white agendas are at one and the same time both the same and distinct. This does not, however, tell us much about *why* priorities may differ across ethnic lines. For this we need to refine our understanding of the causal relationships under-pinning inter-ethnic variance. One line of argument is that the role of ethnicity is something of a red herring since it displaces the key point, namely that ethnic minorities are more likely in any case to be Labour supporters. Identification with Labour, both at a party political level and in terms of general principles and philosophy, means that they are in turn more likely to attach priority to certain types of issue over others. Issues such as housing, health and education are the staple diet of Labour supporters and this is much the same for ethnic minority, Labour-inclined voters. Thus different priorities are really very little to do with ethnically-related fundamentals.

Another, related, line of argument highlights the contribution made by objective socio-economic differences between the white and non-white electorates (Crewe 1983). For example, the substantially younger age-profile of the latter, and the heavier middle-class concen-tration of the former, both serve to give ethnic minority voters a stronger stake in some issues when compared with their white counterparts. It is not uncommon to observe that the age and class characteristics of any electoral sub-group shape their general orienta-tion to key issues such as housing and taxation. Residential patterns are another example of orientation towards issues and, in turn, votes for political parties (McAllister and Studlar 1984: 147).

However, whilst inter-ethnic variance can be traced back in this way, there is always a danger of researchers overdoing things by con-centrating excessively on white versus non-white distinctions. In fact, Labour Force Survey-derived analysis by Robinson (1990) correctly draws attention to fairly wide variations in the socio-economic pro-files of Asian sub-groups: ethnic Indians and ethnic Bangladeshi being prime examples at opposite ends of the spectrum. The upshot of this intra-Asian difference is that there are likely to be different underlying orientations toward political issues which may, in some cases, out-weigh differences between white and non-white electors. An addi-tional risk associated with any social demographic-linked explanation is that this still begs the question of how much convergence is prob-able over time. Ethnic minority voters in that sense are just another illustration of a sectional electorate which, for reasons to do with migration and labour market participation, looks rather different from the rest of the electorate. So much is clear. However, patterns of con-vergence – as well as some tendency toward greater divergence – are the key to understanding why certain issues count for more than others. Rather greater empirical research along these lines is sorely needed if we are to unpick the mystery of issue-salience, and its relationship to issue-voting, among ethnic minorities.

A further line of argument has been that differences of priority are a reflection of the fact that some issues are perceived as linked to race whilst others are not. That is to say, ethnic minority voters are in the business of examining the full range of political issues and interpreting for themselves which issues comply with a race agenda and which do not. This argument ascribes a rather higher level of sophistication to ethnic minority voters, suggesting that any race dimension at play is both selective and variable as a factor in itself. Thus, for example, the issue of education for ethnic minority voters can have meaning both in familiar terms to do with, say, school budgets and class sizes, as well as in terms of multicultural curricula and anti-discrimination policies. A 1991 Harris survey revealed that education was the most significant issue for 41 per cent of Asians (BBC/Harris 1991). This is formidable evidence of issue-salience, driving the issue of racial attacks firmly into second place. However, what we cannot tell for certain is whether the general question of education was interpreted by respondents in racial or non-racial terms. The likelihood is that something of both interpretations is encapsulated in the 41 per cent figure, but distinguishing between them is impossible at this level of analysis. To illustrate issue-recognition is one thing, but to demonstrate what is meant by such salience is another, more complex matter.

### Parallel agendas

Thirdly, and building on the previous remarks regarding sophistication, *white and non-white issue agendas may appear much the same as one another but for the latter group all issues embody some linkage with race and ethnicity*. Ethnic minority voters seem to shadow white voters' concerns and are interested in all the same issues with an equal degree of importance. Such voters are, to a considerable degree, just like white voters and it would be reasonable to claim that the smaller non-white electorate is merely a sectional element of the larger electorate. But the resemblance goes only so far because the similar issue-agenda of non-white voters also comprises a parallel, race-related way of looking at the same issues.

These voters treat issues such as education as involving both non-racial and racial choices at one and the same time. This kind of description would seem to be getting closer to identifying a theory of an ethnically-related way of thinking and behaving politically, the need for which was outlined above. What we are saying, in effect, is that everyday political issues have both racial and non-racial faces. This much is plausible and helps us to understand that there is no easy way to pinpoint what for ethnic minorities is an issue of race. For such an issue can be a reference to either *the* "race issue", as it is commonly dubbed by politicians and the press (e.g. racial discrimination against ethnic minority schoolchildren), or to a race-related aspect of what are otherwise non-racial policy concerns (e.g. hidden racial bias in the educational curricula).

A more helpful way of conceptualizing the two related levels of issue-formation is in terms of the distinction between overt or direct racism on the one hand and covert or indirect racism on the other. Traditionally speaking, the so-called "race issue" has, for ethnic minorities at least, been substantially about the effects of identifiable, direct forms of racial discrimination. In that sense, the question of race stands more or less independently within the social and ideological construction of the issue. It is thus about race first and foremost, irrespective of the wider policy context or environment in which the allegation or grievance is set. This, presumably, is how ethnic minorities interpret powerful public examples of overt bias against non-white people in areas such as policing and job hiring. The only uncertainty is whether an individual black person recognizes such an example to be of importance and worthy of attention. Clearly, some ethnic minorities have differences with others as to the authenticity of specific examples of alleged racial injustice. But, once there is agreement about the significance of a particular example, there is no further uncertainty clouding the question. For example, having immediately been recognized as both salient and authentic, the police shooting of Cherry Groce in Brixton in 1985 represented for many British Afro-Caribbeans a potent reminder of the race issue in a traditional and, sadly, familiar form.

However, comparatively few issues are crystallized in such crude racial terms as the result of a single incident. Indeed, what researchers have been keen to stress is that such an example is by no means the sole interpretation of race in issue terms. The issue is equally about a whole host of anxieties over indirect forms of racial discrimination and hostility. A 1995 survey carried out for a daily newspaper gave credence to the idea that, whatever their sense of optimism or pessimism about race relations, black Afro-Caribbeans cannot afford to forget the high levels of prejudice that all survey respondents – black and white – admit still persists in Britain: 40 per cent of respondents thought that there was "a lot of prejudice", joined by a further 39 per cent who thought that there was "a little prejudice" (*The Guardian* 1995).

From time to time ethnic minorities express doubts about a variety of attitudes, policies and procedures which they feel may be working against their interests. These complaints are essentially about indirect biases and amount to a belief that negative racial considerations are at play in broad aspects of public life. It is also a positivist assessment regarding the extent to which race factors do – rather than ought to – have a bearing on what happens in areas as diverse as pensions, healthcare, and prisons. This, then, is not as close to the traditional interpretation of the race issue, not least because it embodies a range of beliefs about covert attitudes, actions and processes. As conservative commentators frequently remind us, it is pretty hard to convince the electorate at large about the legitimacy of the race issue at this much broader level (Johnson 1991). Moreover, if some critics are to be believed, there are even doubts about the extent to which the ethnic minority electorate share common beliefs about the existence and/or significance of hidden racism.

The important point to stress is that ethnic minority voters accept that many issue areas have a latent race dimension to them, and that a high degree of selectivity is apparent in deciding what additional priority, if any, should be given to otherwise racially-neutral issue concerns. Race is both an issue and a non-issue. The choice between seeing things in racial or non-racial terms is not a haphazard or unpredictable process, but is closely linked to the way in which race is conceptualized in narrow rather than broad terms. Thus criticisms about ethnic minority voters having things both ways would be rather unfair and, in any case, would tend to miss the point about how and why race-related factors come to shape ethnic minority political outlook and behaviour.

## The same agenda, writ small

Finally, *it is frequently suggested that the issue agenda of ethnic minorities amounts to the same as that for the white electorate, but writ small.* The issue agendas of both groups match one another fully, with only small variations of degree being put down to factors such as the legacy of migration. In truth, this view of ethnic minority voters has received backing from some of the data on ethnic minority issue salience and voting behaviour (see Tables 2.1 and 2.2 above). A glance at much of this data reveals heavy, long-term support for the Labour Party among ethnic minority voters. This distribution is accounted for by the skewed class structure of the ethnic minority population, which in turn causes these voters to hold a closer interest in relevant class and party-led issue concerns. The underlying picture remains one of black-white similarity, distorted temporarily by objective class and demographic factors.

In the longer run, so the argument goes, we can expect to see even greater uniformity across the black and white electorates as the former's class structure evolves to match the latter's. The argument is one which tends to veer away from the current, front-end evidence of voting patterns and instead focuses more on longer-term, underlying trends. Even then, there are plenty of conservative-inclined commentators and Conservative Party activists who, looking at current patterns, insist that there is little that is ethnic about the votes of ethnic minorities. Indeed, there is no point in chasing the so-called "ethnic vote" since, it is argued, it has got very little to do with ethnicity as such. These Conservative strategists in particular seem to stress that, insofar as the ethnic minority electorate is to be targeted and courted, it should be treated in much the same manner as the rest of the electorate, of which it is merely a geographically-clustered and socially-discrete element. The extent to which this type of colourblind strategy is translated into campaigning tactics is a moot point, since few candidates of whatever party seem able to resist the temptation of courting ethnic minority votes in an ethnic-specific manner. The question of party strategy and its relationship to ethnicity is a subject taken up later in this chapter.

There is little left for the analyst to explain if black and white agendas *have* converged or are on course do so over time (FitzGerald 1987). If their agendas *are* alike, so, we should expect, will both groups' attitudes be towards the issues they face in common as well as their general political orientation. Ethnic minority voters thus reveal little that is in itself distinct from their white counterparts. Tables 2.1 and 2.2 above reveal a remarkable degree of similarity between black and white voting agendas, save for some limited differences on a handful of issues. However, as noted previously, these data do not preclude Asian and Afro-Caribbean voters from the common perception of an additional race dimension in all of the issues listed, irrespective of whether they are described by pollsters in obviously race-specific terms.

That such a dimension to superficially non-racial issues may exist is not in contention. Indeed, from time to time, examples are thrown up which give us good reason to think that selected issues operate at both levels for those ethnic minorities pushing for wider recognition of ethno-racial bias in mainstream areas of public service delivery such as, say, healthcare and social services. The difficulty is that this level of analysis cannot hope to reveal the full picture of the racialization of issues facing black voters. This is a methodological difficulty that researchers must live with and, moreover, accept cannot be massaged away through speculation or conjecture. All we can do is, first, report the degree of overall similarity that is shown up by survey research, and, secondly, draw modest generalizations about whether race-specific issues *seem* to play a significant part in the priorities of ethnic minority voters.

## RACE AND ETHNICITY AND PARTY STRATEGY

At the heart of contemporary British politics there is an assumption that ethnic minority voters ought to be courted in ethnically-specific ways. The assumption is broadly shared by the three major political parties and generally receives the endorsement of party leaderships keen not to overlook innovative and unconventional approaches to electoral advantage.

Significantly, even the Conservatives who have attempted to project an ostensibly "colourblind" self-image – for example the pointed "Tories say he's British, Labour says he's black" campaign pitch of 1983 – have nevertheless made concessions to ethnic politics. The party's Anglo-Asian and Anglo-Conservative Societies, although wound up in the mid-1980s, clearly signalled the decision of party managers to address these groups of voters – and donors! – using mechanisms that accepted these electors' ethnic distinctiveness. Whilst it may be debatable whether ethnicity counts so centrally for ethnic minority voters as a whole, Conservative Party strategy has been moved by the possibility that it may do so. No doubt the landmark CRC report on the 1974 elections played a big part in shifting Tory strategy, appealing, as it did, to a narrowly-defeated major party that had historically shown no interest in this section of the electorate. Perversely, the acceptance that ethnicity might count for something among this group of voters has largely failed to shape Conservative Party strategy at any broader level, and the party has strenuously avoided making any commitments on ethnic lines that could spill over into its broad appeal to voters at large, white and non-white.

Ironically, for most of the past 10 to 15 years, this willingness, insistence even, on seeing such voters through a sort of ethnic prism seems to go hand in hand with a widely-held desire to leave the race issue on the back burner of party competition. Race and ethnicity in that sense do not seem to command any great significance – arguably since at least early in the 1983 parliament – and yet these concepts count as much as any when it comes to the parties' attempts to gather non-white support. This is a fairly remarkable paradox, to say the least. Furthermore, despite considerable evidence of confusion and muddle over the nature of the issues that are thought to motivate these voters (see previous section), party leaders and strategists remain convinced that a specific race agenda exists and can be exploited for party gain.

In this section we shall look at the origins and reasoning behind this vital assumption. We shall pause to consider whether the parties and non-white voters are well served or handicapped by this central assumption, and whether electoral politics conducted in these terms is capable of delivering beneficial change for ethnic minorities. We shall also consider how this assumption is influenced by underlying views of ethnic minority electoral motivation.

The background to this assumption can be traced back more than twenty years and in particular to the conscious decision by the Labour and Conservative parties to pay more attention to wooing the non-white electorate. A key element in this strategic calculation was the myth perpetuated in the wake of the October 1974 general election that a) the Conservatives' second defeat was attributable to neglect of ethnic minority voters in crucial seats, and b) these voters were an example of a floating vote that could be solicited on ethnic or racial lines (CRC 1975). Neither assertion was supported by much evidence, but they nonetheless proved a powerful force behind the parties' discovery of the "ethnic vote". On the first claim, the CRC study sought to highlight so-called "ethnic marginals", where, it was believed, the size of the non-white *electorate* exceeded the size of the winning majority. This claim was methodologically flawed by the use of 1971 Census estimates of the size of the New Commonwealth and Pakistani origin *population* in these constituencies, making no allowance for calculations of age disqualification (i.e. under-18s), registration rates and turnout. On the second charge, the CRC report made no attempt to substantiate its assertion that the support of ethnic minority voters – whether located in marginal seats or not – was dependent upon the major parties' policies and attitudes towards race and immigration issues. A final nail in the coffin of the CRC's argument was that, despite showing the degree of electoral volatility that had occurred in these marginal seats from first 1974 election to the second, it could not produce any evidence to show that a non-white, differential switch had produced the outcome of seats changing hands. Indeed, it was just as possible to argue the opposite on the basis of the evidence used: that non-white voters had largely stayed put, whilst white voters had changed sides in order to deliver Tory marginals to the Labour Party!

Added to this, an established ethnic minority political leadership received growing media attention from 1976 onwards which, by standing for self-described immigrant interests, gave parties further reason to think about, and do business with, ethnic minorities in ethnic-specific ways. The logic of ethnic leadership meeting with a mainstream party system with virtually no experience of handling or aggregating ethnicity, meant that fertile ground was cultivated by proponents of the new ethnic politics. None of this, of course, particularly helps explain whether such a strategy has been empirically well founded or successful.

Are British political parties justified or prudent in approaching ethnic minorities in this manner? The answer would seem to be that parties do a poor and rather patchy job in relying on such a strategy. Two arguments support this response – one examines the historical-structural context, the other is based on the views of non-white and white voters themselves.

To begin with, it should be recalled that British political parties are not in the *universal* business of trying to attract ethnic minority voters. It is true that some parties *have* flirted from time to time with the notion of seeking the support of this constituency; others, however, have been quite content to let the issue lie undisturbed. The distinction, moreover, is even more striking when you examine the approaches taken by individual politicians. Intra-party variance on this question reveals that the ethnicity of ethnic minorities can often be shunned and embraced at one and the same time.

However, for the most part, political parties have worked fully within the understanding that ethnic minority voters are both attitudinally and geographically amongst the safest constituencies of the Labour Party. As Table 2.3 below makes clear, long-term backing for Labour from ethnic minorities remains strong and remarkably stable. To be sure, even the marked dip in Labour's support at the 1987 poll proved to be a false dawn by the time of the 1992 contest. In any other context, this group of voters would not be described as a particularly worthwhile opportunity for Labour's rivals. Recognizing both Labour's reliance on non-white voters and these voters' strong orientation towards Labour, it has become increasingly apparent that few spoils are on offer to parties competing on this territory. Indeed, Labour's posture toward its ethnic minority supporters has been

TABLE 2.3   Levels of Labour and Conservative support among ethnic minorities, 1974, 1979, 1983, 1987, 1992, 1997 (per cent)

|      | 1974[1] | 1979 | 1983[2] | 1987 | 1992[2] | 1997[2] |
|------|---------|------|---------|------|---------|---------|
| Lab  | 81      | 86   | 83      | 72   | 81      | 78      |
| Con  | 9       | 8    | 7       | 18   | 10      | 17      |

Notes:

[1] October 1974 General Election.

[2] Figures represent recalculated average of Asian and Afro-Caribbean support levels.

Sources: adapted from CRC (1975); CRE (1980); CRE (1984); Harris (1987); Ali and Percival (1993); Saggar (1997).

described in terms of neglect, if not arrogance (FitzGerald 1988). None of this has served to discourage those who are still determined to perpetuate the all-too-hollow "ethnic marginals" thesis (CRE 1994).

In any case, any efforts which have been made across the political parties to marshal ethnic minority support have been unique and unprecedented in the sense that, historically, ethnicity has long counted for little in British party competition. Britain certainly has little tradition of the religious definition or determinisation of party labels and loyalties to be found in many continental European political systems. Equally, the ethno-linguistic character of politics in places such as Belgium, parts of Iberia, and further afield in Canada, appear largely alien to the British system. The extent to which the ethnicity of ethnic minorities receives attention in British politics is thus novel and far removed from the traditional class basis of modern political mobilization (FitzGerald 1985b: 1).

In fact it is not so much the ethnic identity of ethnic minorities that is the subject of attention but, rather, the assumption on the part of politicians that racism and race relations are what count above all else for non-white voters. As we have already seen, this assumption is ill-founded since, according to available, albeit patchy, survey research, ethnic minorities do *not* as a rule prioritize a race agenda over other concerns.

The upshot of this is that it has become increasingly difficult for ethnic minorities to participate in local and national politics without reference to a) their ethnic identity, and b) the wider meaning given to their ethnicity in British politics and society. Critics of this state of affairs would claim that ethnicity has thus become institutionalized and co-opted into mainstream political thinking. This scenario may present a number of opportunities for ethnic minority political leaders and sympathetic white politicians to push ahead and secure tangible gains on behalf of the non-white population. Indeed, much of this kind of advancement has already taken place, especially at local level, enabling Asian and Afro-Caribbean Britons to achieve important breakthroughs in, for instance, accessing public service delivery processes and decision-making (Gyford 1985, Nanton 1989).

On the deficit side, however, there has been something of a steady tightening of the ethnicity straightjacket which shapes major party strategic thinking towards ethnic minority participation. This may not necessarily strike all observers as a drawback, since it successfully tackles the longer-standing complaint of party thinking characterized by colour blindness. The deficiencies become more apparent when we ask to what extent ethnic minorities define their interests in solely ethnic-specific terms. Evidently there is some ambiguity here. Much hangs on the reading of the data though, in general, it is reasonably clear that ethnic minorities are not exclusively obsessed with such an agenda. Whether these voters interpret ethnic-based channels of political action and policy influence as an opportunity or as patronizing and burdensome is a debatable question. It is also a question worthy of extended empirical research in the future.

Putting aside this debate for the moment, there are some important conceptual implications arising from the argument that valuable benefits accrue to ethnic minorities through the current conduct of electoral politics and affiliation with the Labour Party. The most significant of these implications is what *kind* of benefits proponents of this argument have in mind. The most common response has been to restate the view that ethnic minority interests are best served by policy commitments which target unemployment, educational attainment, housing provision, urban renewal, and so on. Many of these policy commitments tend to overlap with traditional Labour and centre-left ideological territory, thereby encouraging the view that the Labour Party is *specifically* best placed to advance non-white interests. However, once more, a complication arises out of the distinction between race and race-related policy concerns on one hand, and various superficially non-racial, mainstream policy concerns on the other. One reading would be to insist that ethnic minorities, by virtue of their socio-economic and geographic location, are likely beneficiaries of a range of public policy commitments that are aimed at improving conditions and opportunities for disadvantaged, less prosperous, urban population groups. Black people are thus not so much the targets of Labour or centre-left policies but, rather, the indirect and disproportionate "winners" from such a policy agenda and its inherent priorities. This interpretation, if widely shared and expounded in Labour thinking and self-image, can serve as a powerful rationale for the party to continue presenting its policies towards ethnic minorities in this generalized way. After all, if it can be argued that Labour's priorities will serve to benefit ethnic minorities indirectly, it becomes increasingly possible to defend a strategy of avoiding making any *direct* appeals to them at all. This defence can in turn appear seductive within a wider electoral landscape that also anticipates – and thus fears – the power of a white "backlash".

Any argument which portrays ethnic minorities as potential beneficiaries of Labour's non-racial policies alone suffers from one overwhelming drawback. Namely, that it is quite misleading to claim that these voters are not courted in ethnic- or race-specific terms. Clearly they are courted in such terms both by parties in general, and in particular by Labour's well-rehearsed display of overt policy commitments to further non-whites' collective interests. Labour, in particular, has come to be regarded by non-white and white electors as the "ethnic minority-friendly party", though, as we shall note below, past experience casts severe doubts on the party's right to such a reputation. In any case, Labour's putatively closer association with non-white interests makes it difficult for the party to continue to insist that the non-ethnic bond between party and group is all that matters. As witnessed in many inner-city constituencies in 1997, Labour's long track record of involvement in various internal ethnic minority concerns demonstrates that its appeal to those voters is not solely a question of its *indirect* appeal on traditional employment and social welfare issues.

Furthermore, almost as if to ignore Labour's structural head start, other parties have periodically made efforts to attract ethnic minority voters, using strategies that both recognise the ethnicity of this electorate and also make play with various related and unrelated factors. These factors can be said to underscore the parties' strategic thinking about the nature of the ethnic minority electorate and are discussed in greater depth below.

Ethnic and racial considerations come into focus even more sharply when we examine the particular appeal that the Labour Party has attempted to project toward ethnic minorities. Despite numerous misgivings within the hierarchy of the national party over any visible association with non-white voters, it is still clear that the party has amassed a variety of policy commitments aimed at maintaining the loyalty of its non-white supporters. The unambiguous thinking behind this position must presumably be that race issues matter and matter significantly to this constituency of supporters. For example, while the party has gone on record in promising to introduce new legislation to promote race equality measures and to expand the legal basis of indirect discrimination. Labour has also indicated that it would take on many of the proposals from the Commission for Racial Equality to expand its powers (Layton-Henry 1992: 119). Elsewhere, it is committed to scrapping the 1981 Nationality Act though, to a very considerable extent, its future plans for immigration policy remain sensitive to the electoral charge that it is a fundamentally weak party on immigration (Saggar 1993, Seyd et al. 1992). Even these plans must be seen in the context of the party's main pledge to remove the discriminatory aspects of the 1981 legislation, as a partial prelude to the *possibility* of wholesale immigration reform. As an early gesture, in May 1997, Labour's Home Secretary announced the scrapping of the 1983 "primary purpose" immigration rules. As the party of government, then, few voters, least of all ethnic minority voters, can have much doubt that Labour will continue in its longstanding policy of backing non-whites' interests in ways that are not just universal and focused only on general socio-economic change. Labour is at the same time squarely behind these interests using policy promises that are ethnically and racially-defined and thus of primary concern to non-white voters.

Does this then mean that the Labour Party deserves the reputation of best-promoter-designate of ethnic minority interests? Arguably not, since far too much is taken for granted in terms of conceptual and theoretical understanding of such interests. For one thing, this perspective necessarily strips the question of race as a political issue down to its barest essentials, relying instead on the idea that formal claims to eradicate discrimination are the same as substantive change. In the minds of many ethnic minorities this simplistic equation may command respect but, equally, among others it may not. One reason for a possible disjuncture is that some ethnic minorities may see the distinction between rhetoric and reality when it comes to questions of race and politics. They may indeed be correct to do so, given all the vacillation and tough talk about race and immigration politics which they have experienced in the past thirty years.

Another, more simple, reason may be that they do not think that this kind of interventionist policy is best suited to addressing British race relations. Seeing, instead, the conflicts thrown up by ethnic and racial pluralism in rather different terms, some non-white voters might entertain some scepticism about the efficacy of legislative and public policy "solutions". You would not need to see these ethnic minority "doubters" as neo-conservatives to conclude that alternative strategies, perhaps based on emphasizing cross-cultural education and compromise, might be the best way forward.

Yet another reason is that Labour's stronger, more activist approach to tackling race relations may be met with indifference and lack of interest by some ethnic minorities. Thus, what for Labour – and indeed progressives in other parties – may be seen as a priority, may not be accepted as such by elements of the target constituency. In other words, it is increasingly apparent that it is difficult, perhaps impossible, to make broad generalizations about the attitude of ethnic minorities as a whole toward race-relations questions. (Indeed, in the following section we shall review some perhaps unexpected evidence to do with ethnic minorities' attitudes to liberal race-relations policies.) This is hard enough but it is even less meaningful to try to make a case for a strong correlation between Labour's policies on race on the one hand, and opinion on race among ethnic minorities on the other. The biggest hurdle would appear to be that there is only limited evidence to show that ethnic minorities attach special – let alone overwhelming – priority to the kinds of policy concern on which Labour's race-specific strategy is based (CRE 1994).

As other parties attempt to make overtures to ethnic minority voters, many cannot avoid pitching their appeal in ways that mimic elements of Labour's strategy. Conservative and Liberal Democrat thinking may remain steadfast in its determination to avoid Labour-style racialization of political discourse, but it is noticeable that both parties have been prepared to utilize reasonably explicit strategies which assume that ethnic minority voters are chiefly interested in race and race-related issues. Both parties, for instance, make great play of the notion that they are committed to rooting out racial discrimination in their own ranks and that anti-discrimination laws have a proper and legitimate role in society. Each of them has had public arguments concerning the persistence of racism among their own party members, and this in high profile campaigns (e.g. the Conservative's tussle over John Taylor's candidacy in Cheltenham in 1992 and the Liberal Democrats' racially-ambiguous messages in local elections in Tower Hamlets in 1994). Both of these episodes demonstrate that neither party can afford to maintain silence in the face of very serious complaints about racism. A part of their response has, presumably, been shaped by the need at least to recognize that potential ethnic minority supporters hold legitimate worries which are directly related to race. Equally, both have accepted, and even made some play with, the argument that ethnic-minority voters are not the only ones concerned about racial discrimination; indeed, white, liberal sentiment on the theme is arguably of some considerable influence in shaping thinking in both parties.

Elsewhere, the Conservatives have made capital over alleged separatist demands made by Black Sections supporters in the Labour Party. With the constitutional blocking of such a proposal in the Labour Party, however, it is worth remembering that the Conservatives' own One Nation Forum exists chiefly to marshal ethnic minority votes and money by an appeal based both on racial *and* non-racial grounds. Equally, the Liberal Democrats have been keen to condemn Labour-style codification of race especially in local government. However, they too retain a formal and informal apparatus to rally ethnic minority supporters, chiefly through aggressive self-promotion of the party's longstanding progressive stance on race and immigration.

Having rightly drawn attention to the remarkable range of shared thinking toward race and electoral campaigning across the major parties, it is of course only fair to acknowledge that there is one area in which Labour's claim to superiority is founded on irrefutable evidence. The opportunities that have been carved out for ethnic minority political candidates over the past 10 years serve to mark the party out as being especially sensitive to its non-white constituency. Geddes (1993) reports that a colossal 85 per cent of all ethnic-minority local government councillors belonged to Labour's ranks. After 1997, all nine ethnic minority MPs are Labour representatives. The remaining ethnic minority "also-rans" in 1997 and 1992 contained a much greater number of Labour candidates who were within reach of victory (though the absolute number of Labour candidates roughly matched the Conservative field). Underlying this track record, Labour has undoubtedly built up a much deeper seam of ethnic minority activists, officials and would-be candidates. It is from this seam that future numbers of successful candidates will emerge at both national and local levels, and we can expect the current picture of party imbalance among non-white representatives to perpetuate into the future (Norris and Lovenduski 1995: 237–48).

The Labour Party, then, is in a curious and rather difficult position. It receives the overwhelming bulk of non-white votes cast and also champions the rights of Britain's ethnic minorities. However, this also means that it is under an obligation to present the ethnic minority electorate with policy commitments that are specifically designed to benefit them. The choice of commitments tends to vary, but at the very least it means that the party has to supplement its broad-based policies aimed at its general constituency of supporters and potential supporters. This, in effect, means that, albeit in a limited and superficial way, Labour must offer a race-specific package of commitments that target non-white voters. The irony is that it is unclear whether the party needs to go to any great effort to massage what is, after all, among one of its safest constituencies. Furthermore, Labour's evident need to show *sensitivity* towards racial and ethnic concerns is founded on very shaky evidence that such issues are the key to retaining non-white support.

Such sensitivity is by no means confined to Labour's ranks and, to some degree, is shared by political parties in general. The willingness of parties to operate in these terms is, of course, partly a consequence of features within ethnic minority community-based politics. Nevertheless, British political parties are unlikely to rid themselves entirely of this style of strategic mobilization and all regard the ethnic minority electorate in some way or another as an important component of electoral competition for the pursuit or retention of office.

## CHARACTERIZING COMMON INTERESTS

If ethnic minority voters are to some degree or another perceived by political parties as the common target, what can be said that best characterizes the interests and mobilization of this group of voters? Research conclusions on this point tend to be somewhat patchy, not least because few commentators have seen the need to map out available evidence at a conceptual level. In this section we shall explore some possibilities and try to assess whether or not political parties base their appeal upon a coherent, and therefore defensible, understanding of ethnic minority political motivation.

There are perhaps three ways in which we can think of ethnic minority voters as capable of having or developing a sense of shared common interest. With each of these characterizations we can see wide variations in the conceptual basis for thinking and acting in a common cause. Some limited degree of similarity is apparent when interpreting survey data and much depends on the extent to which we accept that ethnic minorities themselves are aware of, and influenced by, a race-specific issue agenda.

### Social class

First, *the interests and motivations of ethnic minority voters can be described in socio-economic terms based on class membership and accompanying party identification.* This interpretation is itself founded on traditional class-centred analyses of British electoral behaviour, in which class has been used as a predictor of party choice (Pulzer 1967, Robertson 1984). The point about mapping non-white voting behaviour in class-based terms is that this approach takes account of the continuing concentration of ethnic minorities among lower socio-economic groups relative to their white counterparts (Jones 1993). It is thus not surprising to learn that most ethnic minorities identify themselves with the working class and, in turn, with key institutions related to that class (Layton-Henry 1992: 66). So much is true and helps us explain ethnic minority working-class political orientation. What is more difficult to fathom is the persistently high level of middle-class, ethnic minority support for the Labour Party, with a degree of conviction and loyalty to rival their non-middle-class co-supporters. In this respect, it would appear that they are locking on to an identification as much with their "community" as with anything else (such as class). A rival interpretation might highlight the extent to which middle class ethnic minority support for Labour is the outcome of additional higher education (Price and Sanders 1993). University education for the electorate as a whole tends to push up the likelihood of supporting Labour and, in the case of ethnic minorities, it may be that increasing levels of higher-education participation are fuelling continuing loyalty to Labour, albeit for a range of non-class-related reasons. Table 2.4 tells the story of class-deviant Labour voting among middle-class ethnic minorities over two typical elections.

A very large element of Labour's support among ethnic minorities can be attributed to the skewed class profile of this group. However,

TABLE 2.4 Voting intention by social class, 1979 and 1992[1] (per cent)

1979 General Election

| | White | | | Asian | | | Afro-Carribbean | | |
|---|---|---|---|---|---|---|---|---|---|
| | ABC1 | C2 | DE | ABC1 | C2 | DE | ABC1 | C2 | DE |
| Lab | 20 | 35 | 38 | 42 | 50 | 50 | 41 | 49 | 48 |
| Con | 57 | 40 | 32 | 25 | 28 | 25 | 17 | 11 | 15 |
| Lib | 9 | 5 | 5 | 6 | 3 | 0 | 5 | 8 | 3 |
| Other | 15 | 20 | 25 | 28 | 19 | 25 | 35 | 32 | 35 |
| N | 3,588 | 3,290 | 3,145 | 36 | 32 | 40 | 29 | 37 | 40 |

1992 General Election

| | White (N = 1,879) | | Non-white (N = 857) | |
|---|---|---|---|---|
| | ABC1 | C2DE | ABC1 | C2DE |
| Lab | 37 | 52 | 54 | 78 |
| Con | 47 | 28 | 31 | 8 |

Note:
[1] excludes Lib-Dem and Others.
Sources: BBC/Gallup (1979); CRE (1994).

not all of it can be put down to social class. In looking at the strength of Labour support beyond that accounted for by social class, Heath et al. (1991: 113) argue that: "Perceptions of group interests or processes of group identification are plausible explanations". Therefore, other factors are almost certainly at work, though the impact of race and ethnicity factors may well work *against* certain examples of party choice as for it. For instance, a 1983 Harris survey revealed that 76 per cent of Labour-voting, Afro-Caribbeans justified their choice by citing that "they [Labour] support the working class", followed by a crucial 9 per cent who said that they "did not want the Conservatives in government", and 7 per cent who felt that "they [Labour] supported blacks and Asians". The comparable figures for Asians in the same survey were 64, 8 and 31 per cent respectively (Harris 1983). In a 1996 survey, 31 per cent of Labour-supporting Afro-Caribbeans explained their choice in terms class representation, against just 8 per cent who saw Labour as "best for black people" (MORI 1996). These data tell us that other factors are serving to build anti-Conservative bonds between some non-white voters and the Labour Party. Though smaller in magnitude than the positive link between them, this point cannot be ignored as a long-term key variable stunting the development of greater Conservative identification and/or voting.

This characterization sees ethnic minority voters as creatures of their objective socio-economic environment. Thus, working-class membership is not all that counts, and can be added to the host of other indicators of environment. For example, 1991 Census data show that elements of the black Afro-Caribbean population occupy a generally weaker social and economic position disproportionate to their numbers; aspects of this position include housing tenure, physical housing conditions, lone parenthood, long-term illnesses, unemployment, types of economic activity, and so on. However, on other indicators certain sub-groups within this population were tending to fare rather better than their white counterparts (e.g. in terms of participation in further and higher education, and entry into professional occupations). This picture of differential experience within one group indicates that crude class generalizations should either be avoided or at least seen in their proper context (Owen 1994).

As voters whose loyalties are shaped by environment, ethnic minorities have been strong Labour identifiers and supporters mainly as a consequence of a) their entry into the labour market following immigration, and b) the continuing legacy of manual work among first generation settlers. These two factors have meant that for a long period – and possibly still today – non-white voters have considered themselves to be natural Labour supporters. However, this environment has begun to alter over time, allowing us to gain a handle on changes in labour-market participation patterns. Labour identification has so far waned barely at all, despite the fact that tangible evidence exists to show, for example, steady socio-economic upward mobility among some ethnic minorities, and sharp erosion of job opportunities in older manual industries. Significantly, recent research has high-lighted the strong concentration of ethnic Indians among the former socio-economic pattern, with marked evidence of fairly rapid upward movement seen in some geographically and generationally-localised instances (Owen and Green 1992). Such illustrations of advancement were noticeably missing in the cases of ethnic Pakistani, Bengali and West Indian groups, making the ethnic Indian "stride" seem that much greater. In one way or another, this type of development is likely, in its turn, to be linked to new patterns of party identification. The surprising thing is that so far there has been very little impact upon overall ethnic minority voting patterns. In 1992 Labour's popularity remained as strong as ever at the aggregate level, recovering much of the modest seepage to the right and centre ground that had occurred at the time of the 1987 election (CRE 1994). By 1997 a slight turnaround among Asians was discernable, in contrast to the picture among Afro-Caribbeans where Labour support tightened even further (MORI 1996, 1997). Significantly, a 1991 NOP survey showed that levels of Labour support among ethnic Pakistani and ethnic Bengali Asian voters were barely higher than among ethnic Indians (64 and 63 per cent as against 56 per cent respectively). However, despite this, fully a fifth of the latter group stated an intention to vote Conservative – a noteworthy minority given the date of the survey against a backdrop of poor Conservative standing in many other national polls (Amin and Richardson 1992: 29).

## Issue voting

Second, *ethnic minority party choice can be viewed in strictly rational terms based on accurate knowledge about, and willingness to act on, the issue preferences of non-white voters.* For fairly obvious reasons examined below, this interpretation has been one over which commentators have, knowingly or unknowingly, been most preoccupied. Indeed, it was noted earlier that this model has invited both analytical and speculative attempts to unlock the questions of a) what such preferences are, and b) whether they are sufficiently important to shape electoral choice. Such attempts have usually been poorly thought through and have finished very wide of the mark. In contrast, others have treated the subject with notable distinction. Examples speak for themselves and need not be rehearsed here.

The task for successive researchers has been to profile the issue preferences of ethnic minorities. As we have seen earlier, it is hard to say for certain that ethnic minorities share a common preoccupation with race-related issues (Studlar 1986). Indeed, for the most part, they seem to subscribe to an issue agenda that has considerable similarity with their white counterparts, though, as we have also noted, it is debatable whether or not they perceive there to be a hidden racial dimension to some, most, or all issues. So much for general issues. A rather different picture begins to emerge, however, when we consider the attitudes of ethnic minorities toward those issues which touch on the extent of racial exclusion in modern British society. Here the evidence is complex and it is difficult to draw firm conclusions. Data from a 1985 survey of ethnic minorities in Greater London revealed that a slim majority of Asians felt that black people in Britain were treated the same as white people. Almost 57 per cent of Afro-Caribbeans by contrast reported *unequivocally* that black people were treated worse than others (FitzGerald 1985a: 6). Later (1991) data from NOP confirmed aspects of this pattern: over two-thirds of Afro-Caribbeans thought that non-whites were treated less well than whites by employers, against 42 per cent of Asians and 39 per cent of whites (Amin and Richardson 1992: 44). Table 2.5 below shows a similar pattern opening up across a range of concerns. How is this evidence to be interpreted? To begin with, there is a clear-cut distinction between on the one hand Asians whose attitude towards societal racism is rather similar to whites, and, on the other, Afro-Caribbeans who seem to take a more critical, and perhaps hostile, view. Thus, we may surmise that this profile could lead Asians to a more accommodationist position in British society and Afro-Caribbeans to a line of greater suspicion and possible confrontation. However, the difficulty lies, first, in being certain that these attitudinal differences are *real*, in the sense that ethnic minorities attach weight to such questions in general, and, secondly, assessing the degree to which these views, even if strongly held, actually shape political thinking and behaviour. It would, of course, be implausible to claim that attitudes towards societal racism were irrelevant in moulding political opinion. Indeed, strongly-held and deeply-critical views on this front are almost certainly responsible for skewing basic political instincts and, very possibly, political behaviour as well.

The question is whether causal relationships and levels of cognizance are sufficiently defined to result in beneficiaries and losers among political parties. To put it another way, what reason have we to think that Afro-Caribbean resentment will only be laid at the door of, say, the Conservative Party in particular? A rough glance at the contemporary political landscape might suggest this to be the most likely outcome. However, a number of factors disturb the simplicity of

TABLE 2.5   Treatment of non-whites by authorities, 1991 (per cent)

| | White | Asian | Afro-Caribbean |
|---|---|---|---|
| Employers | | | |
| better | 9 | 3 | 1 |
| worse | 39 | 42 | 67 |
| same | 44 | 44 | 22 |
| Police | | | |
| better | 7 | 2 | 0 |
| worse | 48 | 45 | 75 |
| same | 36 | 40 | 16 |
| Schools | | | |
| better | 14 | 2 | 1 |
| worse | 13 | 15 | 38 |
| same | 61 | 74 | 48 |
| Courts | | | |
| better | 10 | 2 | 1 |
| worse | 24 | 19 | 57 |
| same | 55 | 53 | 26 |

Source: Amin and Richardson (1992).

this picture. First, these would-be voters may be just as likely to internalize their alienation from society and opt not to participate in the electoral process at all. The cost would then be felt just as much, if not more, by Labour, relying as it does on non-white votes in a number of its urban heartlands. Secondly, such electors may conclude that direct action, such as protest politics, perhaps even violence, is a more suitable alternative outlet for their frustration, thereby circumventing the formal electoral process and consequently shunning parties almost randomly. Third, initial feelings of anger that may lay beneath a "culture of resistance" are likely to have faded somewhat by the late 1990s. The result of this might be a higher level of indifference until 1997 towards a Conservative government than might have been supposed. The Conservative Party may console itself by concluding that it is paying a smaller cost for such alienation than it may have a decade earlier or, a little more worryingly, that this is the single largest reason why its efforts to woo non-white voters have achieved so little. Finally, the benefits that might be thought to flow to, say, Labour from the frustration of such would-be voters may be curtailed by the party's ambiguity in presenting itself as the party of the dispossessed "have-nots". These potential supporters still need to be rallied to Labour – and away from the non-participation option in particular – if their pessimistic assessment of British society is to count in electoral terms.

A rational choice-based model also implies that foundations exist for selective issue-voting by ethnic minorities over the policy questions they perceive to affect them alone. Therefore, ethnic minority voters can be relied upon to distinguish between political rhetoric on the one hand and policy deeds on the other. If this is a safe assumption to make, a number of surprising outcomes may result. The best illustration can be seen over immigration policy, an area that over the years has received extended attention by political parties, and where objectively-defined non-white interests have suffered enormously. For instance, non-white voters are liable to receive many of Labour's strongly-principled policy promises with a pinch of salt, remembering that the party reneged twice on clear commitments to repeal Conservative immigration statutes following electoral victory in 1964 and 1974. Ethnic minority voters must be prepared to discount false or unlikely promises. By contrast, they may take a more positive view of the Conservative record on immigration, which in the past has been shown to be something less than the party's tough rhetorical bark. The Heath administration's perhaps surprising decision to allow the entry of significant numbers of expelled British Asian refugees from Uganda in 1972 stands out especially. The Wilson government's rather sordid last-minute attempts to backtrack on commitments to allow in comparable immigrants from Kenya in 1968 is frequently cited by critics as testimony of Labour's blotted reputation.

By separating promises from action, we can perhaps begin to explain how the immigration issue has led to sometimes confusing responses among ethnic minorities. A 1991 Harris survey of Asian political attitudes revealed that a small, though significant, proportion thought that the (then) present immigration controls were either "about right" or "not tough enough" (Harris 1991). Superficially, it may seem as if this group of voters had adopted a stance out of line with its objective interests. However, other factors may apply in their case, since it was not demonstrated by the Harris survey or other comparable evidence that strong immigration controls were, by definition, against Asian political interests. Such a claim is meaningful *only* to the extent that a common bond is shown to exist among Asian voters, who recognize the discriminatory impact of such controls on fellow Asians – and non-whites generally – if not themselves. This group of Asians quite patently had distinguished themselves from others who were more likely to be subjected to tougher controls. Consequently, the Conservative Party's reputation for toughness on immigration control was not perceived as a barrier to pro-Tory sympathy and support.

This is perhaps a generous interpretation since it portrays Asian Conservative supporters as being fully cognizant of notions of objective and revealed interest. It sees them as knowingly undaunted by the blunt and hostile rhetoric that occasionally characterizes immigration debates in Conservative ranks. Neither assumption may be reliable. For one thing, we should remember that these Asian voters, however limited in number and atypical, are just as likely to be bloody-minded and irrational as their white counterparts. After all, the phenomenon of working-class support for Labour in spite of its policies rather than because of them is well-documented in the psephological literature (Sarlvik and Crewe 1983). In addition, these voters may accept that Conservative policies on immigration are hostile to them, but at one and the same time choose to rationalize their party choice on other, non-racial grounds. The Conservatives, therefore, are thought of as potential beneficiaries of non-white votes in terms that bypass, and possibly neutralize, immigration questions or indeed any other race-related issues.

By backing parties that promise them benefits and by taking race as a salient concern in a selective way, ethnic minority voters show that they are not the *natural* constituency of any of the political parties. What then drives some commentators to argue that ethnic minority voters *naturally* veer in one ideological direction or another? This question conveniently leads to a third and final way of conceptualizing common interest among ethnic minorities – namely by reference to voting preference as a cultural manifestation.

## The cultural thesis

Third, *the central motivation behind ethnic minority political outlook can be reduced to cultural forces, albeit ones that are operating in a wider British political and social landscape.* In making such a suggestion, we should recognise that culturally-based arguments have been amongst the most speculative attempts at characterizing non-white political behaviour. That does not in itself render such an approach worthless, but it does mean that the researcher must tread with care in examining what is often a poorly-defined variable.

Putting this argument into context, in the British case it usually takes the form of a characterization of putative "community values", which are said to underpin and subtly unite discrete ethnic minority groups. The British South Asian population tends to be the largest reference point for this claim, a group which, according to 1991 Census findings, approaches 1.4 million. Ignoring any distinctions that may exist within this population, the argument goes on to claim that Asians are subjects of, and subscribe to, a community-wide value system that has various precise features. High among these values are said to be, *inter alia*, respect for traditional family structures, defer-

40

ence to authority both in the home and beyond, importance given to education and socio-economic advancement, support for the institutions of law and order, and willingness to socialize future generations in support of similar values. The testimony of inter-generational immigrant succession, most notably among East African Asians, is sometimes singled out as additional evidence (Bhachu 1985). This set of values forms the nucleus of an outlook that is said to foster a deeply conservative group, which is both suspicious of strong government in certain spheres, whilst supportive in others.

With the image of an inherently conservative group already sketched, it takes only the smallest of intellectual leaps for cultural model enthusiasts to talk of an electoral group that is *naturally* allied with the Conservative Party. Whether what is meant by this thesis is that the group has the potential to become allied to the party in such a fashion is a moot point. The key features of the model are its natural, quasi-deterministic base and the resulting description of an inevitable rediscovery of common interest between group and party. Asian voters, according to the rhetoric, are faced with a choice between a nominal champion of increasingly-outdated immigrant rights (Labour), and a natural home for their true yet hitherto suppressed interests (the Conservatives). Put in these fairly stark terms, commentators and voters alike are encouraged to believe that the passage of time alone will serve to reveal the Conservative Party as a "true home". Labour-voting is thus explained as a structural abberation resulting from a historical legacy which a) acknowledges the group's immigrant past, b) draws a powerful parallel with earlier left-leaning immigrant cohorts (e.g. Jews), and c) sees the Conservatives as instinctively, though foolishly, shying away from courting a potentially valuable constituency.

Asians therefore are viewed typically as a late, though not lost, opportunity for the Conservatives. In particular this group is highlighted for its ongoing adherence to communal, non-individualized ways of thinking and behaving. This last point is highly significant, because much of the characterization thus far attempted has been linked explicitly with the Conservative Party. However, by making inroads into implicitly ideological territory regarding the existence and inherent value of "community", it is not hard to see why aspects of the paradigm have been seized on by both Labour and Liberal Democrat strategists. To be sure, the focus on politically-inspired attempts to rekindle "community values", are close to electoral agendas right across the party system. Therefore, the so-called "model minority" represented by Asians *cannot* be fully absorbed into, or monopolized by, Conservative strategy, since elements of the characterization have a much broader ideological appeal. This factor appears to be especially important to centre-left strategists, aiming to ditch hostages from the past and concentrate on exploiting the Asian example on as level a playing field as possible. Thus, past – and indeed present – Labour identification is interpreted as a sign of a positive bond between party and group, with both occupying similar territory on one reading of the "community values" argument. There is nothing inevitable about seepage of support to the Conservatives, according to this counter-argument. Indeed, Tory presentations of the party as a "natural home" are frequently rebutted as disingenuous ploys to mask covert hostility to non-white participation in Conservative ranks.

In the final analysis, the cultural thesis is remarkable because of the dearth of evidence to support its claims. It is certainly more than conjecture since it makes play of forces and patterns that are widely accepted as existing. Yet it falls far short of a coherent explanation, not least because considerable doubts exist as to what type and level of evidence would be needed to bolster the various assertions made in its name.

Perhaps the single biggest piece of circumstantial evidence comes from the much-cited example of earlier Jewish immigrant succession. Here, it was claimed, was a newcomer group that over time abandoned its close association with the left and found a base, if not a home, in supporting the Conservative Party and participating in its affairs (Alderman 1983). Several generations on, Jews are widely cited for their strong presence in Conservative elite ranks, and their electoral support for the party is taken for granted in many areas. The parallel is just too striking and irresistible for proponents of the cultural model.

Since the vast bulk of the model's supporters are, in any case Conservative strategists, thinkers or commentators, researchers have to be cautious in interpreting much of the haphazard anecdotal evidence. Nevertheless these voices count for something and cannot be entirely dismissed. One reason is that Conservative strategists have been fairly active in trying to attract the support and funds of Asian business leaders. Their efforts have met with limited success and clearly important markers have been established on both sides. It is commonplace for these strategists to go on record as predicting the rightward drift of Asian voters over the medium- to long-term. Such assessments, whilst usually littered with embellishment, are not unimportant since they contain within them a measure of a real investment by a party with countless alternative priorities. It is unlikely that so much would be made of the long-run dividends of this strategy, if those responsible for its implementation were not sufficiently confident of its success. Their conviction may, of course, be grossly mistaken, but it provides a good guide to where and how future efforts to court ethnic minorities are likely to take shape.

Before then strategists from all parties must work within the existing electoral landscape. The here-and-now of ethnic minority voting patterns in 1997 is clear and is likely to remain more or less unshakable in the short- to medium-term. The strong bias in favour of Labour which has persisted throughout successive Tory victories (and one Labour landslide) should not – and cannot – easily be ignored. Perhaps the daunting task facing the right and centre has meant that there is little to be lost by promoting a loosely-defined cultural caricature of potential ethnic minority supporters. Whatever the cause – and indeed meaning – of stubborn Labour loyalty, it is fairly certain that the cultural model will continue to find a convenient outlet as the stuff of Sunday supplement feature-writing. As the saying goes, "watch this space" as political caricature is put up and measured against political reality.

## ACKNOWLEDGEMENTS

I am grateful to the following colleagues for their written and verbal comments on the first draft of this chapter: John Crowley (FNSP, Paris), Anthony Messina (Tufts University, USA), David Sanders (University of Essex), and Ken Young (QMW).

In addition, pre-publication drafts and/or adaptations of this chapter were read to audiences at the 1995 annual meeting of the American Political Science Association (Chicago, September 1995), and at a British Council seminar entitled "Reflections on Two Multi-cultural Societies" (Brussels, January 1996). Working drafts were also presented and discussed at departmental seminars at Salford University and QMW (both February, 1995). I am grateful to various individuals present on these occasions for their informal feedback.

## NOTE

1. The term "ethnic minority" is used to denote people whose recent origins lie in South Asia, Africa and the Caribbean. The term is used more-or-less interchangeably with "non-white" and "black". These terms are designed to encompass a wide range of non-white groups in contemporary Britain. Departures from these terms are properly identified in the paper and are usually used in reference to specific component sub-groups, e.g. "Asians"

and "Afro-Caribbeans". Readers are reminded that no particular socio-logical or political inference should be drawn from the use of these primarily descriptive terms, though the author accepts fully that recent intellectual debates in Britain and elsewhere have centred on the question of terminology and nomenclature in the study of race and ethnicity and political participation.

## REFERENCES

Alderman, G. 1983. *The Jewish Community in British Politics*. Oxford: Clarendon Press.

Ali, A. & G. Percival 1993. *Race and Representation: ethnic minorities and the 1992 elections*. London: Commission for Racial Equality.

Amin, K. & R. Richardson 1992. *Politics for All: equality, culture and the General Election 1992*. London: Runnymede Trust.

Anwar M. 1991. The context of leadership: migration, settlement and racial discrimination. In *Black and Ethnic Leaderships: the cultural dimensions of political action*, P. Werbner and M. Anwar (eds). London: Routledge.

BBC/Gallup 1979. General election exit poll. Unpublished data set, University of Essex, ESRC Data Archive.

BBC/Gallup 1987. General election exit poll. Unpublished data set, University of Essex, ESRC Data Archive.

BBC/Harris 1983. National election issues – Asians and Afro-Caribbeans. Commissioned by *London Weekend Television*, unpublished data set JN49913. Richmond: The Harris Research Centre.

BBC/Harris 1987. Political attitudes among ethnic minorities. Commissioned by *The Caribbean/Africa/Asian Times*, unpublished data set JN98746. Richmond: The Harris Research Centre.

BBC/Harris 1991. Asian poll 1991. Commissioned by *BBC Pebble Mill*, unpublished data set JN99245. Richmond: The Harris Research Centre.

Bhachu, P. 1985. *Twice Migrants: East African Sikh Settlers in Britain*. London: Tavistock.

CRC 1975. *Participation of Ethnic Minorities in the General Election of October 1974*. London: Community Relations Commission.

CRE 1980. *Votes and Policies: Ethnic Minorities and the General Election 1979*. London: Commission for Racial Equality.

CRE 1994. Don't take them for granted. *Connections*, no. 1. London: Commission for Racial Equality, pp. 5–8.

CRE 1984. *Ethnic Minorities and the 1983 General Election: a research report*. London: Commission for Racial Equality.

Crewe, I. 1983. Representation and ethnic minorities in Britain. *Ethnic Pluralism and Public Policy*. N. Glazer and K. Young (eds). London: Heinemann.

Field, S. 1984. *The Attitudes of Ethnic Minorities: Myth and Reality*. Home Office Research Study no. 80. London: HMSO.

FitzGerald, M. 1985a. Preliminary report on GLC sponsored survey of ethnic minority political attitudes in London. Unpublished discussion paper, dated January.

FitzGerald, M. 1985b. Conceptual and methodological problems involved in political studies of Britain's black ethnic minorities. Unpublished discussion paper, dated June.

FitzGerald, M. 1987. *Political Parties and Black People*, 2nd edn. London: Runnymede Trust.

FitzGerald, M. 1988. There is no alternative . . . black people and the Labour Party. *Social Studies Review*, vol. 4, no. 1, 20–3.

Fitzgerald, M. 1990. The emergence of black councillors and MPs in Britain: some underlying questions. In H. Gouldbourne (ed.), *Black Politics in Britain*. Aldershot: Avebury.

Geddes, A. 1993. Asian and Afro-Caribbean representation in elected local government in England and Wales. *New Community*, vol. 20, no. 1, 43–57.

*The Guardian* 1995. Most white Britons say prejudice lives on, 20 March, 1.

Gyford, J. 1985. *The Politics of Local Socialism*. London: George Allen & Unwin.

Heath, A. et al. 1991. *Understanding Political Change: The British Voter 1964–87*. Oxford: Pergamon Press.

Johnson, P. 1991. *The Daily Mail*, 8 July.

Jones, T. 1993. *Britain's Ethnic Minorities*. London: Policy Studies Institute.

Kellner, P. and N. Cohen 1991. Racism: someone else is to blame. *The Independent on Sunday*, 7 July.

Layton-Henry, Z. 1992. *The Politics of Immigration*. Oxford: Blackwell.

McAllister, I. and D. Studlar 1984. The electoral geography of immigrant groups in Britain. *Electoral Studies*, vol. 3, no. 2, 139–50.

Miles, R. 1978. Racism, Marxism and British politics. *Economy and Society*, vol. 17, no. 3, 428–60

MORI 1996. Black Britain. *British Public Opinion*. MORI, July.

MORI 1997. MORI Asian Poll. Unpublished briefing notes, MORI, March.

Nanton, P. 1989. The new orthodoxy: racial categories and equal opportunities. *New Community*, vol. 15, no. 4, 549–64.

Nie, N. et al. 1976. *The Changing American Voter*. Cambridge, Mass: Harvard University Press.

NOP 1991. Survey in Kellner P. and N. Cohen 1991. Racism: someone else is to blame. *The Independent on Sunday*, 7 July.

Norris P. & J. Lovenduski 1995. *Political Recruitment: gender, race and class in the British parliament*, Cambridge: Cambridge University Press.

Owen, D. 1994. Black people in Britain: social and economic circumstances. 1991 Census Statistical Paper No. 6, University of Warwick. Centre for Research in Ethnic Relations/National Ethnic Minority Data Archive.

Owen, D. & A. Green 1992. Labour market experience and change among ethnic groups in Great Britain. *New Community*, vol. 19, no. 1, 17–29.

Price, S. & D. Saunders 1993. Economic expectations and voting intentions in the UK: a pulled cross-section approach. *Political Studies*, vol. XLIII, no. 3, 451–71.

Pulzer, P. 1967. *Political Representation and Elections in Britain*. London: Allen & Unwin.

Rath, J. & S. Saggar 1992. Ethnicity as a political tool in Britain and the Netherlands. In *Ethnic and Racial Minorities in Advanced Industrial Societies*, A. Messina et al. (eds). New York: Greenwood Press.

Robertson, D. 1984. *Class and the British Electorate*. Oxford: Basil Blackwell.

Robinson, V. 1990. Roots to mobility: the social mobility of Britain's black population, 1971–87. *Ethnic and Racial Studies*, vol. 13, no. 2, 274–86.

Saggar, S. 1992. Race and politics. In *Routledge Encyclopedia of Government and Politics*, M. Hawkesworth and M. Kogan (eds). London: Routledge.

Saggar, S. 1993. Can political parties play the "race card" in general elections? The 1992 poll revisited. *New Community*, vol. 19, 693–9.

Saggar, S. 1997. Racial politics and the 1997 general election. *Parliamentary Affairs* (special issue, "Britain Votes, 1997"), vol. 50, September.

Sarlvik, B. & I. Crewe 1983. *Decade of Dealignment*. Cambridge: Cambridge University Press.

Seyd, P. et al. 1992. *Labour's Grassroots: the politics of party membership*. Oxford: Clarendon Press.

Shukra, K. 1990. Black sections in the Labour Party. In *Black Politics in Britain*, H. Gouldbourne (ed). Aldershot: Avebury.

Studlar, D. 1983. The ethnic vote 1983: problems and analysis and interpretation. *New Community*, vol. 11, 92–100.

Studlar, D. 1986. Non-white policy preferences, political participation and the political agenda in Britain. In *Race, Government and Politics in Britain*, Z. Layton-Henry and P. Rich (eds). London: Macmillan.

Troyna, B. 1979. Differential commitment of ethnic identity by black youths in Britain. *New Community*, vol. 7, no. 3.

Verba, S. & N. Nie 1972. *Participation in America: political democracy and social equality*. New York: Harper & Row.

Werbner, P. 1991. Black and ethnic leaderships in Britain: a theoretical overview. In *Black and Ethnic Leaderships: the cultural dimensions of political action*, P. Werbner and M. Anwar (eds). London: Routledge.

Young, K. 1992. Class, race and opportunity. In *British Social Attitudes*, R. Jowell et al. (eds). Aldershot: Gower.

# CHAPTER THREE

# Ethnic minorities and the British party system in the 1990s and beyond

## Anthony M. Messina

## INTRODUCTION

The central purpose of this chapter is to revisit the theme of the representation of ethnic minority interests within the contemporary British party system and the related issue of the incorporation of ethnic minorities into British party politics. Although this theme was prominent in my book *Race and Party Competition* (Messina 1989) and it is one that has been explored, to varying degrees, in other scholarly works that have appeared since 1989 (see, for example, Ball and Solomos 1990, Goulbourne 1990, Layton-Henry 1992, Saggar 1992, Solomos and Back 1995, Norris and Lovenduski 1995), it is well worth revisiting for several reasons. First, since the publication of *Race and Party Competition*, the dynamics of the British party system have substantially changed. Among other important changes, the Labour Party has become much more electorally competitive during the 1990s, and now forms a government. Secondly, recent general elections permit me to reassess some of my earlier arguments pertaining to the relationship between ethnic minorities and the major political parties in Britain. Specifically, we can now evaluate better the merits of my claim that the Labour Party is the most logical and effective vehicle for representing the political interests of ethnic minorities (Messina 1989: 150–77). And finally, it is now evident that substantial controversy and confusion reigns in the scholarly literature about the very concept of ethnic minority political interests and, hence, the representation of ethnic minorities as a political constituency in British politics. The controversy revolves around two disputed issues. First, do ethnic minorities in Britain share a coherent set of political interests? Second, what do we mean specifically when we use the phrase "the political representation of ethnic minorities"?

The central argument this chapter advances is that to the extent that Britain's ethnic minorities are a coherent political constituency – and it is my contention that, to a considerable degree, they are – the political interests of this constituency are best expressed and represented during the 1990s, as they were in the previous decade, through the Labour Party. This argument is founded on three related assumptions, the first two structural and the third subjective. First, the political party remains the most relevant and effective vehicle for articulating and representing ethnic minority political interests. Secondly, the dynamics of Britain's two-party system and the dominant features of its electoral system continue to politically marginalize all but the Conservative and Labour Parties. And finally, of all of Britain's political parties, large and small, Labour remains the most ideologically committed to articulating and promoting the collective interests of non-whites. As I argued in *Race and Party Competition*, these assumptions do *not* imply that the Labour Party articulates and represents non-white political interests exceptionally well. Nor do they imply that Labour's privileged status among non-whites will endure forever, especially given the rapidly changing conditions of two-party competition in Britain. Rather, what they do imply is that, in the current environment of restricted political choice, Labour is, and will probably remain into the indefinite future, the party of and for Britain's ethnic minorities.

## THE POLITICAL REPRESENTATION OF ETHNIC MINORITIES

### The representation of non-white interests

During the last 15 years or so, two schools of thought have come to the fore in the large and burgeoning scholarly literature on the political representation of ethnic minority interests. The first school argues forcefully that there is little, if any, empirical evidence to support the view that non-whites in Britain collectively endorse a coherent and detailed set of policy priorities (Studlar 1986, Studlar and Layton-Henry 1990). According to this perspective, the public opinion survey data on non-white policy preferences reveal two problems for conceptualizing how best to represent the interests of non-whites.

First, non-whites as a group do not express policy preferences that are significantly different from those supported by whites. That is to say, non-whites and whites share similar policy priorities (Fitzgerald, 1987: 55–58). Secondly, the survey data suggest that non-whites are ideologically heterogeneous. Specifically, Afro-Caribbean and Asians in Britain have diverse opinions on issues such as immigration, housing and law and order. Because of these realities, the question of the political representation of the collective interests of ethnic minorities is inherently problematic, since it is far from clear what these shared interests are. Indeed, Studlar (1986: 175) argues that, because the survey data demonstrate "minimal" differences of opinion between non-whites and whites, ethnic minorities are already "well integrated into the mainstream of British politics".

In contrast to the first school, a second and much larger group of scholars *assumes* the existence of a more or less universal non-white political agenda (Mullard 1973, Werbner 1991; 15–37). Supported by little empirical evidence, this alternative school takes for granted that a discrete non-white political agenda can and should be advanced. Although this perspective acknowledges that non-whites are not ideologically or politically homogeneous, this fact does not deter the second school from perceiving ethnic minorities as a policy or political community. Britain's ethnic minorities are a political community primarily because they are defined as such by (white) political elites and governments. Moreover, regardless of their inter-group differences, all ethnic minorities in Britain are primarily "receivers" rather than "makers" of public policy. To put the issue somewhat differently, ethnic minorities largely remain an *object* of British politics rather than fully autonomous political actors capable of effecting political or policy outcomes. As a result of their "object" status, non-whites necessarily share a common political and policy orientation that transcends whatever specific issues may divide them. They are a distinct political constituency *regardless of whether they cohere around a specific set of explicit political or policy goals.*

Which of these two schools of thought is the most persuasive? On the one hand, it is rather too easy to criticize the school that denies that a coherent, non-white political agenda exists within which ethnic minorities as a whole share a common set of interests. First of all, this perspective is not founded on an abundance of empirical evidence. The public opinion surveys frequently cited by this school are relatively few in number and were not specifically or exclusively designed to test the hypothesis that ethnic minorities do, in fact, share a common set of political interests. Moreover, in addition to these problems, the first school conveniently ignores the demonstrated political and social behaviour of non-whites. In particular, it overlooks the activities of

49

some 2,000 ethnic minority voluntary associations in Britain, many, if not most, of which share a common set of policy concerns (Anwar 1991: 44; Cheetham 1988).

On the other hand, the second school of thought is also not without its difficulties. These problems begin, but by no means end, with the fact that this school views the location of ethnic minorities in the British political process through highly subjective and even normative lenses, the question of whether ethnic minorities share common political interests is never seriously examined, primarily because its central preoccupation is how to further these assumed common interests. In contrast to the first school, the second is cognizant that ethnic minority voluntary associations have proliferated during the past 20 years or so. Indeed, from this it extrapolates that non-whites in Britain are gradually cohering into a significant political force (Werbner 1991: 26–34). A possible counter-interpretation of this assumed linkage may be, of course, that the proliferation of ethnic minority associations furnishes evidence that, politically, non-whites are splintering rather than cohering. Moreover, one could reasonably criticize this perspective as naive. Despite numerous predictions over the last 20 years that a unifying, ethnic minority, umbrella political movement will eventually emerge, little progress toward this goal has actually been achieved to date (Studlar 1993: 21).

Despite its problems and contradictions, however, the second school of thought is more persuasive than the first, not least because its broad assumption that ethnic minorities share common political interests is supported by the political behaviour of non-whites, and particularly their voting behaviour. As Heath et al. argue:

> The political behaviour of blacks is not to be explained by their class situation.... They are much more inclined to the Labour Party than white voters in similar class situations, housing, local milieux, and so on.... Perception of group interests or processes of group identification are more plausible explanations.
>
> (Heath et al. 1991: 113)

Put simply, the long history of loyal support for the Labour Party by non-whites across age, class, gender and ethnic cohorts suggests that ethnic minorities *must* share considerable political interests because politically they behave as if they do (Messina 1989: 151–54).

The propensity of non-whites to vote Labour in local and general elections is well documented. Every ethnic minority voting survey that has been conducted since the 1970s verifies that non-whites prefer Labour to its principal electoral rival by an overwhelming margin.

Moreover, ethnic minorities exhibit only token support for Britain's minor political parties. In particular, the non-white Liberal Democratic vote has never exceeded 10 per cent in any general election since 1979 (see Table 3.1).

More importantly, the non-white vote is a specific ethnic vote; social class does not predict the political party preferences of non-white voters to nearly the same extent as their white counterparts (Welch and Studlar 1985). For example, Asian routine non-manual (C1) voters excepted, all social classes within the non-white electorate supported Labour by a ratio of more than three to one over other parties in the 1983 general election. In the 1987 general election no social class gave Labour less than 52 per cent or the Conservative Party more than 33 per cent of the vote. Within the lowest occupational grades (D, E), 9 out of 10 non-white electors in 1983 and more than 8 out of 10 in 1987 voted Labour (Messina 1989: 152–53). These electoral trends have continued into the 1990s. In the 1992 general election only 29 per cent of the ABC1 ethnic minority voters cast ballots for the Conservative Party, in contrast to at least 43 per cent of white voters. Conversely, 78 per cent of C2D ethnic voters endorsed Labour in 1992, as opposed to only a bare majority of whites (see Table 3.2).

The ethnic-specific character of non-white voting behaviour does not, of course, suggest that ethnic minorities in Britain are politically homogeneous. Nor does it demonstrate that non-whites collectively endorse a specific political or policy agenda. One might reasonably ask, what broad group in contemporary British society does cohere around a detailed political programme? However, what it does unambiguously indicate is that ethnic minorities are a well-defined political constituency, a political bloc that is firmly wedded to the Labour Party during good political times and bad, and through changes of Party leadership (Messina 1989: 150–77). Why ethnic minorities in

TABLE 3.1 Ethnic minority voting preferences, 1983–92: per cent.

| Party | Asians | | | | Afro-Caribbeans | | | |
|---|---|---|---|---|---|---|---|---|
| | 1983 | 1987 | 1992 | 1997* | 1983 | 1987 | 1992 | 1997* |
| Con | 9 | 23 | 11 | 25 | 7 | 6 | 8 | 8 |
| Lab | 81 | 67 | 77 | 70 | 88 | 86 | 85 | 86 |
| SDP/Lib/ Lib Dems | 9 | 10 | 10 | 4 | 5 | 7 | 6 | 4 |
| Other | — | — | 3 | 1 | — | — | 1 | 1 |

* Figures for 1997 do not show those not intending to vote, undecideds, etc. (22 per cent, Asians; 21 per cent, Afro-Caribbeans).

Sources: Harris poll, as reproduced in Messina (1989: 152); Ali and Percival (1993); MORI (1997).

TABLE 3.2 Ethnic minority voting preferences by class, 1987–92: per cent.

| Party | 1987 | | 1992 | |
|---|---|---|---|---|
| | ABC1 | C2D | ABC1 | C2D |
| Conservative | 31 | 16 | 29 | 8 |
| Labour | 51 | 65 | 54 | 78 |
| Alliance/Lib. Democrat | 5 | 5 | 12 | 9 |
| Other | 8 | 6 | 5 | 5 |
| Missing values | 7 | 8 | 0 | 0 |

Source: Ali and Percival (1993).

Britain behave as a political bloc is no great mystery. Indeed, as we will argue below, there are obvious structural and subjective incentives for non-whites to support Labour, despite the party's well-known political failings (Fitzgerald 1988). However, these incentives aside, it is intellectually disingenuous to deny that ethnic minorities in Britain share a broad set of special interests when a majority of non-white voters across class, generational, gender and ethnic cohorts endorses one political party, Labour, time and time again. Precisely what these shared political interests are is a question to which we will eventually turn our attention below.

## The elevation of ethnic minorities to political office

Despite the increasing attention paid to the collective political interests of non-whites in recent years, the primary focus of most scholars concerned with the political representation of ethnic minorities in Britain has been and continues to be the physical representation of non-whites in local and national politics and government. Indeed, in this regard, scholars across academic disciplines, normative viewpoints and methodological approaches agree substantially on two points: ethnic minorities are significantly underrepresented at all levels of British politics and government (Geddes 1995); and the underrepresentation of non-whites is a serious impediment to the achievement of racial political equality and the integration of ethnic minorities into British society as a whole (Fitzgerald 1984: 118, Fitzgerald 1990: 46, Norris and Lovenduski 1995: 237–48, Studlar and Welch 1992: 156–57).

There is, of course, no disputing that, at every level of government, relatively few ethnic minorities occupy elected office. For example, although the number of Asian and Afro-Caribbean local councillors has more than doubled during the past decade, the current 350 or so ethnic minority politicians across Britain comprise only 1.6 per cent of all local councillors, or some 3.9 per cent fewer than the percentage of ethnic minorities in the population as a whole (Geddes 1993: 43). Similarly, despite the successful and much celebrated elevation of six non-white parliamentary candidates to the House of Commons in 1992, followed by nine in 1997, Norris and Lovenduski estimate that ethnic minorities are underrepresented in the current Parliament by 30 MPs, assuming non-whites were represented in the Commons in proportion to their presence in the electorate (1995: 106).

What is the larger significance of the physical underrepresentation of ethnic minorities in government and politics? What are its implications for the representation of non-white political interests? The answers to these questions are far from obvious, in part because we have little evidence of the impact that ethnic minorities do have when they attain elected office (Nixon, Chapter 9, this volume; Norris and Lovenduski 1995: 224; Solomos and Back 1995: 200) but mostly because ethnic minorities have never been adequately represented in British politics and government. As a result, we can only speculate about the special influence 36 non-white MPs *might* have on the national political agenda or the collective political clout some 700 or 800 ethnic minority councillors *would* exert on the affairs of British local government.

Indeed, because the answers to these questions are not obvious, it is far from clear that the collective political interests of non-whites would be automatically advanced if 36 ethnic minority candidates were elevated to the House of Commons, or if 700–800 councillors were elected to local authorities across the country. It is not self-evident that the election of more ethnic minority candidates, irrespective of group identification and loyalty, ideological orientation, and political party affiliation would, on balance, accelerate the progress of collective ethnic minority political concerns. In fact, if the policy preferences of whites and non-whites are broadly similar, as some argue, then we can reasonably assume that the equitable inclusion of non-whites in British government would have little, if any, practical policy consequences or advantages for non-whites as a group. On the other hand, the greater physical presence of ethnic minorities in British local and national government might be important *symbolically*. It could, for example, encourage feelings of political efficacy and foster greater political activism among non-whites. However, it would not necessarily effect substantive political change favourable to ethnic minorities (Norris and Lovenduski 1995: 209–10).

If on the other hand, non-whites are a fairly coherent political constituency with important, shared political interests, the representative presence of ethnic minorities in British government could yield substantive political benefits for non-whites, provided that a number of additional conditions were met. First, non-white politicians would have to behave as a cohesive, parliamentary bloc. Ethnic minority politicians would have to act as agents or delegates of the larger non-white constituency and they would have to co-operate to promote the shared interests of this constituency (Birch 1979: 14). Secondly, non-white politicians would require numerous allies among white political elites (Crewe 1983: 220; Studlar 1993: 22). Even at the inflated numbers cited above, non-white political representatives would be dependent upon the goodwill and support of their more numerous white colleagues. Thirdly, and most important, non-white politicians would need an effective means by which to achieve their collective political goals. In particular, they would require an institutionalized political vehicle to articulate, aggregate, represent and implement their shared policy priorities. It seems reasonable to conclude that, in the absence of these three conditions, the election of a representative number of ethnic-minority politicians would probably have more symbolic value than practical political effect.

### Political representation through political party

With regard to the necessary political vehicle alluded to above, it is unambiguously clear that, among all other possible alternatives, the political party is the most important and effective option available to non-whites. In this vein, the arguments I offered in *Race and Party Competition* extolling the advantages of political parties for non-whites are as pertinent to the political conditions of the late 1990s as they were to the circumstances of the late 1980s:

> The election of an increasing ... number of non-whites to political office obviously constitutes progress in the integration of ethnic minorities into the mainstream of British political life. Without the elevation of non-whites to all levels of government, it is difficult to envision how ethnic minority interests can gain a secure place on the national and local public-policy agenda. However ... a tradition of strong political parties coupled with unitary and parliamentary government in Britain virtually requires that non-whites first become influential within the major political parties in order to effect meaningful policy change ... In Britain the power to effect policy change still primarily flows through the major political parties and, increasingly, it is power which is meaningfully exercised only at the level of national politics.
>
> (Messina 1989: 174–75)

Little has changed since 1989.[1] British government remains the quintessential paradigm of strong party government (Norton 1994: 109).

Within this model the Conservative and Labour Parties are still politically dominant and both parties remain highly centralized by the standards of American and continental European political parties and, hence, somewhat impenetrable to small, grassroots constituencies. As a result of these realities, the various political constituencies in Britain must work within the major political parties in order to achieve their political and policy objectives. The fact that non-whites are relatively few in number, not very politically visible nor particularly well organized at the national level, only makes this constituency all the more dependent upon political party to articulate and promote its collective interests.

### Political representation through Labour

For Britain's ethnic minorities, institutionalized political representation almost exclusively implies representation through the Labour Party. Neither the Conservatives nor the Liberal Democrats are as ideologically receptive to the interests (as opposed to the votes) of non-whites and, probably as a consequence, ethnic minorities have in turn historically demonstrated only modest interest in either of the two alternative parties.

### Non-whites and the Conservative Party

The indifference and/or explicit hostility of virtually every tier of and constituency within the Conservative Party to the interests of ethnic minorities is now so well documented that it would appear excessive to underscore the point with yet more empirical evidence (Fitzgerald 1984: 19–29; Gordon 1990: 175–90; Messina 1989: 125–49). Nevertheless, further evidence indeed appears to be necessary since, despite its preponderance, some scholars insist on perpetuating the fiction that the Conservative Party is becoming increasingly receptive to non-whites and sympathetic to the general concerns of this constituency (Bald 1989).

Consider, then, the data presented in Table 3.3, which is drawn from separate opinion surveys of Conservative parliamentarians conducted in 1969 (Frasure 1971: 206) and 1982 (Messina 1989: 129) as well as Conservative Party members in 1992 (Whiteley et al. 1994: 253). What the data unambiguously demonstrate are that Conservative political elites and grassroots members are hostile to the presence of non-whites in British society. How virulent is their racial hostility? Quite virulent, if the findings from a survey of Conservative Party members conducted by Whiteley et al. in 1992 can be taken to apply

TABLE 3.3 Conservative MPs' and party members' attitudes toward the repatriation of immigrants, 1969–92: per cent.

1969: Britain must completely halt all coloured immigration, including dependents, and encourage the repatriation of coloured persons now living here.

|                    | Agree | Disagree | Don't know |
| ------------------ | ----- | -------- | ---------- |
| Conservative MPs   | 38    | 56       | 6          |

1982: Do you favour, oppose, or in some circumstances favour, in others oppose, the voluntary repatriation of Britain's non-white residents?

|                    | Favour | Oppose | Some circumstances |
| ------------------ | ------ | ------ | ------------------ |
| Conservative MPs   | 42     | 26     | 32                 |

1992: A future Conservative government should encourage the repatriation of immigrants.

|                        | Agree | Disagree | Neither |
| ---------------------- | ----- | -------- | ------- |
| Conservative members   | 70    | 19       | 12      |

Sources: Frasure (1971: 206); Messina (1989: 129); Whiteley et al. (1994: 253).

across the whole Party. In their survey of Conservative members Whiteley et al. posed no fewer than 49 questions about "important" political issues. In response to these questions, 30 per cent or more of Conservative members "strongly agreed" on only four positions: immigration into Britain should be tightened (54%); the death penalty should be reintroduced for murder (36%); high income tax discourages hard work (33%); and immigrants should be encouraged to repatriate (32%) (Whiteley et al. 1994: 252–67). On no other issue was the Conservative membership more unified than on the need for tighter immigration controls. Ninety-one per cent agreed and only 4 per cent disagreed that Britain's already stringent immigration controls should be further tightened.

The results of Whiteley et al.'s 1992 survey of Conservative Party members come as no surprise to anyone familiar with the party's long history of antagonism toward non-whites. Previous opinion surveys of delegates to the Conservative Party's annual conference (Fitzgerald 1984) and Conservative parliamentary candidates (Anwar 1984) have yielded more or less similar findings. Despite the empirical evidence to the contrary, Norris and Lovenduski discovered that 44 per cent of Conservative MPs in 1992 believed that Conservative ethnic minority parliamentary candidates lost the party votes (1995: 235).

This seamless opinion-survey evidence of hostility or indifference toward non-whites among Conservatives is buttressed by persistent anecdotal accounts of racism within the Conservative Party at the sub-national level, where even Afro-Caribbean and Asian Conservative Party activists are sometimes the targets of prejudice (Runnymede Trust 1994: 7). Indeed, although the overt racial conflict precipitated by John Taylor's selection as a Conservative parliamentary candidate for Cheltenham in 1990 and his subsequent defeat in the 1992 general election is the most conspicuous and publicly scrutinized example of recent Conservative prejudice at the local level, it was clearly not a rare or isolated incident (Solomos and Back 1995: 113–28). Given this backdrop, is it any wonder that the fear of immigration persists as one of the most important political issues at the Conservative grassroots and only 1 per cent of Conservative Party members are non-white (Whiteley et al. 1994: 48)?

## Non-whites and the Liberal Democratic Party

Unlike the Conservative Party, the Liberal Democrats have a long and predominantly positive history with non-whites and issues of special concern to this constituency. The Liberals opposed, for example, legislative initiatives by both Conservative and Labour governments to restrict New Commonwealth immigration during the 1960s and 1970s. During this period the party consistently supported the construction and enforcement of effective anti-discrimination statutes (Taylor 1980: 107–14). In the current decade the Liberal Democratic leadership has vigorously defended the implementation of positive discrimination policies in public-sector employment and it has specifically promised, if and when it assumes national office, to repeal the racially discriminatory 1981 British Nationality Act and "give statutory force to the Commission for Racial Equality's Code of Practice to ensure that all employers implement equal opportunities in selection, recruitment, promotion and normal working practices" (as quoted in Amin and Richardson 1992: 54). On the basis of this progressive record, it is difficult to disagree with Studlar's conclusion of more than a decade ago that the "Liberals have consistently been the most favourable toward racial minorities of the three traditional parties" (1985: 6).

Why, then, have non-white voters historically been approximately half as likely as white voters to support the Liberal Democratic Party and its predecessors? Political geography and social class have undoubtedly influenced the political preferences and allegiances of Britain's ethnic minorities in a manner that has consistently worked against the establishment of a strong political bond between non-whites and the Liberal Democrats (Fitzgerald and Layton-Henry 1986: 114, McAllister and Studlar 1984). Historically, ethnic minorities have been residentially concentrated in conurbations where Labour has been politically dominant and the Liberal Democratic Party politically or organizationally weak. As Fitzgerald argues the point:

> A cycle, in fact, has built up which is likely to be broken with difficulty. Short of significant changes in the socio-economic and geographical distribution of the black population, it appears that the ... [Conservative and Liberal Democratic Parties], ... [are] at a disadvantage in making overtures to black voters ....
>
> (Fitzgerald, 1988: 21–22)

However, as powerful as these structural variables are, they fail to explain two phenomena adequately: the unwillingness of more non-whites over time to support the Liberal Democrats in general elections (Table 3.1), despite the significant expansion, since the early 1980s, of the overall local Liberal Democratic vote and the number of Liberal Democratic local councillors across the country, including London (Butler and Butler 1994: 443–49); and the stubborn reluctance of ABC1 ethnic minority voters to defect from Labour to the Liberal Democrats (Ali and Percival 1993).

Both of these phenomena can probably be explained by several subjective factors. First of all, it is not clear that non-whites are generally aware of the Liberal Democratic Party's progressive record on immigration and race-related issues. In an opinion survey conducted in 1991, for example, 2 per cent of Asians identified the Liberal Democrats as the "party with the best policy on immigration", a figure no higher among the 17 per cent of Asians who were declared Liberal Democratic voters (Harris, 1991). One possible explanation for this apparent paradox is that the party has not succeeded, for a variety of reasons, in propagating its liberal policy positions among ethnic minority voters (Gifford, Foreword). Alternatively, fearing a possible backlash among prejudiced white voters, the Liberal Democratic Party has not perhaps made committed and sustained efforts to advertise widely its race and immigration policies or to establish links with ethnic minority communities (Solomos and Back 1995: 93).

Secondly, as a party that has historically attracted a substantial percentage of its electoral support from disillusioned "protest" voters and from transient supporters who are *not* well-informed about the party's established policy commitments, the Liberal Democrats may be a less appropriate political option for non-whites than whites (Himmelweit et al. 1985: 159). Classic protest voters are, after all, voters considerably disenchanted with one or both of the major political parties. As a consequence of their disenchantment, these electors are politically available to the Liberal Democrats or other minor parties. It is quite possible, indeed probable given the consistent weakness of the non-white Liberal Democratic vote, that non-whites are relatively satisfied with one or both of Britain's major political parties and, as a result, not readily disposed to defect to the Liberal Democrats. For 90 per cent of ethnic minorities the Liberal Democrats may simply be politically irrelevant.

Thirdly, despite its official national policies, the Liberal Democratic Party and its predecessors do not have an unblemished record on race-related issues (Fitzgerald 1990: 23). Specifically, the party is not seamless in its endorsement of progressive policies. As Amin and Richardson observe:

> On the one hand there is the national leadership with its historic commitments to diversity and tolerance .... One of the features of this outlook is a commitment to introducing a Bill of Rights, as a way of protecting the freedoms of individuals and minorities.
>
> On the other hand, however, local parties sometimes bid for votes from disaffected Conservatives or Labour voters who have absolutely no sympathy for liberalism's core values. There is a strong feeling in East London, for example ... that Liberal Democrats are willing to play the race card by colluding with ... racist views.
>
> (Amin and Richardson 1992: 52)

It is impossible to know how much, if at all, the Liberal Democratic Party's inconsistencies have depressed non-white support for the party. Certainly the contradictions within the Labour and Conservative Parties have been more serious and transparent. However, in contrast to the major political parties, the Liberal Democratic Party may labour under the handicap that it must be consistently and unambiguously progressive on race-related issues. In the absence of a strong pull toward the Liberal Democrats among non-whites, any inconsistencies in the party's progressive race-related record may be disproportionately damaging to its efforts to attract ethnic minority electoral support.

Finally, in addition to the three subjective factors already cited, it is highly likely that the Liberal Democrats' near obsession with policy goals such as the acceleration of European integration and reform of Britain's electoral system is responsible for the party's failure to make significant inroads into the non-white vote.[2] It is not necessarily the case that most non-whites oppose these goals but, rather, both objectives are very distant from the individual and collective concerns of ethnic minorities, as they are also distant from the priorities of most white voters (Studlar, 1986: 170). However, unlike the white electorate which is economically diverse and, specifically, more middle class than the non-white electorate, ethnic minorities are fairly homogeneous socio-economically and overwhelmingly working class. For this predominantly working-class constituency the Liberal Democratic Party's inordinate attention to European and political reform issues can hardly be a positive attraction. On the contrary, it is most probably an electoral liability.

In sum, then, there are several conspicuous, subjective reasons why the Liberal Democratic Party is not the political choice of most of Britain's ethnic minorities, in addition to the well-known structural explanations of class and political geography. Individually and collectively these factors will likely keep most non-white voters at a political arm's length from the Liberal Democratic Party for the indefinite future.

## Non-whites and the Labour Party

In contrast to the Liberal Democratic Party and, to a lesser extent, the Conservative Party, which approach their respective relationships with Britain's ethnic minorities at a decided disadvantage because of the structural variables of class and political geography, Labour, as I argued earlier, is positively advantaged in its relationship with non-whites by these same variables. While recognizing this fact, it would nevertheless be wrong to conclude that subjective factors do not play an equal, if not more important, role in explaining the overwhelming support for Labour among non-white voters.

Probably the most important subjective factor is Labour's advocacy of policies that target the collective social and political condition of ethnic minorities. Since the late 1970s, the Labour Party has adopted numerous policy commitments that are transparently intended to privilege the special concerns and further the collective interests of non-whites. These commitments have periodically included the passage of a new Race Equality Act, which would broaden the definition of indirect discrimination and introduce a new system of contract compliance for all organizations receiving government contracts or public money; repeal of the racially-discriminatory 1981 British Nationality Act and the Carriers Liability Act; and expansion of the investigative powers and authority of the Commission for Racial Equality. What is especially pertinent about these progressive commitments is the fact that they have been made by a political party that is now in government. In other words, these fairly visible promises have been extended by a political party that is expected, sooner or later, to implement them. Consequently, Labour's public promises are undoubtedly more credible and inspire greater confidence among non-whites than similar commitments made by the Liberal Democratic Party. This conclusion is at least partially supported by the opinion survey evidence, which indicates Labour as the preferred party on the immigration issue among Asians by a 22 to one margin over the Liberal Democrats (Harris 1991).

Another significant variable in Labour's favour is that it has clearly established itself since the late 1970s as a party ideologically inclined to identify with non-whites and ethnic minority interests, especially at the national level. Consider, for example, the survey data in Table 3.4 which indicate the fairly liberal attitudes on the part of Labour elites and members towards the issues of non-white repatriation and immigration restrictions. Consider, too, the broad political and social contexts in which these progressive attitudes are held and articulated. Ethnic minorities have historically comprised only a fraction of the overall national electorate. Contrary to the argument of some analysts (Community Relations Commission 1975, Ali and Percival, 1993),

TABLE 3.4 Labour MPs' and party members' attitudes toward the repatriation of immigrants and immigration restrictions, 1969–92 per cent

1969: Britain must completely halt all coloured immigration, including dependents, and encourage the repatriation of coloured persons now living here

|  | Agree | Disagree | Don't know |
|---|---|---|---|
| Labour MPs | 6 | 92 | 2 |

1982: Do you favour, oppose, or in some circumstances favour, in others oppose, the voluntary repatriation of Britain's non-white residents?

|  | Favour | Oppose | Some circumstances |
|---|---|---|---|
| Labour MPs | 2 | 81 | 17 |

1982: Are Britain's present immigration statutes too lenient, too restrictive, or reasonably fair and balanced?

|  | Too lenient | Too restrictive | Fair |
|---|---|---|---|
| Labour MPs | 6 | 68 | 25 |

1990: Restrictions on immigration into Britain are too tight and should be eased

|  | Agree | Disagree | Neither |
|---|---|---|---|
| Labour members | 43 | 41 | 16 |

Sources: Messina (1989: 129); Seyd et al. (1992: 125).

non-white voters have had little, if any, net positive impact on Labour's electoral fortunes in British general elections over time (Messina 1989: 151–60). Non-whites as a group have only modest political resources. No national organization or strong, political pressure groups exist to promote their collective political interests. Moreover, racial hostility toward ethnic minorities is pervasive in white British society (NOP, 1991) and, from time to time, such hostility finds virulent political expression (Messina 1989: 103–25). Yet, despite these numerous and powerful disincentives, Labour elites continue to advocate policies that respect the special social position and political claims of Britain's ethnic minorities (Messina 1989: 132, 171). Labour's ideological heritage as a party of the working class, the socio economically disadvantaged, the politically weak and the socially marginalized reinforces the structural bonds between the party and non-whites alluded to above.

Moreover, Labour's ideological receptivity to non-whites extends beyond its public rhetoric and manifesto commitments. It also manifests itself in the party's inclusion of ethnic minorities among its formal members and its adoption of non-white parliamentary candidates and local authority representatives. For example, ethnic minorities currently comprise 3 per cent of all Labour Party members. While smaller than the proportion of non-whites in the overall electorate, this percentage is three times that of non-white members within the Conservative Party (Seyd and Whiteley 1992: 37).

This base of non-white Labour members has more than symbolic value, moreover, as it is ultimately the pool from which the party chooses its candidates for local government and national parliamentary elections. Indeed, it was from this foundation of non-white members that Labour selected 4 per cent of all its parliamentary candidates in the 1992 general election. This compares with only 1 per cent of Conservative and 2 per cent of Liberal Democratic parliamentary candidates. Five of the six parliamentary candidates elected to the House of Commons in 1992 sat on Labour's backbenches. All nine elected after 1997 are Labour members. The tremendous disparity between the number of Labour and Conservative and Liberal Democratic parliamentarians nationally is replicated at the local level. Of the entire universe of ethnic minority local councillors in Britain, approximately 85 per cent represent Labour, 8 per cent the Conservatives and only 5 per cent the Liberal Democrats. A survey of local councillors in English Metropolitan Districts conducted in 1992 revealed that 32 of 33 sitting Asian and Afro-Caribbean councillors represented the Labour Party (Geddes 1993).

As argued previously, none of the above evidence suggests that Labour's past or current record on race and immigration issues is above reproach. Labour's critics within the Asian and Afro-Caribbean communities are numerous and, on the whole, their complaints about the party are valid. However, to ignore or underestimate the extent to which the Labour Party has significantly discarded the negative policy baggage it adopted during the heyday of the bipartisan "racial consensus" (1964–75) and, since the late 1970s, forged a more positive and progressive relationship with Britain's ethnic minorities is to deny the reality and, ultimately, to forgo the capacity to comprehend the strong bonds that currently tie Labour to its non-white political constituency, and vice versa. In short, the Labour Party mostly remains the political party *of* non-whites during the 1990s, because it is the party ideologically, politically and most publicly *for* non-whites.

## THE POLITICAL INTERESTS OF ETHNIC MINORITIES

What, specifically, do Britain's ethnic minorities expect from Labour? The numerous scholars who have argued that non-whites are generally concerned with many of the same issues as whites are certainly correct. Not surprisingly, non-whites consistently rank the issues of crime, education, the economy, unemployment and housing highest on their list of immediate priorities (Ali and Percival 1993). These are, after all, the core domestic issues of British politics and they are particularly pertinent for the lower socio-economic classes, which incorporate most ethnic minorities. However, the concerns of non-whites are not exhausted by those cited on the aforementioned list. Rather, in contrast to most whites, ethnic minorities are also concerned with several other major issue areas that fall, indirectly or directly, within the purview of politics. These issues include: the general social and racial climate; the condition and effectiveness of the law with regard to racial discrimination; and the application of immigration rules.

Table 3.5 allows a small insight into the differences of viewpoint between whites and ethnic minorities in these issue areas, differences that surely matter for politics. As the data in Table 3.5 illustrate, non-whites are far more tolerant than whites of racially-integrated residential patterns (3 to 2), significantly more enthusiastic about stricter laws barring racial discrimination (5 to 3) and much more supportive of a liberal immigration regime (3 to 1). To be sure, the data in Table 3.5 reveal little about the intensity of these opinions. In particular, nothing in Table 3.5 contradicts the assumption that explicit issues of race and immigration rank below those of the economy, employment, housing, crime, etc. in the minds of most non-whites. However, this caveat does not imply that race-related issues matter

TABLE 3.5    White and ethnic minority attitudes toward race-related issues

1. I would be happy to have people from a different group living next door to me.

|  | Whites | Blacks | Asians |
|---|---|---|---|
| Agree | 62 | 91 | 93 |
| Disagree | 20 | 6 | 5 |
| Neither | 16 | 3 | 3 |

2. Do you think the laws against racial discrimination in Britain are too tough, about right, or not [tough] enough?

|  | Whites | Blacks | Asians |
|---|---|---|---|
| Too tough | 11 | 6 | 6 |
| About right | 48 | 22 | 32 |
| Not tough enough | 31 | 61 | 45 |
| Don't know | 10 | 10 | 17 |

3. Do you think the government should change the [immigration] rules to make it *easier* for any of these groups to come to Britain?

|  | Whites | Blacks | Asians |
|---|---|---|---|
| West Indians | 2 | 16 | 3 |
| Indians and Pakistanis | 2 | 9 | 14 |
| Hong Kong Chinese | 5 | 7 | 3 |
| South African Whites | 4 | 3 | 2 |
| Western Europeans | 4 | 4 | 2 |
| Eastern Europeans | 4 | 4 | 3 |
| Old Commonwealth | 7 | 11 | 3 |
| Arabs | 1 | 2 | 2 |
| All of them | 9 | 25 | 28 |
| None of them | 70 | 33 | 37 |
| Don't know | 6 | 16 | 15 |

Source: NOP (1991).

little to ethnic minorities or that such issues are politically irrelevant. On the contrary, issues of race and immigration do matter very much. In an opinion survey conducted by Harris in 1991, for example, 37 per cent of Asian respondents cited "racial attacks" as the most important issue and 17 per cent cited "immigration". In an opinion survey carried out in 1992, Ali and Percival discovered that non-whites were three times more likely than whites (13 per cent to 4 per cent) to cite race/immigration as an "important" issue (Ali and Percival 1993). Not surprisingly, 58 per cent of all white and non-white voters who cited "race/immigration" as one of the three most important issues in the 1992 general election campaign voted for the Labour Party.

Moreover, in addition to the aforementioned issues, the escalating demands by Britain's ethnic minority population for greater direct political representation and opportunities for political expression cannot be ignored. Although these demands are obviously most salient within the "talking professions" and the non-white middle class, they nevertheless comprise part, if only a modest part, of the general constellation of non-white political interests. It is virtually impossible to know how important the issues of political representation and expression are within the non-white population, since public opinion survey researchers never ask ethnic minority respondents to consider their salience. As a consequence, these issues do not appear on their list of non-white political priorities. However, this glaring oversight of survey research has not inhibited a large number of scholars from concluding that issues of political representation and expression are becoming increasingly important to Britain's ethnic minorities (Saggar 1992: 160–71; Solomos 1989: 140–59; Solomos and Back 1995: 67–92). The long-established Black Sections movement and the more recently founded Black Socialist Society within the Labour Party and the birth of the independent Islamic Party and the Fourth Party, and the Anti-Racist Alliance (ARA) are but a few concrete expressions of the growing concern among non-whites about their collective political status and location in British politics (Amin and Richardson 1992: 34; Runnymede Trust 1994: 4–5).

## CONCLUSIONS

The definition, articulation and promotion of the collective interests of non-whites within Britain's party system is, as I argued earlier, predominantly an issue and a challenge for the Labour Party. For the structural and subjective reasons alluded to above, Labour is uniquely placed to represent the collective interests of non-whites and to accelerate their physical integration into formal British politics. The extent to which the Labour Party remains committed to and ultimately succeeds in fulfilling these ambitions remains to be seen, of course. On this score, the reader may recall that the analysis in *Race and Party Competition* was not entirely optimistic. Specifically, I argued that electorally competitive two-partism, a condition that currently prevails at the national level,

"does not automatically ensure that the interests of even sizeable minorities will be represented politically; even under seemingly favourable circumstances, the concerns of minorities

in a two-party system might be 'aggregated' but not necessarily 'articulated".'

(Messina, 1989: 102).

For broad electoral reasons and under specific pressures from illiberal
white voters, Labour's leadership has perhaps become more timid in
advertising its previous promises and fulfilling its stated commitments
to non-white voters as it progressed toward national power. However,
political timidity does not necessarily exclude the possibility of effective action. Nor is the fear of a white backlash likely to motivate
Labour to disown its loyal non-white constituency. To put the issue
simply, the late-1990s are not the mid-1960s (Messina 1989: 21–52).
Labour's current relations with non-whites, however imperfect and
tempestuous they may be, are probably more stable than any the party
enjoys with any other group or political constituency in British
society.

Indeed, if anything, these relations have only deepened with time, in
part as a consequence of the tremendous investment of political energy
and loyalty an entire generation of ethnic-minority political activists
have made in the Labour Party (Shukra Chapter 6 in this volume), as
well as the not inconsequential investment the party has made in this
unique political constituency. With respect to this mutual investment,
it would be folly to underestimate the positive sea change that has
occurred over time in the political leverage of non-white members and
activists within the Labour Party, especially at the local level (Solomos
and Back 1995: 171–201). To acknowledge that ethnic minorities now
enjoy greater, albeit limited, influence within the Labour Party than
thirty or twenty years previously is not to deny that Labour could do
more to accommodate the concerns and promote the shared interests
of non-whites. Nor is it to assume that Labour's relations with its
ethnic minority constituency can and necessarily will only improve.
Rather, it is simply to recognize that, despite current tensions, ethnic
minorities are less the "object" of Labour's policies and electoral strategies than they once were. The entry of increasing numbers of non-
white members into the Labour Party (*The Economist* 1995: 33–34)
combined with the political advance of a small but expanding group
to positions of prominence within its parliamentary and non-
parliamentary wings have strengthened the political bonds between
Labour and non-whites. The interests and influence of ethnic minorities as a collective political constituency are to an unprecedented
degree now structurally embedded in the Labour Party and its policies.

Whether Labour's political relationship with Britain's ethnic minorities grow stronger or less strong in the long-term may ultimately
depend less upon the policies or racial posture of its political rivals

than the trajectory of the collective interests of non-whites. Specifically, the question may be reducible to one of whether or not Labour can find the right balance to satisfy the expectations of non-whites both to be well represented in terms of policy outcomes and to be properly included physically in politics and government. As argued above, the two objectives are not the same. Indeed, since the late 1970s, the Labour Party has been much more conscientious and successful in promoting policies, at the local and national levels, that specifically benefit non-whites, than in integrating ethnic minorities into the party's decision-making machinery and British politics as a whole (Messina 1989: 160–71). While, for the reasons cited above, the Conservative and Liberal Democratic Parties cannot compete very well with Labour on the plane of implementing policies specifically framed to benefit ethnic minorities, they can compete more effectively in elevating greater numbers of non-whites to positions of political prominence. The second task is more or less a matter of political will and selective individual recruitment (Norris and Lovenduski, 1995: 237-48). The first task also requires political will, but it is, above all, an issue of ideological commitment, a plane of party competition on which the Labour Party enjoys a decided comparative party-political advantage.

## NOTES

1. The relative stability of British constitutional arrangements through the late 1990s is, of course, subject to future change. The commitment of the Labour Party to devolve considerable political authority to regional assemblies in Scotland and Wales could, for example, alter the political context and reshape the political interests and strategies of ethnic minorities.
2. I am grateful to Shamit Saggar for raising the issue that some ethnic minority activitists are currently emphasizing the importance of the European Union in their larger campaign for equality. Whether or not this campaign ultimately succeeds remains to be seen.

## REFERENCES

Ali, A. and G. Percival 1993. Race and representation: ethnic minorities and the 1992 elections. London: Commission for Racial Equality.
Amin, K. and R. Richardson 1992. *Politics for All: equality, culture and the general election 1992.* London: Runnymede Trust.

Anwar, M. 1984 *Ethnic Minorities and the 1983 General Election*. London: Commission for Racial Equality.

Anwar, M. 1991 The context of leadership: migration, settlement and racial discrimination. In *Black and Ethnic Leaderships: the culture dimensions of political action*, P. Werbner and M. Anwar (eds). London: Routledge.

Bald, S. R. 1989. The south Asian presence in British electoral politics. *New Community* 15 (4), 537–48.

Ball, W. and J. Solomos (eds) 1990. *Race and Local Politics*. Basingstoke: Macmillan.

Birch, A. H. 1979. *Representative and Responsible Government*, London: Allen and Unwin.

Butler, D. and G. Butler 1994. *British Political Facts*. London: Macmillan.

Cheetham, J. 1988. Ethnic associations in Britain. In *Ethinic Associations and Welfare State: services to immigrants in five countries*, Jenkins, S. (ed.). New York: Columbia University Press.

Community Relations Commission 1975. *Participation of Ethnic Minorities in the General Election of October 1974*. London: Community Relation Commission.

Crewe, I. 1983. Representation and ethnic minorities in Britain. In *Ethnic Pluralism and Public Policy: achieveing equality in the United States and Britain*, N. Glazer and K. Young, (eds). London: Heinemann.

*The Economist* 1995. Old Tricks and New Faces. 9 September 33–34.

Fitzgerald, M. 1984. *Political Parties and Black People: representation, participation and exploitation*. London: Runnymede Trust.

Fitzgerald, M. 1987. *Black People and Party Politics in Britain*. London: Runnymede Trust.

Fitzgerald, M. 1988. There is no alternative … black people and the Labour Party. *Social Studies Review* 4 (1) 20–3.

Fitzgerald, M. 1990. The emergence of black councillors and MPs in Britain: some underlying questions. In *Black Politics in Britain*, Harry Goulbourne (ed.). Aldershot: Avebury.

Fitzgerald, M. and Z. Layton-Henry 1986. Opposition parties and race policies, 1979–83. In *Race, Government and Politics in Britain*, Z. Layton-Henry & P. B. Rich (eds). London: Macmillan.

Frasure, R. C. 1971. Constituency racial composition and the attitudes of British MPs. *Comparative Politics* 3 (1) 201–10.

Geddes, A. 1993. Asian and Afro-Caribbean representation in elected local government in England and Wales. *New Community* 20 (1) 43–57.

Geddes, A. 1995. The "logic" of positive action? Ethnic minority representation in Britain after the 1992 general election. *Party Politics* 1 (2) 275–85.

Gordon, P. 1990. A dirty war: the new right and local authority antiracism in *Race and Local Politics*, W. Ball & J. Solomos (eds). Basingstoke: Macmillan.

Goulbourne, H. (ed.) 1990. *Black Politics in Britain*. Aldershot: Avebury.

Harris Research Centre 1991. Asian Poll 1991. Richmond: The Harris Research Centre.

Heath, A. et al. 1991. *Understanding Political Change: the British voter 1964–87*: Oxford: Pergamon Press.

Himmelweit, H. T. et al. 1985. *How Voters Decide*. Milton Keynes: Open University Press.

Layton-Henry, Z. 1992. *The Politics of Immigration*. Oxford: Blackwell.

NOP 1991. Runnymede Trust poll. London: NOP Social and Political.

Norris, P. and J. Lovenduski. 1995. *Political Recruitment: gender, race and class in the British parliament*. Cambridge: Cambridge University Press.

Norton, P. 1994. *The British Polity*, 3rd edn. New York: Longman.

McAllister, I. and D. T. Studlar 1984. The electoral geography of immigrant groups in Britain. *Electoral Studies* 3 (2) 139–50.

Messina, A. M. 1989. *Race and Party Competition in Britain*. Oxford: Clarendon (Oxford University) Press.

MORI 1997. "Asian voting: preliminary results". Unpublished briefing notes, February 1997.

Mullard, C. 1973. *Black Britain*. London: Allen and Unwin.

Runnymede Trust 1994. The Runnymede Bulletin 280 (November).

Saggar, S. 1992. *Race and Politics in Britain*. Hemel Hempstead: Harvester Wheatsheaf.

Seyd, P. and P. Whiteley 1992. *Labour's Grassroots: the politics of party membership*. Oxford: Clarendon (Oxford University) Press.

Solomos, J. 1989. *Race and Racism in Contemporary Britain*. Basingstoke: Macmillan.

Solomos, J. and L. Back 1995. *Race, Politics and Social Change*, London: Routledge.

Studlar, D. T. 1985. Waiting for the catastrophe: race and the political agenda in Britain. *Patterns of Prejudice* 19 (1) 3–15.

Studlar, D. T. 1986. Non-white policy preferences, political participation and the political agenda in Britain. In *Race, Government and Politics in Britain*, Z. Layton-Henry and P. B. Rich (eds). London: Macmillan.

Studlar, D. T. 1993. Ethnic minority groups, agenda setting and policy borrowing in Britain. In *Minority Group Influence: agenda setting, formulation and public policy*, P. D. McClain. (ed.). Greenwood, Conn.: Greenwood Press.

Studlar, D. T. and Z. Layton-Henry 1990. Non-white minority access to the political agenda in Britain. *Policy Studies Review* 9 (2) 273–93.

Studlar, D. T. and S. Welch 1992. Voting for minority candidates in local British and American elections. In *Ethnic and Racial Minorities in Advanced Industrial Democracies*, A. M. Messina et al. (eds). Westport, Conn.: Greenwood Press.

Taylor, S. 1980. The Liberal Party and immigration control: a study in policy deviance. *New Community* 8 (1) 107–14.

Welch, S. and D. T. Studlar 1985. The impact of race on political behaviour in Britain. *British Journal of Political Science* 15 (4) 528–39.

Werbner, P. 1991. Black and ethnic leaderships in Britain: a theoretical overview. In *Black and Ethnic Leaderships: the cultural dimensions of political action*, P. Werbner and M. Anwar (eds). London: Routledge.

Whiteley, P. et al. 1994. *True Blues: the politics of Conservative Party membership*. Oxford: Clarendon (Oxford University) Press.

# PART TWO

# Political parties and "race politics"

CHAPTER FOUR

# Ethnic minority participation and representation in the British electoral system

## *Michel Le Lohé*

The Census of 1991 indicated that the ethnic minorities accounted for 5.5 per cent of the population of Great Britain. This same land mass (which excludes Northern Ireland) elects 84 members to the European Parliament, 641 members to the Westminster Parliament and almost 25,000 persons to serve as representatives on the principal local government authorities. If the ethnic minorities were to be represented exclusively by members of their own communities then one would expect that there would be about five MEPs and 35 MPs whose origins were either Asian or black. The reality is that there are no MEPs and only nine MPs with any claim to membership of the ethnic minority communities. In terms of this kind of representation then the ethnic minorities are grossly underrepresented.

There is, however, a striking difference in Asian representation at the local government level. In the seven local authorities outside London where the Asian population exceeds 10 per cent, Asians provide 13 per cent of all councillors. This is just 1 per cent lower than the average Asian population in these authorities – thus the representation is almost exactly proportionate. It is, however, not proportionate in the partisan sense since 64 of these 65 councillors are Labour. The pattern of Afro-Caribbean representation is similarly overwhelmingly Labour, but the level significantly lower.

The chapters in this book by Adolino and Geddes give further insights into Asian and black representation in local government and the remarkable level of Asian representation at this level is considered in detail later in this chapter. It remains true that the ethnic minority populations, like many other groups in society, are not proportionately present as representatives in the Parliaments at Strasbourg and Westminster. So far as participation is concerned, it is also true that all members of the ethnic minority communities are, with few exceptions, able to vote in all the elections which take place in Britain. This has considerable significance and there is a consequent leverage in electoral politics which adds greatly to the influences exerted, outside the electoral system, through various lobbying and pressure group activities. In fact one of the impressive features of British electoral politics is the extent to which some members of the ethnic minority communities have become politically active and the degree to which those communities have been turning out at the polling booths.

## REPRESENTATION IN THE HOUSE OF COMMONS

Prior to the General Election of 1987 there were no ethnic minority Members of the House of Commons. It is conceded that before that time three Bombay-born Parsees had been elected, but those who stood after World War II initially had no success whatsoever despite the growing ethnic minority electorate. There was a major setback when, in 1970, Dr David Pitt, a respected member of the Greater London Council, lost an apparently safe Labour seat at Clapham. The swing against him was 10.2 per cent, far higher than the average anti-Labour swing of 4.1 per cent in the other 41 Inner London constituencies and well beyond their range, which was between 2.1 per cent and 6.7 per cent. Prejudice amongst white voters lost a good Labour candidate a fairly safe Labour seat.

David Pitt's misfortune worked against the adoption of ethnic minority candidates for it could be quoted as an argument (or an excuse) for not selecting them. It would have been in the interests of those promoting the adoption of black and Asian candidates to deny the "Pitt effect" but that would also have been to deny the existence of racial prejudice. The secrecy of the ballot protects the bigot from exposure.

Between 1970 and 1983 none of the three main parties adopted ethnic minority candidates for even marginal parliamentary seats, though they did adopt one or two for hopeless contests, and the numbers adopted began to rise. In 1979 their total was five, but in 1983 it was boosted to 18, with 17 in hopeless contests, but one in what was classified, notionally, as a marginal. It was notional because boundaries had been redrawn, creating the completely new seat of

Hertfordshire West for which an electoral history was simulated to assess it as a Labour marginal (BBC/ITN 1983: 80). The GLC councillor Paul Boateng was adopted, but this was Labour's worst election for half a century and the Labour marginal proved to be, in reality, a safe Conservative seat. Whilst all Labour candidates lost votes and the simulation lacked the certainty of an actual result, it again seemed that Mr Boateng had fared rather worse than expected. He came third and the swing, albeit notional, of 12.8 per cent against him compared unfavourably with that of 6.8 per cent in the remainder of Hertfordshire. It seemed clear that if there were to be successful candidates they would need to be adopted for safe seats.

The main parties are sometimes criticised for not adopting ethnic minority candidates in safe seats but there are two reasons why these criticisms are not justified. First the selectors in the constituencies are, to a great degree, autonomous and there are few circumstances where the national leadership can impose candidates. Secondly, on average only 59 incumbents choose to retire at each general election (Norris and Lovenduski 1995: 187) and opportunities for "new blood" are limited.

The breakthrough came in 1987 with three black candidates adopted by Labour for safe seats and an Asian, Keith Vaz, standing for the marginal Leicester East. Two of the black candidates had been adopted following the deselection of sitting white Labour Members at Hackney North and Tottenham whilst the third, Brent South, selected Paul Boateng. These three were successful, although there was a small loss of votes which, because these were thoroughly safe seats, had no effect on the outcome.

Leicester East, however, was not safe for Labour, yet their share of the poll and the size of the vote rose significantly more than that in other urban East Midland constituencies where the Labour candidate was white. Keith Vaz received a share of the poll which was 5.3 per cent greater than the model of comparable constituencies would suggest (Le Lohé 1989: 168). The most plausible explanation for this success is that Keith Vaz benefited from an increased level of participation by Asian electors (approximately a quarter of the total), because the Labour candidate was a particularly strong one and he was also Asian. Support organised by the Asian community more than compensated for any possible loss amongst white voters and produced a highly significant gain for Mr Vaz and the Labour Party.

The proposition then suggests itself that higher rates of participation by the ethnic minorities may be achieved with ethnic minority candidates, which may compensate for white voter prejudice against them. Clearly one element in this equation will be the relative sizes of the white and the ethnic minority communities. Prejudice will have a greater impact, where the electorate is overwhelmingly white, but where there is a significant non-white electorate the impact of prejudice is greatly reduced and there may be a substantial and compensatory effect.

This proposition is supported by the results of the General Election of 1992. On this occasion the three black Labour winners in safe seats were joined by Piara Khabra following the deselection of Sid Bidwell at Ealing Southall. These four were successful and, additionally, Mr Vaz's 1987 margin of 3.4 per cent increased to a very safe 22.8 per cent. The sixth ethnic minority candidate who succeeded was the Conservative Niranjan Deva who had been selected for the safe vacancy at Brentford and Isleworth. The swing to Labour at Brentford was somewhat greater than in comparable constituencies and this is probably explained by white prejudice, but the seat was safe enough and the Conservatives had their first Asian MP since Sir Mancherjee Bhownagree won in 1900.

The proposition is also supported by the performance of two losers in marginal seats. At Cheltenham the Conservatives adopted a black barrister in a seat that would be lost with a swing of only 4 per cent and which had an ethnic minority population of only 2 per cent. The ethnic minority population at Langbaurgh in Cleveland was less than 1 per cent but Labour needed a swing of only 2 per cent to reverse the 1987 result. Since 1987 the incumbent Conservative had died and Ashok Kumar won the seat for Labour at the by-election in November 1991. Labour claimed that the Conservatives emphasised the race of the Labour candidate (*The Guardian* 9 November 1991) and Dr Kumar himself said that he was sure his colour had lost him votes in the by-election (*The Times* 9 November 1991). When it came to the General Election of April 1992 Dr Kumar performed less well than the average Labour candidate (compared with 1987) and failed in this marginal, whilst John Taylor performed less well than the average Conservative similarly failing to hold that seat.

Finally, the pattern of steady growth continued with the results of the 1997 General Election. In this election, all five of Labour's ethnic minority incumbents were re-elected, in each case extending already strong winning majorities. In the case of some such as Grant, Boateng and Abbott, larger than average swings (within Great London) to Labour were recorded, indicating either a positive incumbency factor or the absence of any racial lialibity factor. These five were joined by three newcomers, one of whom, Kumar, had briefly served between 1991 and 1992 as a Labour member. The post-1997 total therefore stands at nine MPs. The Labour monopoly was the result of the dismal performance of Nirj Deva, the only ethnic minority Tory candidate defending a notional majority, and the marked absence of any further ethnic minorities in remotely promising Tory-held seats. Deva's worse than typical result reinforced at least the impression of lingering voter prejudice, despite his high profile attempt to lobby a significant local Asian electorate to the Conservative cause.

The conclusion is that prejudice amongst white voters will cause ethnic minority candidates to lose some support and this appears, not unexpectedly, to be greatest where the ethnic minority population is smallest. This may be a consequence of several factors but in the reverse instance, where there is a substantial ethnic minority population, the effect of this prejudice may be rendered nugatory by ethnic minority electors. However it is not to be assumed that electors will switch partisan allegiance for reasons of racial solidarity or that, for example, Muslim voters will give a Hindu candidate unequivocal support. Yet, whatever the balance, it seems that safe seats will stay safe. If the Conservative candidate at Beaconsfield was Asian, the seat would not be lost, nor would Barnsley Central be lost to Labour if their candidate was black. The same problem of white prejudice is found in the elections to local authorities, but there is also a whole range of features not seen at Westminster which produce significant differences.

## REPRESENTATION IN LOCAL GOVERNMENT

At this level there are three basic factors which make it more likely that representation of the local ethnic minority will become representation by that community. These are the electoral system (in certain areas), the smaller size of the electoral areas and the concentration of the ethnic minority populations.

First is the fact that local government elections have several features which are quite different from Parliamentary elections. Some, such as the fact that all councillors are elected for a fixed term of four years, have no consequences for ethnic minority representation, but one feature is quite significant. This is the existence of multi-member divisions as opposed to the single-member divisions which are used for Parliamentary elections. It is therefore necessary to set out the different electoral systems and identify where the system is helpful, or otherwise, to the cause of electing members of the ethnic minorities.

All the county councillors are elected in single member divisions every fourth year, the last occasion being in 1994. Almost two-thirds of the district councils have complete renewal every four years but they differ from their County Councils in that they usually have mixtures of single-member and multi-member divisions. These district councils had their last elections in 1995 but the London boroughs which also have a mixture of single- and multi-member divisions were last contested in 1994. Finally all the metropolitan districts, like Birmingham and Bradford, and about a third of the ordinary districts have three councillors per ward, but they normally retire in rotation with a single member being elected in each of three consecutive years.

These complex variations have consequences for black and Asian citizens because the multi-member system causes the political parties to look for a larger number of possibles and to put up a slate of candidates. When a party has to put up a slate of, perhaps, three candidates it becomes more aware of the need to make a balanced appeal to the electorate. Consequently when three candidates have to be put forward, there is a greater likelihood that a woman, or a member of an ethnic minority group, will be included on the slate.

The second factor which has significance for the success of ethnic minority candidates is the numerical size of the electorates involved. This combines with the third factor, known in the United States as "ghettoization" which prevents the dilution of the black vote. Asian and black people tend to concentrate in relatively small areas and, where those areas are also electoral areas, the minority can become the majority or come near to it. Where this happens, the community is more able to elect a representative from amongst its own members. When the election is for a much larger area the electoral power of the "ghetto" is diluted. This point, about the size of the electoral areas, can be illustrated even using one of the big cities where the system is unhelpful. For example, at Sheffield the average electorate in the wards which elect city councillors is about 14,000, that of the Westminster constituencies is about 70,000 and the Sheffield European Parliamentary constituency had 476,530 electors. A concentration of a "minority" population of around 7,000 in one ward has the potential, if organized, to become the majority, but with a Parliamentary constituency that same 7,000 is diluted to a mere 10 per cent of the electorate and within the Strasbourg constituency it is diluted to 1.5 per cent. The critical factor, particularly in the local government wards, is the extent to which there is an effective organization.

Electorates in the biggest Metropolitan cities tend to be around 10,000 electors[1] in each ward and, unless there is a major boundary revision, they elect just one person to the city council. These two factors together create difficulties for the election of ethnic minority councillors, but there are two equally important factors which can overcome these barriers. These are the mobilization of the ethnic minority electorate and the activation of that community as members of the local political parties.

Whilst there are several instances of individuals from the ethnic minorities winning elections in areas where there is an absence of any concentration of Asian or black people, most ethnic minority councillors, in fact, get elected where there is a concentration. Several of our biggest Metropolitan cities actually have only small ethnic minority populations which, even though they may be concentrated in particular wards, do not produce ethnic minority councillors. This is probably the explanation for the absence of any ethnic minority councillors, at the time of writing, in Liverpool.[2] Despite the widespread awareness of Toxteth and Liverpool 8, the city is predominantly white. There is a concentration of black electors, but only 1.7 per cent of the city's population is black and the figure for South Asians is even less at 0.5 per cent.

In Liverpool, then, the electorates are relatively large, the councillors are elected one at a time and the ethnic minorities are relatively small. Additionally the potential countervailing factors of mobilization as voters and of activation as party members do not seem to have developed sufficiently.

## COUNTERVAILING FACTORS

So far as the mobilization of voters is concerned there is an earlier stage which is getting those who are qualified put on the electoral register. The legal position is that all who are qualified must complete form A which is distributed annually and may be fined up to £1,000, if they refuse to do so. In order to encourage registration, many authorities produce instructions in several South Asian or other appropriate languages and the Association of Electoral Administrators has a code of practice emphasizing their responsibility to seek out and register all who are qualified.

Research into non-registration in five areas where there were concentrations of ethnic minority residents was conducted in 1986 (Le Lohé 1987). Investigators found 588 persons who were not registered at that address which amounted to 16.9 per cent of those living in these areas. However 321 were new at that address and claimed to be registered elsewhere and 64 were not qualified by nationality, which left 203 for further inquiry. These who had failed to register, either accidentally or deliberately, comprised 48 Asians, 109 blacks and 46 whites. A total of 1,020 Asians, 1,297 blacks and 1,172 whites had been interviewed, hence we had found levels of 4.7 per cent, 8.4 per cent and 3.9 per cent non-registration in these groups. Although there was a higher level of intentional non-registration by black respondents, there was no real difference between the levels amongst Asians and whites and registration does not appear to be a serious barrier.

Once on the electoral register there is the need to know where to go to vote and how to complete the ballot. Polling cards give the location of the polling station, but far more important is the availability of friends and helpers to get voters to the polling stations. Inside the station the notes for guidance are usually available in a range of languages and spoilt papers are relatively rare.

In Bradford there was a time when the turnout of the Asian electorate was at a very low level, indeed it was recorded at 4.5 per cent in 1966 (Le Lohé 1990: 66). However when Asians stood as candidates, either as Independents or with party labels, they made major efforts to get the Asian community to vote for them. Another stimulus came with the insecurity produced by racists contesting the elections and the publicity associated with Enoch Powell's speech in April 1968.

The consequence of these stimuli was a political awakening with an enormous increase in voter participation. A study of Central Ward Rochdale, where the Liberals broke new ground with an Asian candidate in May 1968, revealed that the Pakistani community was committed both to the Liberal party and to going out to vote. The teller's returns at Castlemere polling station show that 53 per cent of Asians had voted, compared with 41 per cent of "Others" (Le Lohé and Goldman 1969: 445).

In 1969 at Manningham Ward Bradford, the Liberal candidate was Dr Qureshi and Labour, hoping to retain the seat, had the support of Mr Khan who was the Secretary of the Pakistan Immigrant Welfare Association. These two certainly mobilized the Asian community which achieved a turnout vote far higher than that of the rest of the electorate. The greatest concentration was at polling station LG, where almost half the electors were Asian, and here the Asian turnout level was 58.2 per cent as against 28.7 per cent of the white electorate (Le Lohé 1975: 96).

This pattern of relatively high voter-participation, higher than that of the white neighbours, has become the normal standard where there is a substantial Asian community. However, where it is not so substantial, the levels appear to be about the same as their neighbours, for, at Waltham Forest a study of eight polling stations, where Asians averaged 15 per cent of the electorate, found the Asian turnout slightly below that of the non-Asians (Anwar 1994: 29). This, however, was 1990 and a factor in that year was the general rise in local election turnout right across the country as a response to the introduction of the Poll Tax. Normally the white turnout in inner city areas is quite low and the Asian turnout is typically twice as high. A particularly impressive example of this was observed by this author during the 1984 European Assembly election at Bradford when the Asian electors proved to be better Europeans than the Europeans with a turnout rate of 42.3 per cent, twice that of their neighbours and higher than that of any of the United Kingdom's constituencies.

The second, and probably the more important, countervailing factor is their participation in the local political parties. Candidates are selected by the local membership and, although there is some minimal control by the need for endorsement at a higher level, selection is the crucial stage. In the vast majority of cases the choice at the selection conference is more decisive than the choice of the voters because most seats in the Commons and the Council Chambers are safe. Of the 651 MPs elected in 1992 no less than 481 had majorities exceeding 10 per cent of the vote which means that 74 per cent are defined as safe (*Times Guide* 1992: 279). There can be greater volatility at the council level when the electors take mid-term revenge upon the party in power at Westminster, but in most years the majority of council seats report the result as "no change". In 1994 there was little change in the London boroughs – for example at Greenwich 5 of the 60 seats and at Wandsworth only 3 of the 61 seats changed hands. Even in 1995, when the Conservatives suffered massive losses, the number of seats which changed hands was relatively small. In that year in ten of our major cities[3] 336 councillors were elected but for 249 of them there was "no change".

The local Labour parties in the inner city wards frequently had very few active members, very little organization and considerable complacency, but they provide all the ward councillors. The first-generation immigrants tended to settle in these working class areas and when individuals in this "new working class" decided to become politically active they tended to become involved with the Labour Party. Some early attempts to become councillors were as Independent candidates (Spiers and Le Lohé 1964) and, whilst these certainly made the main parties aware of the potential of the ethnic minority vote, they also made ambitious individuals aware that the established parties were the better option. The best option in the inner city wards where they lived was the Labour Party, and for many, as working-class and union members, it was a natural choice. In some wards their membership was welcomed, in others it was discouraged but the potential for "taking over" the party was clearly obvious.

There are several instances of older white Labour politicians being deselected and replaced by members of the ethnic minorities. Sometimes the deselected white will be the source of allegations about the "Muslim Mafia" with anecdotes about a selection conference at which most of the participants could not speak English. Ambitious politicians are said to have recruited friends and paid their membership fees in order to control the selection process.[4] However, apart from allegations of "rigging" and "stuffing" it would actually be a natural consequence of the concentration that the local parties should have a majority of members who belong to the ethnic minorities. It is not surprising that some of the Conservative or Liberal candidates in these inner city wards are Asian or black and it is not necessarily evidence of "tokenism" that they are fighting in safe Labour territory. They are all locally-chosen candidates but, normally, it is only the Labour candidates who win.

Abnormal results at Bradford and Pendle in 1995, which raise interesting questions, are referred to later in this chapter, but the fact is that the overwhelming majority of Asian or black councillors are Labour and they win in areas of concentrated ethnic minority settlement. It is also a fact that many of them suffer from white voter prejudice, but they still win. The important factor in their success is the concentration, which produces not only a countervailing support at the polling station but also opportunities to provide the candidates. Where there is dispersion and dilution, both countervailing factors are missing and success is rare if not quite unknown.

The hypothesis, then, is that Asian and black candidates are less likely to succeed because of white prejudice, but they will still win in safe seats. Representation by the ethnic minorities is most likely where they are concentrated, because as voters they compensate for white prejudice and beyond that because they can dominate the parties' selection conferences. Relatively small electorates and a multi-member system will favour ethnic minority representation whereas large single member wards are unhelpful barriers which may be overcome by the countervailing activity of the community at the ballot box and the selection conference. The elements in this hypothesis are not necessarily quantifiable but they can be considered by examining electoral performances in different places at different times.

## THE EVIDENCE OF WHITE PREJUDICE

Because it gives white selectors an argument against them, some Asian and black candidates would wish to deny that white prejudice exists at the ballot box. The fact is that it is variable from place to place, but it can be demonstrated by election results in multiple systems apart from evidence collected by the pollsters. A National Opinion Poll finding had 35 per cent of the population admitting a degree of racial prejudice with an interesting breakdown by political party with those proposing to vote Conservative at 39 per cent compared with 29 per cent Labour supporters (*The Independent*, 14 December 1990).

When parties put up more than one candidate it sometimes happens that one candidate has an Asian name and the other has not. Asian names are distinctive, and a voter who, frequently, has little knowledge about the candidates would be aware of the Asian candidate's ethnic origin. If that voter is white and prejudiced, then the Asian, in "harness" with a white colleague of the same party, would not receive that voter's support and overall would receive fewer votes than the other candidate. Such situations occurred extensively in the London borough elections of 1994. Before examining the results of those elections it has to be pointed out that all people with Asian names are not Asian and that many people with "English" names are black, but the average voter would not know that and would make a judgement upon any available publicity and upon the name on the ballot paper. The extent of white prejudice would also depend upon the relative size of the white community in the ward as opposed to that of the ethnic minorities who might compensate for the prejudice.

In the elections to the London boroughs in 1994 most wards returned two or three councillors and the main parties had slates of two or three candidates. Some of these candidates had Asian names and stood "in harness" with others of the same party. For example, at Queensbury Ward, Brent, the Conservative candidates were Eric McDonald and Navin Patel. Where there were two candidates like this there are three possible outcomes, the rarest being one in which both candidates receive exactly the same number of votes. Occasionally the Asian named candidate gets more votes than the other, but most frequently the Asian name has fewer crosses against it on the ballot paper.

Another situation arises when there are three, not two, councillors to be elected and a "two and one" slate arrangement is possible. In such instances there is a wider range of outcomes including "neither ahead nor behind" situations with the Asian named candidate winning more votes than the bottom-placed person, but fewer than the top-placed person. There are several other combinations which can be simplified into "ahead", "behind" or 'neither". There is also the situation where all the candidates are Asian and no comparisons are then possible, and these, twos and threes, involved a total of 35 candidates. Including these all-Asian slates, and those which were neither ahead nor behind, there were 330 candidates with names which marked them out as of Asian, or possibly African, origin. They were involved in contests in 249 wards in 29 of the 32 boroughs. The discrepancy between the number of candidates and wards arises because more than one candidate for the same party could be a contestant. In 30 per cent of these contests the non-European-named candidate was neither ahead nor behind, in 58.4 per cent such candidates trailed, but in 11.6 per cent of contests they were in the lead. This imbalance between leading and trailing looks like the consequence of white voter prejudice.

It is possible to offer a measure of this situation, though this relates to a specific election and in specific places. Reference was made to Councillors McDonald and Patel at Queensbury Ward in Brent. McDonald got 1,041 votes and Patel 1,018, so the difference was not very great and could be expressed by saying that Patel received 97.8 per cent of his white colleague's vote. In Roe Green Ward (also in Brent) two other Conservatives won. Chunilal Chavda got 1,460 votes and Peter Golds 1,444, which means the Asian-named candidate had 101.1 per cent of the white vote. The Queensbury type of result is more common than that at Roe Green, since taking half the London boroughs, there were 27 Conservative results where a comparison could be made and the figure exceeded 100 per cent in only 4 of them, although in one instance both candidates achieved the same vote producing the 100 per cent figure. There were 57 instances with Labour candidates, 6 with an Asian name ahead and 51 behind, whereas the comparable figure for the Liberal Democrats is 2 ahead and 17 behind.

Ranking these 103 results from the three main parties and taking the median figure, suggests that an Asian-named candidate would run at 93.3 per cent of the vote of a white colleague with the range from 64.9 per cent to 116.9 per cent and that across the two middle quartiles from 88 per cent to 97.4 per cent. There is some small difference between the parties: the Liberal Democrat median is 92 per cent, the Labour 93.4 per cent and the Conservative median is 95.3 per cent.

Circumstances will vary greatly and it is simply intended here to suggest a tentative figure for an average loss of votes through white prejudice. All that it amounts to is that the average loss is about six votes out of a hundred which would lead to a loss only of highly marginal seats. Safe seats would stay safe and only about half the marginals would be in danger. On the other hand, even that would not be the situation if there was a substantial ethnic minority community which would have the potential to compensate for white prejudice.

This pattern was clearly demonstrated at Leicester where 11 of the 28 wards had candidates with Asian names. In three of these both Labour candidates were of Asian origin and succeeded, but in the other eight the Labour "slate" was a combination of both Asian and white. In these eight wards the white Labour candidates received

13,595 votes and their Asian partners received 13,583 or 99.9 per cent of the white total. The results within this overall pattern of parity, however, show some interesting variations. At Spinney Hills which, according to the 1991 census has an ethnic minority population of 82.5 per cent, the Asian candidate received a vote equal to 105 per cent of his white colleague. Labour actually won ten of these wards and, with one exception, their Asian candidate's weakest performance was where less than half the population was from the ethnic minorities. The exception was at Belgrave where two Asians challenged as Independent Labour candidates. Impressive Asian performances also occurred with two established councillors, including Mrs Vaz whose son is a local MP.

Also at Leicester the Liberal Democrats had Asian-plus-white partnerships in four wards. These included three of the four which have the largest ethnic minority populations and in these three the Asian ran ahead of his partner. It was only where that population was down to 50 per cent that the white partner ran ahead. There are no wards with more than 50 per cent from the ethnic minorities in Nottingham and in all ten situations of Asian-plus-white the white was ahead. Seven of these involved the Labour Party and all seven Asians were elected, even though they trailed their white partners with an average of 89 per cent of the white's vote. The other three instances were with Conservative partnerships and the Asians there equally suffered from white prejudice.

Although no seats were lost in Nottingham there were a few instances elsewhere where the trailing Asian was not only left behind, but also left out of the council. It may be that the Conservative candidate John Warren, at Chamberlayne Ward Brent, was particularly popular and had personal support which helped him to second place with 1,197 votes between the white Labour candidate with 1,251 votes and his partner Asish Sengupta with 1,151. The third place also went to a white Conservative with 1,162 votes, but before one concludes that the Labour candidate lost it through racial prejudice, we would need to be certain that the leading Labour candidate Jonathan Godfrey had not won the seat through personal popularity. This seat was a gain from the Conservatives and it would be better to state that Labour did not lose a seat but simply failed to win one. There were three other instances where Asian Labour candidates failed to join their white Labour partners in gaining seats in the London boroughs and only one in which a seat was genuinely lost. One Conservative seat was lost, but an outstanding Labour candidate beat the two white Conservatives as well and it would not, therefore, have made any difference to the result if they had all three been white. In three other wards the Liberal Democrats won seats from Labour, but failed to win the last seat with the Asian partner. Here, however, it was clearly a case of strong Liberal Democrat candidates, who happened to be white, edging out Labour.

The final point on this matter should be that it was frequently only a few votes that were missed; for example, in the four Labour wards the missed votes were 46, 21, 80 and 139. The conclusion must be that ethnic minority candidates only fail to win seats, or perhaps lose them in the very few instances of very close contests and in many, many contests these candidates are remarkably successful.


## ETHNIC MINORITY SUCCESS RATES

In most elections over the last three years ethnic minority candidates seem to have been particularly successful. This statement is made with some caution because it is only possible to measure success rates when both the candidate and councillor populations are known. It is only possible to be reasonably sure over a large number of results by using Asian names. In one or two council contests one might know which candidates are Afro-Caribbean, but that requires considerable local knowledge. It is possible to enquire from the authority how many councillors are Afro-Caribbean, but after a short lapse of time even the elections officers will be uncertain about candidates, indeed they may never have known about them at the time.

Enquiries from each of the London boroughs indicated that 215 (11.2 per cent) of the 1917 councillors might be regarded as being from the ethnic minorities. These comprised 144 South Asians, 66 Afro-Caribbeans and 5 Others said to be Vietnamese, or Lebanese or Turkish Cypriots. Of these 215 no less than 194 were Labour, leaving 15 Conservative and 6 Liberal Democrats. There are probably minor errors in these figures but one can only record the data that is given.

There are two ways to assess what this data means in terms of success. One is to compare the proportions of councillors elected with the proportions in the population as a whole and this will be considered presently. The second is to compare the proportion of candidates who succeed in different populations and for that purpose only those with distinctive Asian names may be used.

Labour winners with Asian names numbered 130 out of a total of 179 candidates. Thus Labour Asian candidates had a success rate of 72.6 per cent. Labour won 1,043 seats with 1,914 candidates giving an overall success level of 54.5 per cent, but we should subtract the Asians from these figures to have two groups, one of Others and one of Asians. The success rate of the Asians at 72.6 per cent is then slightly greater by comparison with the new figure of 52.7 per cent for the others. It was a good year for Labour, and the other parties were relatively short of success. Conservative Asians succeeded in 11 instances with 93 candidates (11.8 per cent) but non-Asian Conservatives were more successful with 508 wins with 1,747 candidates which equates to 29.1 per cent. The Liberal Democrats had an Asian candidate success rate of only 7.0 per cent but their non-Asians achieved a rate of 20.0 per cent.

As Labour candidates, then, Asians were significantly more successful than the non-Asians who were also Labour. Yet we also know that when fighting the same wards, side by side, the Asians tend to attract slightly fewer votes than their white running mates so it must be that the Labour Asians are contesting better Labour seats than the bulk of the non-Asian Labour candidates. This has come about through the selection process, with Asians gaining adoption for some of the better seats, typically those in the inner cities which are not only safe Labour but also the places of residence of the concentrated ethnic minority communities. It also follows that Conservative and Liberal Democrats when they choose local people will be contesting poor ground and their low success rates are therefore not unexpected.

The same pattern is observed outside London, particularly where there are concentrations of people of Asian origin. At Leicester the 14 Labour Asian candidates achieved a success rate of 92.9 per cent which was better than the 76.2 per cent of the non-Asians, and similarly at Nottingham seven Asian Labour candidates achieved 100 per cent which was also better than the 91.7 per cent for the non-Asian Labour candidates. The five Liberal Democrat Asians at Leicester had nil success but the non-Asians achieved a success rate of 16.3 per cent. There were no Asian Conservative candidates at Leicester and there were no Asian Liberal Democrats at Nottingham where three Asian Conservatives failed completely, which was only slightly worse than the white record, since only one Conservative was elected. In these two cities the complete council was being elected but elsewhere it was often only one third who were returned in places such as Birmingham, Blackburn and Bradford. At Birmingham Labour Asians with 100 per cent success beat the non-Asian rate of 77.1 per cent and at Blackburn Asians with 100 per cent had a higher rate than their Labour partners 82.4 per cent figure. The Conservatives and Liberal Democrat Asians all had inferior records compared with the non-Asians in these places but at Bradford the pattern was changed by one remarkable Conservative Asian gain. At Bradford this one candidate put the Conservative rate up to 25 per cent which was above the white rate of 11.5 per cent and the Labour Asian rate was unusually cut to 75 per cent whereas the non-Asians achieved 84.6 per cent. There was also the quite exceptional result at Pendle but here Asian Liberal Democrats were defeating Labour's Asians.

So, Asians who are Labour Party candidates, with the odd exceptions, are much more successful than whites who stand for Labour. Conversely those who stand for the Conservatives or the Liberal Democrats are generally less successful than whites. This conclusion is based upon the proportion of Asian candidates who were successful. An alternative measure of ethnic minority success can be made by comparing the proportion of councillors from the ethnic minorities with their proportions in the relevant population.

The 1991 census gives the proportions of the population which may be related to the proportions of councillors who have been classified as Asian, black or white. Taking all the authorities shown in the census as having a white population which is less than 90 per cent produces 15 authorities outside London and 25 London boroughs. There are some minor problems in matching the census data with the reported origins of the ethnic minority councillors, which arise partly because the census' ten-fold classification includes Chinese and Other others who may not be qualified to stand as councillors. For this reason those two very small groups in the population described as belonging to the ethnic minorities and equally a very small group of councillors also reported as being from the ethnic minorities (e.g. "Turks and Vietnamese") have been ignored.

The following tables compare the two broad groups of Asian and black populations with their numbers as councillors. In Table 4.1 there are eight councils in which the Asian population exceeds 10 per cent. The Asian population at Wolverhampton is weakly represented, but all the others are roughly in balance, except that Asians in Slough have been outstandingly successful in gaining seats in the council chamber. Amongst those where the Asian population is less than 10 per cent there is also outstanding Asian success at Nottingham and to a lesser extent at Coventry. However, overall, the Asian communities have achieved a situation in which their numbers in the population are reflected in the council chambers. The number of Asian councillors would be 112 if it mirrored the population perfectly and it is 108. The significance of this reality must not be understated. The other remarkable feature is that 105 of these councillors were Labour with only two Liberal Democrats and one Conservative.

So far as the black population is concerned the pattern is different. In the first place the population is much smaller and is on average only 2.9 per cent, with the largest figures at Birmingham and Wolverhampton but with six figures of less than 2 per cent. Five of these six had no black councillors although all of them (except Pendle) "deserved" one; there were four other authorities where there were

TABLE 4.1  Populations and representation outside London (percentages)

| | Asian | | Black | |
|---|---|---|---|---|
| | Population | Councillors | Population | Concillors |
| Birmingham | 13.5 | 13.7 | 5.9 | 3.4 |
| Blackburn | 14.2 | 10.0 | 0.4 | 0.0 |
| Bradford | 13.6 | 12.2 | 1.1 | 0.0 |
| Coventry | 9.3 | 13.0 | 1.6 | 1.9 |
| Kirklees | 8.3 | 5.6 | 1.8 | 0.0 |
| Leicester | 24.7 | 23.2 | 2.4 | 0.0 |
| Luton | 13.6 | 16.7 | 4.9 | 6.3 |
| Manchester | 5.9 | 4.0 | 4.6 | 3.0 |
| North Beds | 5.6 | 5.7 | 2.8 | 0.0 |
| Nottingham | 4.8 | 12.7 | 4.6 | 5.5 |
| Pendle | 9.7 | 7.8 | 1.0 | 0.0 |
| Preston | 8.3 | 3.5 | 1.2 | 0.0 |
| Sandwell | 10.6 | 11.1 | 2.4 | 0.0 |
| Slough | 22.6 | 30.0 | 3.8 | 0.0 |
| Wolverhampton | 12.3 | 5.0 | 5.1 | 0.0 |

Sources: for the populations the 1991 Census; for councillors the author's research.

no black councillors at all. Black councillors were reported in small numbers at Birmingham, Luton, Manchester and Nottingham and, in 1995, Coventry acquired its first black councillor, but Wolverhampton which "deserved" three still had none. The total, if it mirrored the population, would have been 32 councillors but it was only 14, all of whom were Labour.

The pattern within London is broadly similar although the Asian community is not as successful in the outer boroughs as it is in the inner. In the inner boroughs a "mirror" would suggest 62 Asian councillors and there are 60, although Table 4.2 shows both weakness and strength. There are two boroughs with over a quarter of the population of Asian origin and they have approximately this proportion elected to the council. There are five boroughs where there is a deficit in Asian councillors. Three of them, Kensington, Wandsworth and Westminster are solidly Conservative with only about a quarter of their seats held by Labour. The other two which are deficient in Asian councillors are Lambeth, which had none following the election in May 1994, and Camden, which only had three Asians. These five boroughs have a combined deficit of 12 councillors, but the balance is almost regained by the exceptional success at Haringey, Lewisham and Tower Hamlets.

By contrast Asians do not achieve a rough parity in the outer boroughs where their proportions are much higher, with more than half this group exceeding 10 per cent. Ealing has parity with 15

TABLE 4.2   Populations and representation (percentages)

Inner London Boroughs

| | Asian | | Black | |
|---|---|---|---|---|
| | Population | Councillors | Population | Councillors |
| Camden | 7.9 | 5.1 | 5.5 | 1.7 |
| Hackney | 7.7 | 6.7 | 22.0 | 13.3 |
| Hammersmith | 4.2 | 4.0 | 10.2 | 4.0 |
| Haringey | 8.1 | 13.6 | 17.1 | 10.2 |
| Islington | 4.9 | 7.7 | 10.6 | 7.7 |
| Kensington | 5.1 | 1.9 | 5.8 | 1.9 |
| Lambeth | 4.8 | 0.0 | 21.8 | 6.3 |
| Lewisham | 3.1 | 9.0 | 16.3 | 13.4 |
| Newham | 25.7 | 23.3 | 14.4 | 5.0 |
| Southwark | 3.8 | 3.1 | 17.7 | 7.8 |
| Tower Hamlets | 25.7 | 30.0 | 7.7 | 0.0 |
| Wandsworth | 7.0 | 4.9 | 10.7 | 3.3 |
| Westminster | 7.9 | 1.7 | 7.6 | 0.0 |

Outer London Boroughs

| | Asian | | Black | |
|---|---|---|---|---|
| | Population | Councillors | Population | Councillors |
| Barnet | 11.4 | 5.0 | 3.6 | 1.7 |
| Brent | 24.1 | 13.6 | 16.5 | 10.6 |
| Croydon | 7.6 | 5.7 | 7.6 | 2.9 |
| Ealing | 21.8 | 21.1 | 7.1 | 0.0 |
| Enfield | 6.1 | 1.5 | 6.2 | 0.0 |
| Greenwich | 5.3 | 9.7 | 5.4 | 8.1 |
| Harrow | 19.9 | 4.8 | 3.7 | 1.6 |
| Hillingdon | 9.1 | 4.3 | 1.7 | 0.0 |
| Hounslow | 19.1 | 25.0 | 2.7 | 3.3 |
| Merton | 7.9 | 0.0 | 5.8 | 3.5 |
| Redbridge | 15.1 | 11.3 | 4.3 | 0.0 |
| Waltham Forest | 12.1 | 17.5 | 11.3 | 0.0 |

Sources: for the populations the 1991 Census; for councillors the author's research.

councillors, and Hounslow (also with 15), Greenwich and Waltham Forest have more than achieved parity, but all the others trail. The two weakest are Harrow and Brent which, by contrast with the achievers, did not have Labour majorities, although they had large Asian electorates.

The proportions of councillors who are black are consistently smaller than the proportions of the populations who are black. In both the inner and the outer boroughs their numbers are less than half what might be expected and, taken together in these 25 boroughs, the actual figure of 65 black councillors was 83 fewer than the proportion in the population that indicated parity. There were nine inner and two outer boroughs where the black population exceeded 10 per cent of the total, but every one of them had a smaller proportion of black councillors than the proportion in the population, producing a deficit of 53 black councillors. The principal sources of the deficit were Lambeth, Newham, Southwark, Hackney, Waltham Forest, Ealing, Wandsworth and Westminster. Only Greenwich was above "quota" and only Hounslow had achieved parity.

The broad picture, then, is that the Asian communities have been more successful in producing councillors than their black counterparts. It might be noted that the proportion of the population which is eligible to contest elections is actually smaller than the proportion of the Asian or black populations, because the age profile exhibits a disproportionately large number of young people who are excluded on grounds of age. The Asian community has achieved a position close to parity in these 40 authorities, but the black community trails badly. Perhaps, however, the most remarkable fact is that in these 40 authorities the proportion of Labour representatives with 310 councillors is 93.4 per cent and that of the Conservatives 4.5 per cent and Liberal Democrats 2.1 per cent. The extent of this party-based imbalance is perhaps not fully appreciated. It is certainly a fact that needs to be driven home in the popular coverage of race-and-representation themes.

These areas of substantial ethnic minority populations contrast with areas where there are only small groups and individuals. Yet individuals do win places on councils in areas which are overwhelmingly white. Two such areas were analyzed, the first comprising the 27 local authorities in East Sussex, Hampshire and West Sussex, the second the 29 local authorities in the five northernmost counties of England (Cleveland, Cumbria, Durham, Northumberland and Tyne and Wear). Both areas have populations of about 3 million with 1.3 per cent from the ethnic minorities in Central Southern England and 0.6 per cent in the North.

In the 1995 elections there were 2,040 candidates, including six who had Asian names, involved in the elections in the North; 1,082 of these succeeded, including three with Asian names. In so far as 0.3 per cent of candidates were Asian and 0.3 per cent of councillors are Asian the evidence is that they succeeded just as much as any other candidates. The three who succeeded were all Labour and included Dr Ashok Kumar who won the 1991 Langbaurgh by-election and sat in the Commons until 1992 and again in 1997. Yet he had attracted a smaller vote than his white running mate at Southfield Ward as had the other Middlesbrough Asian candidate in Marton Ward. The Census indicates that the ethnic minority population in the North is overwhelmingly Asian, but it is the absence of a substantial Asian community which is probably the explanation for the deficit between the 0.6 per cent of the population and the 0.3 per cent of council membership.

The Southern study area differs in that the ethnic minority population, though still small, is twice that of the North and also in that the North is dominated by Labour but the South is not. Since the search for candidates amongst the election results was restricted to Asian names, the relevant population becomes Asian only and amounts to 0.9 per cent of the total. There were seven candidates with Asian names, three Labour, three Liberal Democrat and one Conservative but only two of the Labour candidates were successful. One of these was Mohammed Qamaruddin who became the first Asian councillor at Crawley, which is the authority with the largest proportion (6.4 per cent) of Asians in all these 27 councils.

The total number of candidates in this area in 1995 was 2,051, of whom 747 were successful, giving a success rate of 36.4 per cent which is slightly better than the Asian rate of 28.6 per cent. Yet in terms of having 0.3 per cent of council seats the Asian community at 0.9 per cent is not really successful. However, it should be remembered that this is a snapshot year and some councils which returned only one third in 1995 have Asian councillors elected in earlier years. This is unlikely to be a misleading snapshot, although if more whites convert to Islam and follow Labour Councillor John Truscott at Southampton with a change to a Muslim name, the true Asian position would be exaggerated.

## CONCLUSION

To return to the hypothesis, there is some evidence that the size of the electorate and the electoral system has an impact. It is actually possible to demonstrate this where the same areas are used for both county and district elections. At Leicester the same wards which return city councillors in multiples are also divisions returning single councillors to the county council. In 1993 six divisions returned Asians to the county council, but in 1995 these same places plus four others returned Asians to the city council, which does suggest that multiple vacancies are helpful.

Similarly there is some evidence that where the electorates are less numerous, such as at Pendle where the average is 3,733, the chances are better, but these influences are largely obscured by the countervailing factors. The community at Pendle has awakened only recently, but those in Luton or Slough have more experience and political organization and it is not possible to ascribe the success at Luton simply to the multiple-member system. That part of the hypothesis must be left as unproven.

The part of the hypothesis which suggested that success would be found where there were concentrations of the ethnic minority populations and that they would be overwhelmingly Labour is quite definitely proven, although at this point reference must be made to 1995 results in Bradford and Pendle which would seem to suggest that Labour might be losing its dominance.

At Pendle, an authority including the east Lancashire towns of Nelson and Colne, Labour lost three seats in a year when Labour triumphed widely across the country. In two of these seats an Asian Liberal Democrat gained a seat from an Asian Labour candidate. The most remarkable of these gains was at Whitefield Ward where it was a straight fight between Councillor Ali (Labour) and Mr Rasool (Liberal Democrat), the latter winning in a record turnout of 61 per cent. Since that election, the Liberal Democrats with an Asian candidate have taken another seat from Labour and now have an overall majority including three Asians, whereas Labour now has only one Asian councillor.

It would be wrong to suggest on this basis that Labour is losing ground, even though there has also been remarkable Labour setbacks in Bradford where two wards were involved. In one "super-safe" Labour ward, Bradford Moor, a Muslim Conservative did not quite gain the seat against a Labour Muslim, but he achieved a swing of 22 per cent against Labour, whereas the swing elsewhere was 4 per cent from Conservative to Labour. A precise explanation of this very anomalous result cannot be given, but it is noted that the sitting Labour councillor, the only Sikh on the council, was deselected and replaced by a Muslim. The influence of ethnicity *within* Asian communities is a factor with obvious potential impact although it is often hard to gauge its true trajectory in electoral contests such as this.

At Toller Ward the sitting Labour candidate, a distinguished white woman, was also deselected and replaced by a Muslim man, Sajawal Hussain. This ward was also regarded as a safe Labour seat, but the Conservative candidate, Arshad Hussain, gained it and provoked a major Labour inquiry. There were statements that Labour Party activists had put up Conservative posters and had helped to swing the seat against their own party. It would seem that the adherence to the Labour Party was rather superficial and that connections and kinship within the Muslim community were more deep-rooted.

Scrutiny of the marked registers at Toller indicates that almost half the 11,562 electors had Asian names, but these made up 68.3 per cent of those who voted, as opposed to the 29.1 per cent of whites who voted. There was nothing untypical in this, the only remarkable event being that there was an impressive swing from a bus company employee to a successful businessman. It is perhaps also relevant to point out that Sakhawat Hussain, who nearly won Bradford Moor for the Conservatives, was also a successful businessman whereas his opponent was a less prosperous retired teacher. Perhaps successful businessmen have the resources and the contacts which allow them to mobilize support more effectively.

Labour will clearly continue to provide most of the ethnic minority councillors and once elected they do have the advantage of forming a politic elite in their own community. As incumbents they may deliver to their communities, and it is noted that there was a Labour incumbent in only one of the four instances of loss at Bradford and Pendle.

The Conservative Party had a minor breakthrough in Bradford which may, or may not, have some significance for the future. That party's belief that the Asian community has the values of natural Conservatives is explored in this book by Saggar. One hesitates to make long term forecasts, but the best chances of success for Asian or black Conservatives in local elections probably depend upon a Labour Government at Westminster achieving a high level of unpopularity. It should not be forgotten that the unpopularity of the Wilson Government in the late 1960s saw the Conservatives in control of cities such as Liverpool, Newcastle and Sheffield.

Finally, the point must be made that significant change has come over time. Parity between the proportions of the population and the proportions of councillors may now exist in many places, particularly for Asians, but this is a relatively new phenomenon. In 1978 this author found that there were 35 ethnic minority councillors in the London boroughs. In 1990 it was reported that there were 179 (Geddes 1003: 54). Enquiries following the 1994 borough elections raised this figure to 213. Asians increased from 21 in 1978, to 35 in 1982, to 69 in 1990, and to 145 in 1994. The black community has also progressed, for example Catherine Cruikshank became the first black on Tameside Council when she captured a seat from the Tory leader in 1995, but black people are still trailing the Asian community. In some respects this is surprising, since the black communities are just as concentrated as the Asian communities and successful leaders have emerged from within the black organizations. There is evidence that black people are less ready to turn out as voters, but ambitious persons could certainly improve upon this with organization and take council seats.

It does now, however, seem that Asian people participate fully in British politics both as voters and as councillors and progress towards parity in the House of Commons is to be expected.

## NOTES

1. The average electorates in the bigger Metropolitan District range from 18,699 at Birmingham down to 9,367 at Manchester.
2. In recent years there have been only two ethnic minority councillors for Liverpool wards. One was Petrona Lashley who was elected for Granby ward in 1991 but did not defend her seat in 1995. The other was Judith Nelson who represented Anfield ward between 1987 and 1992.
3. The ten places were Bradford, Birmingham, Derby, Leeds, Leicester, Manchester, Newcastle, Nottingham, Sheffield and Wolverhampton.
4. *The Economist*, 9 September 1995 reported several examples of allegations of Asian entryism in parliamentary constituencies at Birmingham, Glasgow and Manchester.

## REFERENCES

Anwar, M. 1994. *Race and Elections*. Monographs in Ethnic Relations, No. 9, University of Warwick.

BBC/ITN 1983. *Guide to the New Parliamentary Constituencies*. Parliamentary Research Series, London.

Geddes, A. 1993. Asian and Afro-Caribbean representation in elected local government in England and Wales. *New Community*, vol. 20(1) 43–57.

Le Lohé, M. J. and A. Goldman 1969. Race in local politics. *Race*. vol. x(4) 435–47.

Le Lohé, M. J. 1975. Participation in elections by Asians in Bradford. In *British Political Sociology Yearbook*, vol. 2, I. Crewe (ed.). London: Croom Helm.

Le Lohé, M. J. 1987. *A Study of non-registration among Ethnic Minorities*. University of Bradford.

Le Lohé, M. J. 1989. The performance of Asian and black candidates in the British General Election of 1987. *New Community*, vol. 15(2) 159–70.

Le Lohé, M. J. 1990. The Asian vote in a Northern City, in *Black Politics in Britain*, H. Goulbourne (ed.). Aldershot: Avebury.

Norris, P. and J. Lovenduski. 1995. *Political Recruitment, Gender, Race and Class in the British Parliament*. Cambridge University Press.

Spiers, M. and M. J. Le Lohé. 1964. Pakistanis in the Bradford Municipal Election of 1963. *Political Studies*, vol. xii (1) 85–92.

The Times 1992. *Guide to the House of Commons*. 384.

CHAPTER FIVE

# Ethnic politics and the Conservatives in the post-Thatcher era

## Paul B. Rich

The Conservative Party in the 1990s continues to have a checkered and uneasy relationship to ethnic minority politics in Britain. It has been generally reluctant to incorporate black and Asian politicians in any significant numbers and has preferred to keep ethnic minorities at arm's length. Although on occasions the Conservative Party in the late 1970s and 1980s was seduced to play the "race card" in party politics, there have been signs of a newer tendency towards the incorporation of small and relatively compliant sections of the Asian and Afro-Caribbean middle class elite. This process has proceeded gradually with the party leadership anxious to avoid as far as possible letting race and ethnicity becoming a sectarian issue within the party like that of "Black Sections" in the Labour Party in the 1980s. The issue of race has threatened to unmask underlying tensions between the party leadership in Central Office and constituency organizations fiercely determined to preserve their political autonomy. It is unlikely that the party will make any major new initiatives in this area for the foreseeable future and will probably prefer to go down the road of increasing the number of female Tory MPs in Parliament rather than black or Asian ones.

It might seem that the picture in the 1990s is simply one of a major political party being signally unwilling to take any major initiative to advance ethnic minority political representation. However, the issue of Europe has served as a major diversion for the party's ideological right and has helped facilitate the rise of a language of Englishness centred on London and the South East. As this chapter will argue, developments under John Major's leadership confirmed a trend that was already visible in the early to middle 1980s of the party slowly cutting itself adrift from an older discourse of race and moving towards a language of ethnic nationalism. The party has progressively ceased to be a Unionist Party of the whole of the United Kingdom and become instead largely a party of English nationalism. It is still as yet too early to see what the implications of this process will be for the politics of race and ethnicity. The intense debate on closer European unity, however, indicates that, as the Conservative Party has become an increasingly Anglocentric political machine, it may possibly choose to play in the future a racial card in the pursuit of a populist path of political mobilization.

## FROM MARGARET THATCHER TO JOHN MAJOR

The Conservative Party that John Major inherited as leader in 1990 had been infused over the previous eleven years with a militant brand of quasi populist politics committed to wide-ranging privatization and the rolling back of the frontiers of the state. Margaret Thatcher's legacy was not simply one of leadership style but of political culture as well. The previous social democratic consensus of the 1960s and 1970s was replaced by a neoliberal consensus, although outside the confines of the political elite this was only partially supported by the electorate at large. (Crewe 1993: 18–21; Whiteley et al. 1994: 185–203). Mrs Thatcher was widely credited with injecting a language of race into British politics and for some analysts "Thatcherism" became synonymous with a "new racism" that threatens, if unchecked, to lead to a policy of deportation (Miles and Phizacklea 1984). As I have pointed out elsewhere, this is a considerable exaggeration since the actual discourse of the Conservative Party's ideological right was largely in terms of preservation of the nation rather than the race, though "nation" in this context could to some extent be interpreted as a euphemism for a "white" British nation (Rich 1986: 45–72).

From the middle of the 1970s onwards there were some additional themes that began to complicate this relatively simple picture of a former imperial party bogged down in "traditional" racial symbolism. Some 70 per cent of the non-white population lives in metropolitan areas and has developed considerable voting power in a number of urban constituencies – 41 per cent of the black population, for example, live in London alone. Some evidence suggested that up to 13 of the 17 seats Labour won in the October 1974 general election had been in constituencies where the margin of the Labour victory was less than the number of black voters. For the first time, the black electorate began to have some limited political significance and encouraged the Conservative Party's rather opportunist managers to strive to win over at least a portion of the black vote. In January 1976 a Department of Community Affairs was established in Conservative Central Office with the objective of establishing better relationships with certain targeted groups including ethnic minorities. An Ethnic Minorities Unit was established inside the Community Affairs Department, now under the directorship of Andrew Rowe, and this led in turn to the establishment of an Anglo-Asian and Anglo-West Indian Conservative Societies These societies still peripheralized ethnic minority issues from the mainstream of Conservative Party politics and indeed indicated that the party's tradition of paternalistic benevolence was by no means burnt out. They had the effect, nevertheless, of bringing in a small number of new faces to party conferences such as Narindar Saroop, a Conservative councillor for Kensington and Chelsea (Sewell 1993: 62–63).

The Anglo-Asian Conservative Society was the more successful of the two societies and eventually had some thirty branches before its work became hampered by ethnic political divisions rooted in South Asian politics. Narindar Saroop brought in a Sikh, Professor Mohinder Paul Bedi, as Deputy Chairman, and Bedi then went on to challenge Saroop for control of the Association, backed by a well-organised group of Sikhs committed to an independent Khalistan. They more or less took over control of the society and Conservative Central Office became worried that this might lead to adverse publicity overseas. In December 1986 a working party under Sir Peter Lane decided to dissolve the society and replace it with an advisory body called the One Nation Forum. The party leadership was determined to prevent anything like a "black sections" issue emerging and so kept membership to the Forum strictly by invitation from the party chairman.

The One Nation Forum appeared to get off to a good start and some analysts considered that it was likely to be more influential than the previous Anglo-Asian and Anglo-West Indian Conservative Societies (Sewell 1985: 65). In the wake of the 1981 Nationality Act the issue of immigration effectively dropped out of British politics and failed to have any sort of impact in the 1983 general election. It seemed to be a good time for Conservative Party managers to start trying once again to court sections of the black and Asian vote (Saggar 1992: 128). The policy was also in part directed towards trying to shift fairly widespread perceptions of the Conservative Party as a white political party in the wake of Mrs Thatcher's comments in January 1978 of the "British people's fear" of being "swamped" by "alien cultures" as well as the embarrassing poster in the 1983 election of a black man with the caption "Labour says he's black, we say he's British". In the early 1980s racial tensions had also significantly increased with inner city disturbances in the St Paul's district of Bristol, in Brixton and in Handsworth and Conservative Party managers became interested in trying to separate immigration from race issues in British politics. With the first having been more or less settled, there now seemed to be an opportunity to deal with the latter by capitalizing on the fact that the alleged unity of ethnic politics in Britain was largely fictitious (Werbner 1991: 113–141). Some Conservative strategists thought that it might be possible to win over sections of the Asian business and professional elite who were widely thought to come from cohesive family-based cultures that were "naturally" conservative.

As Shamit Saggar has argued elsewhere in this volume, there are considerable problems with this cultural thesis for Conservative support among Asian voters, particularly as it appears to hang on an analogy with shifting political preferences among Jewish voters. It may be the case that many Asian voters have begun to abandon support for Labour as they adopt more secure lower-middle-class and middle-class occupations in British society (Anwar 1990: 314, Srinivasan 1992: 71). However, the conception of an intrinsically Conservative Asian "communalism" is also a rather dubious ideological prop for Conservative political allegiances, since it can also be used to sustain a Labour or Liberal Democratic political creed. The cultural explanation for Asian political support for the Conservatives is thus at best a very thin one, and shifts attention away from the brokerage role of particular Asian political leaders and the advantages that are seen to accrue from forging a political pact with the Conservatives. The calculations for these are manifold, since they may be based on local political issues as well as complex status gradients typical of the Asian petty bourgeoisie in Britain which might see itself as working class in the British context, middle class within the Asian community and upper class *vis-à-vis* the home country in South Asia (Srinivasan 1992: 72).

This project to attempt a partial de-racialization of the Conservative Party in any case has achieved only limited success. As Table 5.1 shows, the party has continued to field only a very small number of parliamentary candidates in general elections, with just one being elected in the 1992 General Election (and losing 1997).

The establishment of the One Nation Forum in the mid-1980s highlighted the issue of ethnic minority representation in the party and probably aided the nomination of a small number of black and Asian candidates over the following few years. At this time the Conservatives were still riding high on the crest of popular electoral support while Mrs Thatcher was engaged in restructuring the contours of

TABLE 5.1  Ethnic minority candidates and MPs elected

| Year | Conservative Party | | Labour Party | | All Parties | |
|------|------------|-----|------------|-----|------------|-----|
| | Candidates | MPs | Candidates | MPs | Candidates | MPs |
| 1974a | 0 | 0 | 0 | 0 | 6 | 0 |
| 1974b | 0 | 0 | 1 | 0 | 3 | 0 |
| 1979 | 2 | 0 | 1 | 0 | 12 | 0 |
| 1983 | 4 | 0 | 6 | 0 | 18 | 0 |
| 1987 | 6 | 0 | 14 | 4 | 28 | 0 |
| 1992 | 8 | 1 | 9 | 5 | 22 | 6 |
| 1997 | 13 | 0 | 14 | 9 | 44 | 9 |

Note: 1974a is February 1974, 1974b is October 1974.
Source: Norris et al. 1992: 93.

British party politics. The Thatcherite vision owed much to the idea of the resurrection and regeneration of the British nation state; the Conservative Party was envisaged as being a party of the enterprising and successful who were at the forefront of a strategy of economic liberalisation no matter what their class or ethnic background.[1] The strategy appeared to be working for a large part of the 1980s and ensured the success of the Conservatives in the 1987 general election.

Mrs Thatcher overestimated the loyalty of her own supporters and proved eventually to be intractable on two major issues in the late 1980s, the Poll Tax and Europe. Both these issues damaged the unity of the party and threatened to produce divisions between the party leadership and constituency associations. In the case of Europe, particularly, the prospect of closer integration into a supra-national political entity centred on Brussels heightened a mood on the political right of a growing threat to English national identity. For some this signalled a retreat into an increasingly insular isolationism that proved surprisingly successful in setting the political agenda in the course of the 1990s. At the same time the preoccupation with "race" issues continued to drop out of mainstream political discussion. In the 1987 election, for instance, only 1 per cent of voters considered that "race" was one of the most important political issues, while in the 1992 election they surfaced only indirectly with the Labour Party being perceived by many electors as being weak on a number of issues, including immigration (Saggar 1993a: 694).

This progressive marginalization of race issues in British politics did not prevent sections of the Conservative right periodically attempting to goad the party leadership into taking up the issue. At the 1989 party conference, for instance, the Chairman of the Monday Club, Jonathan Guinness, saw the issue of repatriation of New Commonwealth immigrants as a political life-line for a government that appeared to be "on the ropes" as far as more general economic issues were concerned.[2] The appointment of a centrist and establishment figure, David Waddington, as Home Secretary the same year suggested that the government was uninterested in heeding such advice, while the defeat of Margaret Thatcher at the end of 1990 and the emergence of John Major as prime minister indicated if anything a pronounced turn back to One Nation Toryism. On issues of race, John Major earned the grudging respect of political opponents such as Ken Livingstone and Bernie Grant for, as a councillor in Lambeth twenty years previously, he had secured the expulsion of twelve local Conservatives for racism (*Daily Telegraph* 29 November 1990).

The party leadership around Major soon found themselves involved in fresh political controversy following the nomination of a black barrister, John Taylor, for the Conservative seat of Cheltenham. Taylor's nomination was clouded in racial slurs from the very start when it provoked considerable opposition in a predominantly white constituency. One leading Conservative Councillor, Peter Galbraith (a cousin of the Earl of Strathclyde), publicly declared: "I don't think we should give in to a bloody nigger even though Central Office have foisted him upon us" (*Daily Telegraph* 6 December 1990). Even though there is little evidence to suggest that Central Office did play a major role in Taylor's nomination, the resulting uproar did little to help the local party which was defending a majority of only 4,896 over the Liberal Democrats in the 1987 election. The local Conservative branch chairman, Monica Drinkwater, expressed shame and regret at Galbraith's remarks, but failed to bridge deep divisions within the constituency association that undoubtedly helped the Liberal Democrat candidate, Nigel Jones, to defeat Taylor in the 1992 election against the national political trend. There were allegations that a section of the party actively campaigned for Taylor's defeat and held a party to celebrate it on election night (*Brighton Post* 21 May 1992). One prominent member of the local Conservative Association was reported as saying that "He (Taylor) should have stood where there were more Coloureds. He's not appropriate here" (*The Voice* May 26 1992).

The Cheltenham affair confounded those observers who had hoped that Taylor's nomination would lead to a more active policy of nominating blacks and Asians as MPs. It suggested that, contrary to the mythology of an interventionist Central Office, the actual state of affairs at Conservative headquarters was far more haphazard and uncertain. During the Thatcher years, Conservative Central Office had been run down and marginalized as greater attention was paid to the outpourings of various think tanks on the ideological right. When John Major succeeded Mrs Thatcher in 1990 it seemed for a brief period that this trend might start to be reversed under the skilful chairmanship of Chris Patten, who had plans for developing the Conservative Research Department and the Centre for Policy Studies into a single think tank geared towards the promotion of an "opportunity society" (*The Times* 7 February 1991). However, any moves in this direction were postponed until after the approaching election in which Patten lost his seat in Bath and left British politics to become Governor of Hong Kong.

Patten's successor, Norman Fowler, was prevented from developing Central Office as a major arm of political debate as it emerged that the party had got into debt to the tune of some £19.2 millions after the 1992 election. Fowler began a radical reorganization of the whole headquarters structure in order to increase its efficiency as well as direct its resources towards key marginal seats. By September 1993 the total number of employees at Central Office had been cut from 400 to 250. The basic tripartite structure of the party of elected representatives in London and Strasbourg, constituency associations and the central office structure remained essentially intact. The party has continued to avoid any further centralization on the lines of a continental-style right-wing populist party, though such a transformation seems likely after the heavy defeat at the polls in May 1997.

Under John Major, the Conservatives have preferred to fall back upon traditional "One Nation" Conservative rhetoric as far as policy towards ethnic minorities, and for the most part the Powellite right has kept quiet. This was well reflected, for example, in a parliamentary debate in June 1992 on a motion of Roy Hattersley criticizing the government for initiating policies to reduce the disadvantages suffered by ethnic minorities. The debate provided a good opportunity for One Nation Conservatives to demonstrate their influence in the party. The tone of the Conservative response in the debate was set by the new MP for Aylesbury, David Lidington, who in a maiden speech declared:

> Racial problems are difficult to resolve. The challenges are not for the Government alone, but for voluntary societies and individuals – the mainstream of British cultural and social life. The prize that we shall seek to gain is great. I wish to help, as far as I am able, to build a society in which any man or woman, whatever his or her colour, racial origin or ethnic background can feel at home in the United Kingdom and has a willing attachment and loyalty to the institution's history and traditions of this nation. I also wish them to feel that their contribution to our mainstream national life is valued and welcomed by other and different traditions (Hansard 1992: col. 180).

This re-stated the One Nation Conservative ideal in terms of a sort of solar system vision of different ethnic cultures, each of which was "valued and welcomed" by the "mainstream" of the national culture like planets revolving around a dominant sun. It did little to indicate what the future of the national culture was as a whole beyond its continuing commitment to tolerance of diverse cultures and attachment to dominant institutions and historical myths. To this extent, it accurately reflected the reluctance (or inability) of the party to engage in any serious debate over the future of British national identity and its general fear of seeing this linked in any way to the issue of race and ethnic minority identity.

Indeed, it would be fair to conclude that the whole question of ethnic and race issues were put on hold in the Conservative Party under John Major. They have generally been seen as minor concerns compared to more general questions of economic management, Europe and "sleaze". The party has drifted on with little or no sense of direction or major interest in the issue, though as the last part of this chapter shows, such trends have confirmed a continuing process of black and Asian disaffection with the party after a brief period in the 1980s when some advances appeared to have been made. The general implication has been indeed that neither side on the Conservative debate on Europe in the 1990s considered the position of ethnic minorities all that important to the question of what defines British national identity. Ethnic issues in effect fell by the wayside as "Euro-phobes" and "Eurosceptics" engaged in battle for the soul of the party. This might seem in some respects rather odd since it appears at first glance a fairly obvious terrain on which to play the race card. The "Eurosceptics", however, probably feel that for the time being at least the issue of Europe is of sufficient magnitude as to warrant a single-minded focus upon it to the exclusion of race and immigration issues.

## THE ISSUE OF EUROPE

The debate over Europe has nevertheless had some impact on the issue of race and immigration in British politics. In the 1950s and 1960s immigration emerged as a looming threat for opinion on the right, while the question of British membership of the EEC was successfully contained as the generally technical (and rather dull) issue of "Europe". The Conservative debate on immigration was in some respects an outgrowth of older debates on colonial self-government and decolonization. Black immigrants were by and large seen as "alien" and "different" (just as they had under the doctrine of indirect rule) and could only be admitted into Britain in controlled numbers. No-one doubted, however, the essential cohesion and identity of the "British government" and "British society" into which the immigrants were settling, and it was assumed that by a steady process of cultural accommodation (some used the American word "assimilation") the immigrant communities would in time be "absorbed" into British society. There is, therefore, no equivalent in Britain to the French project of linking immigration to nation building, since the dominant national myth (to the extent that there has been one) has been a national tradition of toleration requiring no systematic efforts to promote anti-racism (Weil and Crowley 1994: 112)

There was one lone political seer in the form of Enoch Powell, who as early as 1974 began to warn of the longer-term implications of belonging to the EEC. However, whereas Powell had helped to galvanise a distinct "Powellite" faction on the right in the Conservative Party on immigration issues and free-market economics in the late 1960s, the same thing did not occur on the issue of Europe (Schoen 1973). Driven to despair by the reluctance of the Heath leadership to respond to his arguments, Powell voted Labour in 1974 and departed from the Conservative Party for Unionist politics in Ulster. There appeared to be no room for a De Gaulle figure in British politics. In the process, he deprived the Conservative right of coherent intellectual leadership on the European issue for the following decade, and it was not indeed to be until the early 1990s that a small group of "Eurosceptics" began to emerge to organize Conservative opinion on the issue.

By the late 1980s, the contours of the earlier debates on both Europe and immigration/race had changed only marginally. For the Conservative right the emerging issue of Europe increasingly appeared to be the threat to the very identity of British society and politics. It is one they believe that can only be fought off by the mobilization of a strong body of patriotic sentiments. As Timothy Garton Ash has pointed out, much of the debate over "Europe" has really been about Britain as it has become caught up in a tortured process of national self-examination (Ash 1995). Seen in the context of the wider processes of European integration, this is not particularly surprising. The progressive expansion of the European Union has undermined the orthodox concept of sovereignty linked to the unit of the nation state. Sovereignty has, instead, become an increasingly tradeable resource at the level of political elites among the fifteen members states of the EU, though for electorates it is a matter of considerable anxiety, as concepts of national identity become divorced from the political sphere. (Hedetoft 1994: 13–46). This battle for control over the definition of sovereignty threatens to destabilize Western European politics unless

104

some generally acceptable compromise set of formulas can be worked out that ensures a division of sovereign powers between the EU on the one hand and the various member states on the other.

Short of such a compromise being established, Western European politics have become defined around identity politics, as battles rage over the nature and definition of the various component groupings of the EU. It is in this context that the Anglocentric right wing of the Conservative Party made a bid to define the terms of debate over the politics of Englishness in the 1990s, though in a manner that was largely devoid of explicit reference to issues of race. The leading Tory Eurosceptic, Michael Spicer, for example, has seen sovereignty as a simple absolute, with Britain either having it or not. By this yardstick, Maastricht was nothing less than "a torpedo fired at the keel of British democracy" (Spicer 1992: 14). Similar sentiments echoed around the Conservative right, many of whom thought they had at last found an issue that would secure a renewed momentum for the Conservatives after the departure of Mrs Thatcher. They proved sufficiently strong to leave John Major with a majority of three in November 1992 in a Commons vote on the Maastricht Treaty, following a vigorous defence of the policy of staying in Europe. "National self-interest is not about striking attitudes", he declared, "but about striking deals which are in our own interest" (*The Times* 5 November 1994).

The following year, an attempt was made by a right-wing MP to try and link the issue of national identity with that of race and immigration. In a widely reported, if notorious speech, Winston Churchill attempted to inject a further dose of Powellite rhetoric into the British body politic. Churchill's speech to the Association of Jewish Servicemen was notable for its linkage of immigration to an English rather than a specifically British identity and perhaps indicated how far the Conservative right has travelled on the issue since the "rivers of blood" of Enoch Powell in 1968. In an attack specifically on John Major, Churchill declared:

Mr Major seeks to reassure us with the old refrain "There'll always be an England!" He promises us that, 50 years on from now, spinsters will still be cycling to church on Sunday morning. More like the Muezzin will be calling Allah's faithful to the high street mosque (*The Times* 29 May 1993).

Churchill's speech also went back to the issue of numbers of immigrants by claiming that under existing legislation the immigrant population was increasing each year by over 59,000 a year or a figure greater than the total size of the town of Grantham (pop. 31,095) (*The Times* 1 June 1993). Such emotive language failed to do much to rally the Tory right wing around the issue. Churchill soon found himself disowned by the party leadership while Charles Wardle, the Home Office Minister, accused him of getting his facts wrong. In addition, papers like *The Times* saw the speech as giving comfort to "militant anti-racist campaigners" who had been left for some years without an issue to fight for (*The Times* 31 May 1993).

Some analysts have seen the speech as confirming the fact that the government was still under pressure from its right wing to be tough on immigration controls (Layton Henry, 1994: 293). However, a rather more important consideration is that Churchill's political isolation on the immigration issue indicates that, so far at least, the debate over nationhood in Britain has not lived up to predictions that it would connect up with issues of race (Saggar 1993b: 35). By the early 1990s the electorate appeared only marginally interested in the immigration issue, and appeared far more concerned about Europe. While there had been little stress on race issues in the 1992 election, it is possible to detect underlying racial themes as secondary issues in the campaign, linked specifically to Labour's capacity to govern (Saggar 1993a: 697). The Conservative right *could* have chosen to continue with the racial theme in British politics, though the dominant issue was increasingly that of Europe, following the signing of the Maastricht Treaty in 1992. Churchill's sub-Powellite rhetoric was a diversion from what was felt to be the far more central issue of protecting British – or more specifically English – national sovereignty and the fitness of the Conservative Party as the only party capable of protecting these from the tentacles of the Brussels bureaucracy. This theme became increasingly evident in the motions submitted for the 1992 party conference. Luton South Conservatives, for example, called on the government to ensure that "the shackles of state socialism so successfully rolled back after the past 13 years are not re-imposed by a Federal Europe" while another called for "an end to interference in the nooks and crannies of British life by unelected bodies overseas" (*The Times* 19 September 1992).

There was an increasingly Gaullist tone to British politics in the 1990s as the European issue started to exert a growing impact on electoral attitudes, though one that lacked anything like a Gaullist political leader following Mrs Thatcher's departure at the end of 1990. It has become increasingly clear that the right has the advantage in a number of respects where Europe is concerned, but it has so far failed to be galvanized by a charismatic political leader capable of disciplining the rebellious ranks of the party's right around a clear political agenda. Instead the right-wing attacks on the party leadership over Europe have tended to contribute to a general sense of party malaise as it has performed poorly at by-elections and local elections and undermined the authority of John Major. The Conservative right, therefore, has failed to exploit fully the electoral opportunities provided by Europe. In 1995, for example, 74% of all voters supported a referendum on whether Britain should join a federal Europe (69% Conservative and 74% Labour) while 71% of voters supported a referendum on joining a single currency (65% Conservative and 74% Labour). The fact that Labour voters are more insistent than Conservative voters on a referendum on these two issues suggests that the Conservative Party probably has a considerable opportunity to take a hard-line stand on the issues and try to wean voters away from a Labour Party that is "soft" on the issue (*The Guardian* October 10 1995). There was some attempt to do so during the 1994 European elections, when the Home Secretary, Michael Howard, tried to play the race card by accusing the Labour Party of seeking to dismantle domestic immigration controls in favour of those accruing from Brussels, so leaving the country open to having up to 8 million foreign nationals coming to settle from elsewhere in Europe (*The Guardian* 27 May 1994).

The resurgence of quasi-Gaullist rhetoric has given an added momentum to the drive on the Tory right to try and define a new sense of national purpose. Even though John Major managed to see off his right-wing Eurosceptic critics in the summer of 1995, the longer-term ideological challenge remains and is likely to resurface with particular bellicosity in the wake of a Conservative general election defeat. John Redwood, the defeated leadership candidate, for instance founded a new Conservative Policy Forum as a think-tank to formulate policy in support of the ideal of a sovereign national entity still strongly controlled from London and Westminster. It also sought to return to the Thatcherite strategy of devolving limited power to consumers through market processes and is resolved, if need be, to reject future rulings from the European Court of Justice.[3] Elsewhere on the right, though, there is a rather different ideological tendency expressed in the form of a revamped economic libertarianism. This revives Thatcherite demands for a massive roll back of the state and echoes similar rhetoric across the Atlantic among Republicans in the United States such as Newt Gingrich. One luminary among this latter group, the Tory MP Alan Duncan now a party vice-chairman, would like to see public expenditure halved from some 43% of GNP to a mere 20% (*The Times* August 16 1995).

These debates between neo-Gaullists and economic libertarians suggest that the Conservative right in the 1990s has generally been preoccupied with issues of the economy and political sovereignty and have for the most part avoided issues of race and ethnic culture, unlike the Powellites in the late 1960s and 1970s. It is by no means evident that this situation will continue. As the debate over the Asylum Bill has shown, some Conservative managers still see some political mileage to be gained from the issue of immigration. In the course of the 1990s the number of asylum seekers to Britain rose astronomically from 4,000 in 1988 to 44,840 in 1991, though falling back to 22,370 in 1993. The issue was initially dealt with in the 1993 Asylum and Immigration Appeals Act which imposes tight conditions on would-be asylum seekers and has invoked the anger of the UN Human Rights Committee. Since it takes an average of 32 weeks to process individual cases, the backlog of cases had increased considerably to 55,255 at the end of 1994. The then Home Secretary Michael Howard proposed publishing a "white list" of countries deemed to be safe, while the Bill would cut back the appeals process to 42 days from the current period that can run up to 18 months (*The Guardian* May 21 1995). Reducing the number of asylum seekers was likely to be politically popular and accorded with the government's general desire to cut back on welfare spending, though in the course of the Bill's progress through Parliament the government studiously sought to avoid unnecessary confrontation by reprieving some 13,000 would-be refugees who would have been deprived of benefits (*The Independent* 12 January 1996).

Critics of the Asylum and Immigration Bill such as the Bishop of Liverpool roundly condemned it as a measure that would harm domestic race relations (*The Times* October 26 1995), though it is clear that some Conservative Party managers saw political capital to be made from it. The former Director of Research at Conservative Central Office, Andrew Lansley, reportedly said that "immigration, an issue which we raised successfully in 1992 and again in the 1994 Euro elections campaign, played particularly well in the tabloids and has more potential to hurt" (*The Guardian* December 5 1995). The Conservative Party may well find, indeed, that the control of immigration at the European level is an increasingly sensitive political issue in domestic British politics, raising as it does the question of sovereignty in an acute form. A number of members of the EU have found that it has been in their interest to work for a centralizing policy in Brussels in order to avoid an unchecked plethora of divergent policies at the national level. This approach in many respects contradicts the central tenet of subsidiarity, though it may be that in the longer term administrative harmonization is of greater importance than short-term electoral advantage (Butt 1994: 188).

## BACK TO BASICS?

The steady drift of the party in the early 1990s into a rhetoric of Englishness has done little to boost its standing among black and Asian minorities. The small progress that was achieved during the 1980s was not really capitalized upon and there is evidence of a further decline in support. A survey by the CRE in 1992 of 30 constituencies in England and Wales selected from 113 seats where the ethnic minority vote was over 5% of the total found that 77% of the Asian vote and 85% of the Afro-Caribbean vote went to the Labour Party, while the Asian vote for the Conservatives fell from 15% in 1987 to 11% in 1992 and for Afro-Caribbeans it fell from 17% to 8% over the same period (Geddes 1995: 275–85). By 1997, there was limited evidence to show a small Tory revival among Asians (25 per cent) though not among blacks (8 per cent) (MORI 1987).

At the local government level, some of the small gains made as a result of the work of the One Nation Forum in the 1980s have been undermined in the course of the 1990s. In Birmingham, for instance, the Forum managed for a period to establish a fairly successful branch chaired by a man of Greek origin, Demetrios Marcus. This grew to some dozen members and met every six weeks to consider issues and send reports to Central Office. Conservative candidates continued to do rather poorly in local elections, reflecting the fact that the party was still seen by the black and Asian electorate as largely white, middle-class and suburban. On occasions, however, the race factor helped Conservative candidates to increase their vote. In the Sparkbrook ward in Birmingham the Labour leader of Birmingham Council, Dick Knowles, had his majority cut by an Asian Tory candidate A.U. Hassan in 1992 (Solomos and Black 1995: 160–1). In the May general election two Asian Tories, Choudhary and Riaz, made quite spectacular inroads into Labour majorities in Bethnal Green and Bow and in Bradford West respectively.

Elsewhere, the Conservatives found that the small support they could garner from ethnic minorities came from rather curious groups of political marginals who tended to look to the party as a place of refuge after bitter infighting between rival groups on the left. In Brent, for example, the local Tories made a tactical alliance with a small African community that formed itself into the Brent Democratic Labour Party after falling out with the local Labour Party. Led by the politically volatile Nkedi Amalu-Johnson it was seen by some local Tories as preferable to the "loony left", although it was generally viewed with considerable suspicion by Conservative Central Office (*The Times* 11 August 1991).

At the same time, the Conservative Party's devolved structure has ensured that some constituencies still secure the support of political activists from the far right. In Torbay, a former National Front activist, Mark Cotterill, joined the local Conservative Association in January 1993, even though he had been the agent for the NF candidate in the same constituency in the 1992 election. Despite protests from the liberal wing of the party, including the party's one Asian MP at that time, Nirj Deva (Brentford and Isleworth), Central Office declared itself powerless to intervene in the affairs of a local association (*The Times* 15 August 1993).

The reluctance of Central Office to intervene in local affairs ensured that perpetuation of efforts at the local level to play the race and immigration card where it was felt it might retrieve some electoral support. In local elections in Leicester in 1994 there were complaints by local Liberal Democrats over racist literature disseminated by the Conservatives against the building of a mosque, a Sikh *gurdwara* and a Hindu temple on a new housing estate in Humberstone. One of the documents concerned stated "if places of worship are considered necessary in the Hamilton Development, they should be restricted to the religious groups serving the needs of the local community and not outside groups" – presupposing that any ethnic minority community was by definition an "outside group" (*The Independent* 6 March 1994). Similarly, in the case of the London borough of Newham, Conservative candidates contested two wards under the banner of "Conservatives Against Labour's Unfair Ethnic Policies" in an attempt to wean away support from the far-right British National Party (*The Independent* 14 April 1994).

These examples of playing the race card did little to maintain the limited black and Asian support for the party that had been secured during the 1980s. In the mid-1990s the Party became embarrassed by a number of well-publicized resignations of prominent black supporters complaining of restrictions on their career ambitions. In October 1994, a black civil servant, Joyce Sampson, resigned from the party after 12 years to join the Labour Party, complaining that there was a "glass ceiling" in the party for people from an ethnic background (*The Independent* 14 October 1994, *The Guardian* 14 October 1994). In the same month all the Asian members of the Conservative Association in Small Heath in Birmingham resigned after the chairman, Qayyam Chaudhary, alleged that there was a barrier against his trying to stand as an MP and that complaints to Central Office went unanswered (*The Independent* 17 October 1994).

These defections brought adverse publicity on the party at a time when opinion polls indicated it was facing major electoral defeat. They tend to undermine the efforts of John Major to improve the party's image on race. In May 1996 for instance, he attacked the ethnic composition of the House of Commons and called for more black and Asian MPs (*The Guardian* May 29 1996). Major's rhetoric though was not matched by any significant political reforms. Only in the last few months of the government was it finally decided to reverse previous opposition to multiculturalism and antiracism in schools and to work with the CRE on ethnic monitoring schemes and a programme to tackle ethnic stereotyping (*The Guardian* September 6 1996).

By the time of the general election in May 1997 the party had not really succeeded in altering its image towards the broad bulk of black and Asian voters. Its attempt to develop a strategy early in 1997 to attract ethnic minority votes failed to produce any significant results. Its one Asian MP, Nirj Deva, ran a campaign in Brentford and Isleworth that was based mainly on local issues rather than on national party policy (*The Guardian* April 17 1997).

## ELECTORAL COLLAPSE AND THE RISE OF HAGUE

The spectacular electoral collapse of the Conservative Party in the general election of May 1 1997 has radically altered the political land-scape in Britain. The unprecedented Labour majority of 179 in the House of Commmons left the Conservative Party without any repre-sentative from the Asian or Afro-Caribbean communities following Nirj Deva's defeat. The swift departure of John Major and the suc-cession of the relatively inexperienced political novice William Hague has led some commentators to suggest that the party may well be in terminal decline (Gray 1997). Such predictions may prove to be rather premature; even if the Conservative Party did split up it will almost certainly be replaced by some other political alignment on the right of British politics with a standpoint on issues of race. Indeed, such a party might well prove to resemble a continental-style populist party such as the French Front National with a keen desire to play the race card.

So even if the Conservative Party in its present form is destined to be out of power for a considerable number of years, it would be fool-hardy for analysts to dismiss it as of little or no consequence for ethnic minority politics in Britain. While political debate in the party, at the present time of writing, continues to be dominated by European issues, there is still a subcurrent of concern about its relationship to ethnic minorities. This sub-text was vividly illustrated by Hague's own appearance shortly after his emergence as leader at the Notting Hill carnival in the summer of 1997 in what can only be interpreted as a bid to appear at least "respectable" to ethnic minority voters.

The present concern of some sections of the party to appeal to some

111

Asian and Afro-Caribbean voters raises the more general question of what motivates such attempts when the party has been more or less forced to retreat back to its suburban and county heartlands in Southern England and the Home Counties. A survey of its record since the 1970s indicates three main phases of Conservative political concern on race. The first phase, as Saggar has recently pointed out, was motivated by a simple electoral calculus in the wake of the October 1974 election. The CRC report on black and Asian voting in the election indicated that a number of potentially vital marginal seats were at stake if these voters voted *en masse* for Labour. Conservative efforts centred on the Anglo/Asian and Anglo/West Indian Associations in the mid- to late-1970s can thus be seen as part of an attempt to win over at least sections of the black vote at a time when the party was on the defensive (Saggar 1998).

This phase ended with the victory of Mrs Thatcher in 1979 and a second phase of involvement with race began. Given that the issue of immigration was now widely seen as politically settled in the wake of the 1981 Nationality Act, the Tory involvement with race via the One Nation Forum can be interpreted as a sop by Mrs Thatcher to her liberal critics at a time when they were being marginalised on most other fronts. On this issue at least Mrs Thatcher was willing to appear as something of a One Nation Conservative and significantly, the CRE was not abolished as some of her right wing critics would have liked. The black and Asian vote no longer mattered as much as it did in the 1970s and the Tory interest in the issue was mainly an ideological one. This was still a rather slender sort of liberalism since the party refused to accept the basic tenets of multiculturalism. Mrs Thatcher entertained Ray Honeyford, the controversial headmaster and critic of multiculturalism at Number 10 while the 1988 Education Reform Act marked a commitment to the continuation of a largely mono-cultural form of educational curriculum in state schools.

The removal of Mrs Thatcher from power at the end of 1990 ushered in a third phase of Conservative concern on race under John Major which looks as though it may well continue in a similar form under Hague. Major's interest in promoting a relatively liberal platform on race was partly linked to his own personal hostility to racists in the party from the days when he was active in politics in Brixton. However, his continuing interest in the race issue suggests that he saw it as one notable way of establishing his own personal identity in British politics at a time when he faced continual eclipse by rival factions battling for the Party's soul over Europe. As evidence increasingly emerges of a weak and indecisive leadership in the Major government, it is clear that race was at least one terrain where Major could imprint a mark of his own and confirm his authority as leader of the government.

There are signs of a similar use of race by William Hague who, in the early months of his leadership, was faced by a rather different challenge in the form less of Europe than the referendum on devolution. In a nation-wide tour to try and bolster up his reputation, Hague ensured a well-publicised meeting with Asian businessmen and small traders in Balsall Heath and Handsworth in Birmingham. Here he reiterated the party's long standing belief in the idea that Asians epitomise conventional Conservative commitments to family values, hard work and private enterprise (*The Guardian* September 24 1997).

Once again, ethnic minorities, especially those from South Asia, were being used as symbols to embody the identity of a party that is in many respects in serious question given the apparent threat to the long-term cohesion of the Union with Scottish and Welsh devolution and the domination of the middle ground of British politics by the new Blair government. This need by the Tory leadership to turn to black and Asian voters respresents a remarkable shift from the position of thirty years ago when the axis of debate in the Conservative Party was defined around Enoch Powell's 1968 "rivers of blood" speech. Black and Asian communities — in those days usually termed simply "immigrants" – were then seen as a direct threat to a British or English culture whose identity was not really in question. The Conservative Party was by implication seen in the Powellite analysis as the true embodiment and defender of all that was held most dear in this racialised definition of Englishness (Rich 1986).

It would be premature to conclude that the older debate within the Conservative Party stretching back to the 1960s over immigrant numbers and their potential to undermine British/English identity is entirely over. There are indications that subterranean currents still exist within the party which are committed to a racialised conception of British (or more specifically English) ethnic identity. The long standing division within the party between the economic libertarian wing and the Tory traditionalists looks set to continue though they may emerge in somewhat different forms. Under Mrs Thatcher the former wing tended to prevail and there was relatively little emphasis on the need for preserving communal and national identities. In the 1990s, by contrast, free-market Conservatism came increasingly to rely on the latter tradition of community as resistance mounted to the market disrupting and undermining communities (*The Guardian* July 3 1995).

The rhetoric of the Tory traditionalists has failed to inject anything significantly new into the debate on British and English national identity. Right wing rhetorics of national identity generally fall back upon a body of collective virtues and a shared framework of historical understanding, though they also contain the potential for confusing

113

cultural with political life and equating a political community with the culture of the dominant ethnic or national group (Parekh 1994: 502). Much will depend upon the degree to which these cultural traits become politicised and linked to a coherent populist ideology of nationhood. Many political parties on the right in Europe make populist overtures towards the idea of preserving nationhood and generally avoid going down the path of fascist parties of the extreme right and systematically linking nationhood with race. To this extent, they avoid giving a systematic lead to racism, which remains rather diffuse and inarticulated as it fails to gain acceptance at the level of mainstream political debate. Michel Wieviorka has termed this *infraracism* and has argued that it is the weakest of four main levels of racism in Europe. It can be contrasted with the second level of *split racism* where racism is still weak but tends to have a rather more obvious prominence as a central political issue. The final two forms represent more politicised versions of racism and are termed *political racism*, when political debate give a greater degree of unity to racist ideology and *total racism* where the state becomes based on racist principles (Wieviorka 1994: 183–4).

The British Conservative Party has remained for the most part at the first of these four levels of racist discourse. It has avoided giving any systematic focus to racist tendencies among some of its supporters, though on occasions local Conservative associations have been willing to play a racial or communal card in search for votes in local elections. Under John Major's leadership, the party's official rhetoric in regard to ethnic minorities was unashamedly One Nation Toryism, in striking contrast to other policy issues where the party leadership vacillated as it has sought drastic cuts in such areas as education and welfare. The diffuse nature of the racism within the party survives mostly as a series of tribal prejudices that are fortified by the extremely small black and Asian participation in most local associations (certainly outside major city areas) and by the preoccupation of the party's ideological right since the late 1980s with the issue of Europe.

Such prejudices may well be able to survive at the local within the Conservative Party, especially if the modernisation and restructuring of the party under Hague ensures some devolution of authority to elderly constituency associations. They are only likely to surface in a more virulent form if the party faces continuing splits over such issues as Europe and devolution and opts for a more populist path under a new leadership anxious to champion some form of isolationist little Englandism.

## NOTES

1. Mrs Thatcher was keen to see the recruitment of suitable black and Asian candidates by the Conservative Party and later described the defeat of John Taylor at Cheltenham as a "very sad result" (*The Sun* 10 April 1992).
2. *The Voice* 17 October 1989. The Young Monday Club also urged repatriation "as a matter of policy". *Asian Herald* 2 November 1989.
3. John Redwood, "Building a strong foundation" (*The Times* 16 August 1995).

## REFERENCES

Anwar, M. 1990. The Participation of Asians in the British Political System. In *South Asians Overseas*, C. Clarke, C. Peach & S. Vertovec (eds). Cambridge: Cambridge University Press.

Ash, T. G. 1995. Catching the wrong bus? *The Times Literary Supplement*, May 5, 3–4.

Commission for Racial Equality, 1994. *Don't Take Them For Granted*. London: CRE.

Crewe, I. 1993. The Thatcher Legacy. In *Britain at the Polls*, A. King et al. (eds). Chatham House, Chatham House Publishers.

Geddes, A. 1995. Ethnic Minority Representation in Britain in the 1992 General Election. *Party Politics*, vol. 1, no 2, 275–85.

Gray, J. (1997) Tories are on the brink *The Guardian* September 22.

Hedetoft, U. 1994. The State of Sovereignty in Europe: Political Concept or Cultural Self Image. In *National Culture and European Integration*, Zetterholm, S. (ed). Oxford: Berg, 13–46.

Layton Henry, Z. 1994. Britain: The Would-Be Zero-Immigration Country. In *Controlling Immigration: A Global Perspective*, W. A. Cornelius et al. (eds). Stanford: Stanford University Press, 273–94.

Miles, R. & A. Phizacklea. 1984, *White Man's Country*. London: Pluto Press.

Parekh, B. 1994. Discourses on National Identity. *Political Studies*, vol XLII, 492–504.

Philip, A. B. 1994. European Union Immigration Policy: Phantom, Fantasy or Fact?, *West European Politics*, vol 17, no 2, 168–88.

Rich, P. 1986. Conservative Ideology and Race in Modern British Politics. In *Race, Government and Politics in Britain*, Z. Layton Henry & P. Rich (eds). London and Basingstoke: The Macmillan Press, 45–67.

Saggar, S. 1992. *Race and Politics in Britain*. Hemel Hempstead: Harvester Wheatsheaf.

Saggar, S. 1993a. Can political parties play the "race card" in general elections? The 1992 poll revisited. *New Community*, vol. 19, no. 4, 693–99.

Saggar S. 1993b. Black Participation and the transformation of the race issue. In British politics, *New Community*, vol. 20, no. 1, 27–41.

Saggar S. 1998. A late, though not lost, opportunity: ethnic minority electors, party strategy and the Conservative Party. *The Political Quarterly*, forthcoming.

Schoen, D. 1973. *Enoch Powell and the Powellites*. London and Basingstoke: The Macmillan Press.

Sewell, T. 1993. *Black Tribunes: Black Political Participation in Britain*. London, Lawrence and Wishart.

Solomos J. & L. Black 1995. *Race, Politics and Social Change*. London: Routledge.

Spicer, M. 1992. *A Treaty Too Far*. London: Fourth Estate.

Srinivasan, S. 1992. The class position of the Asian petty bourgeoisie. *New Community*, vol. 19, no. 1 (October), 61–74.

Weil P. & J. Crowley. 1994. Integration in Theory and Practice: A Comparison of France and Britain. *West European Politics*, vol. 17, no. 2, 110–124.

Werbner, P. 1991. The fiction of unity in ethnic politics: aspects of representation and the state among British Pakistanis. In *Black and Ethnic Leaderships*, P. Werbner & M. Amwar (eds). London: Routlege, 113–141.

Whiteley, P., P. Seyd, J. Richardson & P. Bissell. 1994. Thatcherism and the Conservative Party. *Political Studies*, vol. XLII, 185–203.

Wieviorka, M. 1994. Racism in Europe: Unity and Diversity. In *Racism, Modernity and Identity on the Western Front*, A. Rattansi & S. Westwood (eds). Oxford: Polity Press.

# CHAPTER SIX

# New Labour debates and dilemmas

## Kalbir Shukra

### INTRODUCTION

The history of Labour's position on race and immigration is well documented as constituting one half of a restrictive bipartisan consensus (Solomos 1989, Layton-Henry 1984, Carter et al. 1987, Tompson 1987, Shukra 1995b). On the question of "black"[1] political participation, Labour has been contradictory. Whilst seeking black support, it rejected black claims for representation and recognition (Shukra 1990a). The construction of New Labour in the 1990s only exacerbated matters. Although it works with its black lobby in the form of Black Socialist Society (BSS), the party also stands accused of challenging, investigating and undermining the recruitment, membership and activities of thousands of its black supporters.

Black participation within the Labour Party has been a contentious issue since ethnic minority voters were first identified as a coherent political constituency (Messina, this volume). Ethnic minority voting patterns first came to prominence when two close-run general elections in 1974 and a series of research studies highlighted the importance of marginal votes. While mainstream political parties wooed black electoral support in the 1970s (Saggar, this volume), black party members argued for greater representation (Shukra 1990a). However, it was not until 1981 that black people began to make an impact with their demand for political influence in return for votes. The explosion of anger in urban areas in 1981 provided black activists with political leverage while the rising fortunes of the Labour left in local government produced opportunities to place black representation on the

117

mainstream political agenda. Amid the growing weight of black demands and the creation of new opportunities to voice them, existing Labour Party members took the initiative to establish an unofficial national Labour Party Black Section (LPBS) in 1983.

During the ten years which followed, the Labour Party refused to recognise LPBS. LPBS members, nevertheless, operated as if their group was legitimate, often with the support of their local Labour Party branches. Consequently, the relationship between LPBS and the Labour Party leadership was marked by conflict and tension. However, in 1993 Labour leaders and officials worked with a handful of black party members to install an official "Black Socialist Society" (BSS). It was heralded as the most significant step forward for the party on ethnic minority representation since the election of four black Labour MPs in 1987. BSS appeared to symbolize a serious working compromise between Labour's National Executive Committee (NEC) and black party members. This chapter will consider how and why that settlement occurred.

BSS embodied a range of different hopes and aspirations amongst black party members. It was perceived as a forum in which black Labour Party members could discuss issues pertaining to black communities; a mechanism through which black members might influence party policy; a machine to recruit new black members; and a base from which new black political careers might be launched. Not only were these objectives similar to those of LPBS, but I will show that BSS soon ran into difficulties which were remarkably close to the LPBS experience.

The tensions and contradictions which characterized the development of Labour's relationship with its black members were rooted in their mutual efforts to accommodate each other's objectives (Shukra 1990a). While the Labour Party was primarily motivated by a need to maintain the support of black voters without alienating white people, black party members made significant electoral gains in the 1980s by pressurising the party for rewards in the form of representation at every level of the party (Geddes 1993). Having secured black voters in the 1980s, the party leadership changed its focus on to white ones. This chapter identifies the key debates and dilemmas which emerged from the changes and developments in this relationship in the 1990s and places them in the context of political and ideological change. In doing so, this contribution highlights how the impact of the changes can be seen in the loss of critical debate about the relevance of the Labour Party to black communities, the conditional support offered to BSS by the Labour Party leadership, the shift in emphasis from anti-racism to equal opportunities in management and a move away from militant community mobilizations towards support groups organised around victims of racism and their families. In sum, what will emerge is an analysis of what became of LPBS and of black politics generally.

## THE DEMISE OF LABOUR PARTY BLACK SECTION

LPBS flourished in the early 1980s in the context of street rebellions which heightened the influence of black activists arguing for recognition from the mainstream. The rise of left-led Labour councils, with which this coincided, enabled, first, black representation to be pursued in local Labour Parties and, secondly, authorities and resources to be allocated to ethnic minority groups. The 1987 General Election bore the fruit of LPBS' work in the form of four black Labour MPs and the concomitant legitimacy to black political activity through mainstream party politics. However, there was a significant change in the socio-political landscape after 1987 which contributed to LPBS' entry into a protracted period of decline and the emergence of the Labour Party's BSS.

After the 1987 General Election, LPBS found itself lacking new ways of maintaining electoral pressure on the Labour Party and became ineffective in using situations where the black vote appeared insecure to put pressure on the Labour leadership. Instead, it maintained a low profile. In areas such as Bolton and Bradford, for example, it was no longer LPBS, but the newly formed Islamic Party, which stole the headlines with political demands. The headlines read "Muslims seize chance to find equality in Labour heartland" (*Independent* 1990), "Bolton's Muslims find a mouthpiece" (*Guardian* 1990) and "Disaffected Muslims backing the Islamic Party could cost Labour seats in Bolton" (*Independent* 1990). Similarly in Vauxhall, it was the "independent" candidates who put pressure on the Labour Party and not LPBS. According to the columns of *The Caribbean Times* (1989): "The party's national executive is believed to be running scared of the challenge being offered by the two independent candidates for the seat."

Rather than increasing pressure on the Labour Party, LPBS found itself under more pressure than ever before to operate within a framework acceptable to the Labour NEC. This was partly the result of the other main change in the political climate: the retreat of the Labour left. This affected LPBS right into the 1990s because from 1985 the organization's leadership was associated with the Labour left.

> We're very intimately connected with the fortunes of the left. If the left suffers, on a very practical level, we don't get the same amount of resolutions to Conference ... That's the main

119

worry to me ... As you know, at the moment the left is somewhat divided as to the strategy.

(Wongsam 1990)

As Mike Wongsam (National Chair 1990) suggested, the future of a LPBS reliant on the Labour left looked bleak at the turn of the decade. However, the post-1987 LPBS began to look away from the Bennism of the 1980s. When the left tried to regroup at the Chesterfield conference called by Tony Benn in 1987, its split on how to respond to the cuts facing local government was reflected in the different positions taken by LPBS councillors. The division weakened the left, which appeared to flounder in the face of official policies recalling the days of the 1975 Social Contract. The political retreat of the left meant that left supporters in LPBS began to see themselves working to "prepare the ground for the new rise of the left ... based on alternative economic policies and not simply on constitutional matters" (Wongsam 1990). This retreat signalled an opportunity for the growth of cultural and religious reactions to racism, ethnic mobilizations and alienated responses such as the Asian youth revolts witnessed in Bradford in 1995.

Since much LPBS work was based historically around local authorities, the changing political climate in local government also affected LPBS. The defeat of the left and Kinnock's crackdown on "loony left", "high spending" councils, meant that LPBS councillors of the 1990s operated in the context of pressure on all Labour councils to prove themselves as responsible, moderate, low-spending, market-led managers of public funds. In trying to demonstrate their moderation, many councils made efforts to play down race relations work, maintain a low Poll Tax/Council Tax level, defeat the town hall unions and make swingeing cuts in jobs and services. Pressure on councillors increased as they feared that the emergence of politically-restricted posts under the Local Government Act 1988, might force many black councillors, who worked for neighbouring authorities, to choose between job and political office.

Financial changes in local government in the early 1990s, including the introduction of the Poll Tax, Council Tax, Compulsory Competitive Tendering and various financial constraints, turned the work of councillors into a series of decisions about what services to cut; how many workers should be made redundant; which jobs would be lost and which departments closed. The lack of resistance to these measures from black and white councillors alike suggested black councillors would increasingly find themselves arguing for the closure of one service to a local black community preferred to another. Ironically, this could only exacerbate the ethnic rivalry which the LPBS "black" identity sought to counter. I shall return to this question later in the chapter.

The participation of women in LPBS also altered after 1987. Out of the more politically-experienced black women in the organization, only Martha Ossamer demonstrated a firm commitment to LPBS. Linda Bellos and Sharon Atkin were no longer actively involved and Diane Abbott prioritized her parliamentary duties. Ossamer urged the younger women activists to organise as a sub-group called "Women in Black Section" (WIBS) but it made little impact. WIBS conferences were held irregularly and were poorly-attended events which focused on policy matters specifically as they related to black women and the election of officers in WIBS, LPBS and the Labour Party. Although LPBS rules required that 50 per cent of the positions on LPBS Executive Committee be held by women, the key committee positions after 1987 tended to remain in the hands of men.

The final development which affected LPBS after 1987 was the increase in racism and repression in Britain. Highly publicised drug scares were used to justify police raids and harassment. Racist attacks and murders were on the increase (Skellington et al. 1992: 60–66). New panics were created in the form of "Yardie" scares and fears of "Muslim fanatics". Meanwhile black people died in police custody and immigration controls were tightened. In the political sphere, there was a growing concern with "Englishness" – as represented by Norman Tebbit's remarks about cricket tests, anti-immigration interventions from Winston Churchill and the short-lived election of a BNP councillor in Tower Hamlets.

It was in this changing social and political climate that LPBS found the Labour leadership increasingly intolerant. In its death agony the pressure group abdicated its key objective of official recognition in order to accommodate to the party leadership. The result was a negotiated compromise in the form of BSS. Why were LPBS members prepared to concede to the party leadership on the question of official recognition? This can only be understood in the context of the changing fortunes of rival ideological traditions within the party and the construction of New Labour.

## NEW REALISM TO NEW LABOUR

In her book, *Black Tribunes*, Terri Sewell (1993) identified the late 1980s and 1990s as a period of "New Realism" in the Labour Party. This is misleading, because an analysis of ideological shifts within the Labour Party reveals that the renewed struggle for cleansing the party of left-wing influence and a Labour left policy of retrenchment began much earlier under the leadership of Neil Kinnock in the mid-1980s. In 1985, Kinnock attacked Militant-led Liverpool council for its resistance to ratecapping. He proposed a "dented shield strategy" regarding local government cuts which involved justifying expenditure cuts on the basis of defending the most "deprived" (Shukra 1990a). In the wake of the 1986 Greenwich by-election in which defeat was blamed on London's left-led council policies, the Labour leadership stepped up its campaign against Militant, the "loony left" and gay activists. At the same time, Kinnock indicated that tolerance of LPBS was coming to an end. He sent out warning shots of disciplinary action against separatist activity and followed this up by insisting that the black prospective parliamentary candidates ensured that they did not support LPBS policy where it differed from Labour Party policy. Following Labour's defeat in the 1987 General Election, Kinnock maintained his tough stance against fringe tendencies within the party. Thus the NEC imposed white candidates in the 1988 Kensington by-election and the 1989 Vauxhall by-election where LPBS was relying on black candidates to win. The heady days of "municipal socialism" from which LPBS grew, appeared to be over. The only additional facet of the anti-left campaign after the 1987 election defeat was the launch of a policy-review exercise which marked a continuity in the leaderships of Neil Kinnock, John Smith and Tony Blair and had the effect of diluting and then reversing many Labour policies. By November 1995, Tony Blair was able to take his message to a Confederation of British Industry conference where he claimed that Labour had changed irreversibly and accepted the market economy.

In the 1990s, LPBS experienced more trouble when a sitting black candidate, Crispin St. Hill, was defeated in nominations for the 1990 Mid-Staffordshire by-election. Further, LPBS's target of gaining 30 black prospective parliamentary candidates for the 1992 general election failed to materialize and LPBS chair Narendra Makanji lost his council seat in Haringey (Shukra 1990b). In the context of these losses, LPBS concentrated on surviving as a caucus within the Labour Party and shelved its concern for black representation for fear that members might be expelled from the party. This was exposed in the 1989 Vauxhall by-election, when LPBS was caught in a dilemma because two black independent candidates, Rudy Narayan and Reverend Huey Andrews, decided to stand for election in response to the Labour leadership's imposition of a white candidate, Kate Hoey. The question facing LPBS members was should they support a white Labour candidate or a black independent one? LPBS refused to support either of the black candidates because they were anxious about the risks entailed in any challenge to the party leadership. They anticipated expulsion from the party, and sought to limit any damage to their prospects of gaining official recognition within the party. National vice-chair, Kingsley Abrams, noted after the event that "While the NEC's actions were evidently racist, we could do nothing but protest in the media" (Abrams 1989).

LPBS retreated in the face of Labour's 1990s not-so-new realism and came to accept a pragmatic approach to the question of its own constitutional recognition within the party. Its original demand for recognition as a section within the party was replaced by a growing acceptance that a Socialist Society option was more feasible. Prior to 1987, even the idea of discussing how socialist society status for LPBS might be negotiated was rejected out of hand. After the general election, however, there were a growing number of dissenting voices. Paul Sharma and Bill Morris initiated a debate during 1987–8 which took place largely through press and television interviews. Although LPBS National Committee at the 1988 AGM treated the idea as a betrayal of the organization's fundamental principles, Bernie Grant MP picked up the idea and surprised conference delegates with his own version of a way forward. Grant claimed that Neil Kinnock's representative had approached him to lead negotiations that might end the LPBS controversy. Grant asked conference to give him a mandate to go ahead and enter into dialogue. Grant's greater authority within LPBS as an MP who had continued to work closely with LPBS after being elected to Parliament may have contributed to the support which he gained from the delegates, but also important was the enduring climate of realism and retreat. LPBS had declined to the point that attendance at its own conferences had dwindled to only 50 delegates in 1988. In this context there was growing recognition that a new direction was needed. This was finally resolved through the establishment of BSS.

Not only was the ideological climate within the Labour Party strikingly different when BSS was created, but its development needs to be read in the context of Tony Blair's construction of New Labour. While Kinnock's new realism was designed to address the perceived problem of left-wing influence within the party, John Smith in 1993 introduced measures to reduce trade union influence, notably through one member/one vote. Tony Blair extended the Kinnock and Smith reforms through a bigger project to "modernise" the party. In his first year as party leader, Blair confronted and triumphed over remnants of the left and trade unions. He announced plans to replace Clause Four of the constitution, which declared the party in favour of nationalization, with a passage that committed Labour to a market-dominated economy. Then he used his victory to declare the birth of "New Labour" and launched a review of all party policies. The old Labour left, TGWU and Britain's largest trade union, UNISON, campaigned and voted against the change of Clause Four. They viewed the old clause as the bedrock of Labour's socialist principles. In defeat, the individuals, campaigns and organizations which opposed Blair's alterations contemplated what role they could play within New Labour. With Blair's strategy offering a serious opportunity to oust the Conservatives from government, his opponents continually came up against two questions. First, at what cost were they prepared to support New Labour to gain parliamentary power? Second, would they support New Labour's market-led ethos, communitarian values and managerial approach to social issues (Shukra 1995c)? That New Labour was not prepared to tolerate dissension which might reduce its electoral chances was clear. It is against such dilemmas that the responses of black party members need to be interpreted.

## WHY A BLACK SOCIALIST SOCIETY?

LPBS members concentrated a large proportion of energy debating the way forward for their organization. The direction they should take was often a contentious issue within LPBS and the source of many splits and realignments. However, a turning-point was marked by the debate at LPBS 1990 AGM which was unusually amicable. The dispute was posed by activists in discussions and meetings, sometimes as a split between left and right factions, and sometimes as divisions between purists and pragmatists. The left, or the purists, were seen to be those wanting to maintain the demand for a LPBS whereas the right, or the pragmatists, called for a Socialist Society formation as a way forward.

The way forward debate originated as a question of how to achieve official recognition in the party constitution. The dominant position within LPBS up to 1988 was one of demanding no less than constitutional recognition as a section, along the lines of the Women and Youth Sections. This position shifted shortly after the 1987 General Election to one of LPBS being prepared to consider proposals from the Labour leadership if they met LPBS' general criteria. At the same time, LPBS did not expect the party leadership to respond seriously to the 1988 Labour Party Conference instruction that the NEC draft proposals for the establishment of an organization for black people modelled on Labour's Socialist Societies. Indeed, fearing that they might be left out of such proposals even if they were forthcoming, LPBS' 1989 AGM in Leicester reaffirmed Grant's 1988 negotiating position which was followed by a proposal to the NEC in July/September 1989. The proposal which finally went to the party conference in 1989 was, however, for a Black Socialist Society which would include whites with voting rights. Refusing to support any proposal which allowed for white membership, LPBS successfully lobbied against this motion at Conference. Consequently all of the proposals put to conference regarding a black group within the Labour Party were rejected.

This resulted in a LPBS recall conference in January 1990 to consider two possible courses of action. The choice was posed as one of continuing to demand a national section as before or to propose fresh negotiations based upon the position endorsed at the Leicester conference. Several more recall meetings resulted in a proposal to the 1990 LPBS AGM to negotiate on the basis of what subsequently became known in LPBS circles as "three principles": unitary organisation; autonomous representation; black-only organization. Despite a debate on this matter at LPBS conference, the negotiating position was adopted and this was reflected in the results of officer elections. The newly-elected national officers of LPBS were returned on the basis that they would pursue a Socialist Society option. The office of Chair was contested between Abrams and Wongsam. Wongsam's election gave him a clear mandate to go ahead and seek official recognition within the Labour Party on mutually acceptable terms.

The way forward debate in 1990 differed primarily in that it occurred in a more defensive political climate. Lack of political leverage, pressure from Walworth Road and the need to keep the organization together, combined to place a greater urgency on LPBS' need to resolve the matter of recognition. At the LPBS 1990 AGM, Grant articulated one of the underlying fears of many LPBS activists. He pointed out that the general political mood was one of retreat and that the left was weak. His view was that LPBS' weakness meant that it was time to be "pragmatic" and assess what would be achievable in such a climate. The endorsement of this perspective at the 1990 AGM indicated that LPBS was lowering its horizons even on the question of its very existence and the form of official recognition it would pursue. The original demand for a section was replaced because it was no longer considered feasible.

By 1991, such pressures were exacerbated by the continued decline in activity within LPBS and the climate within the Labour Party generally (LPBS 1991). At its 1991 AGM, the LPBS leadership proposed a list of priorities for the year ahead, which conference agreed. These included continued negotiations to establish a Black Socialist Society within the Labour Party; to continue as LPBS in the Labour Party; to establish a Constitution Writing Sub-Group of the LPBS National Executive Committee with a brief to draw up a constitution for the proposed Black Socialist Society; and to begin organizing meetings with a view to low-key discussions with other black organizations about the establishment of a Black Socialist Society. This reflected the ascendancy of the view that LPBS should continue to operate under its current constitution, actively develop a Black Socialist Society within the Labour Party and seek to win political leadership of it. Speaking on behalf of LPBS Executive Committee, Mike Wongsam explained to the conference that the move should be seen as a tactic that – in the light of the defensive political climate – was "one of the necessary steps that we need to take in order to ensure the future existence of this organization ..." Therefore, the most immediately pressing activities to be pursued by LPBS activists were to encourage CLPs to support the draft constitution drawn up by a team of LPBS members for a Black Socialist Society and ensure that LPBS members participated in Labour Party consultation exercises related to the establishment of the Society.

The main anxiety shared by LPBS members appeared to be one of how far LPBS could survive after the establishment of a Black Socialist Society. At the 1991 AGM it was acknowledged by Mike Wongsam – summing up on behalf of the Executive Committee – that enabling the development of a Black Socialist Society would mean developing an organization that would replace LPBS' influence within the Labour Party. LPBS entered the 1990s in decline, with only 20 people attending its 1992 AGM, and its leadership attempting to metamorphize the organization into a tendency within the anticipated Black Socialist Society. When BSS was finally set up in 1993, the LPBS project was virtually abandoned. Its members joined BSS and helped to set up local BSS branches.

The original members of LPBS had moved in a variety of different directions: some had become councillors, others were MPs but most were increasingly distancing themselves from the organization. However, BSS offered the opportunity of renewing links on their common ground of official Labour Party territory. LPBS critics such as Paul Boateng MP, Paul Sharma and Bill Morris were all happy to work in a Black Socialist Society which was supported by trade unions and Walworth Road. Nevertheless, the involvement of LPBS members in BSS was viewed with suspicion. Key members of the first BSS national committee were LPBS members: Kingsley Abrams, Palma Black, Marc Wadsworth and Jatin Haria. This produced what one Labour Party Officer described in an interview as "mistrust" (Hakim 1995). Piara Khabra, MP (1995) expressed a highly cynical view and went on to describe BSS as composed primarily of LPBS members and "professional politicians fighting among themselves". For Farzana Hakim (1995), Labour Party Development Officer (Ethnic Minorities), the election of fresh faces to BSS National Committee in 1995 promised a new, positive relationship with the Labour Party. However, LPBS member Palma Black expressed a less than happy view in columns of *The Asian Times* (1995):

> They hatched their plans at a "secret" meeting at Labour Party Headquarters on March 30, facilitated by the Labour Party Development Officer (ethnic minorities) Farzana Hakim, called to decide a slate for the BSS National Committee and an "acceptable" candidate for the BSS seat on the Labour Party National Executive Committee (NEC). This was a deliberate move to block Black Section supporters who established the BSS in the first place, from being re-elected.

An initial facade of unity behind the banner of BSS concealed a number of underlying differences. These quickly emerged in the form of a series of ongoing debates which are considered next.

## THE "BLACK" QUESTION

In recent years usage of the term "black" has come to be contested in political and academic circles (Modood 1988, Hall 1992, Shukra 1995a). After more than a decade of uneven usage and activist acceptance of it as a "political" term denoting people of African, Caribbean and Asian origin or descent, Tariq Modood (1988) articulated a significant challenge in the late 1980s on the basis that the majority of Asians do not accept the term. At the same time the Commission for Racial Equality (CRE) withdrew its support for the term "black" to be used to refer to Asians (Modood 1988). Nevertheless, LPBS retained a commitment to using "black" as an umbrella concept. BSS was soon troubled by a debate about the name of the organization but it also retained the term "black" to denote an Asian as well as African-Caribbean membership. Given the level of debate and discontent, why was usage of the term "black" not abandoned in political circles? The answer chiefly lies in the evolution of the term.

The concept of political blackness was reconstructed in the context of changing political strategies. Whereas in the 1960s and 1970s "black" identity was a tool for mobilizing self-reliant "communities of resistance" to racism (Sivanandan 1988) LPBS in the 1980s used it in a narrower sense to refer to co-ordinating ethnic groups in a bid for resources and representation in the mainstream. In this way LPBS changed "Black as a grassroots struggle ... to black as a parliamen-

127

tary struggle" (Sivanandan 1983: 4). Consequently, African-Caribbean and Asian unity was reduced to achievements at the level of internal party matters, organizational questions and electoral gains. As such, LPBS represented a rupture from "black radicalism" and was central to what I have described in detail elsewhere as the reconstruction of black radicalism in the form of "black perspectivism" (Shukra 1995a).

Although the battle for "black" was won in BSS, the struggle between ethnicists and black perspectivists continued. Prominent Asian members of BSS maintained their argument for the title "Black and Asian Socialist Society" on the basis that some Asians do not identify with the term "black" and they complained to the party and members of Labour's NEC. BSS chair, Jatin Haria, claimed that Asian BSS members manufactured the issue with the ultimate aim of splitting the society so that the party would feel obliged to offer an Asian-led breakaway group a seat on the NEC too (*The Voice* 1995a). Amongst those contesting the name of the BSS were Piara Khabra MP, Keith Vaz MP and Paul Sharma. There was a deep irony in the Asian MPs' defence of an Asian political identity, because, while they feared that what they perceived as Asian interests might be overlooked, they did not stand up against the criminalization of Asians within the party. Asian Labour Party members in constituencies including Birmingham and Manchester had found their proactive demands for a share of representation and resources criminalized. This occurred through the construction of what Solomos and Back identify as "racialized codes and discourses" which associated "black politics with patronage, criminality and corruption ... often relating to particular racialized collectivities (including Asian, Muslim, Pakistani, Indian)" (Solomos and Back 1995: 101).

Solomos and Back made an important breakthrough with their case study of black politics in Birmingham. They identified how patronage politics went unchallenged by the party whilst it was used to secure the position of key white politicians, but created an outcry when the same patterns were emulated by Asians. In the 1990s the Labour Party NEC investigated allegations of Asian membership "abuses" in Manchester and notions of an "Asian Mafia" in Birmingham. In 1995 the party suspended 5,500 black members while it investigated claims that black (mainly Asian) members were mass-recruited to vote for black people in the selection of parliamentary candidates (*The Voice* 1995b). What amounted to the criminalization of Asians in mainstream politics appears to lend support to Modood's suggestion that Asians face a specific new form of racism that some black perspectivists do not appreciate. Yet the very politicians who advocated Modood's arguments kept a low profile on alleged anti-Asian practices.

## RECRUITMENT AND REPRESENTATION

From the mid-1970s, the Labour Party grew increasingly conscious of the value of recruiting black members, but it was left to LPBS to create the machinery that would register and recruit them in the 1980s. The Labour Party consistently claimed to welcome black members and enjoyed the electoral benefits of LPBS activities. Internal disputes between the Labour leadership and its black caucuses were primarily related to party leadership concern that the consequences of a larger and more organised black party membership might be unpalatable. Recent examples of this tension can be found in the allegations and counter-allegations of irregularities in membership lists and voting which were made in Manchester, Birmingham, London, Bradford, Glasgow and Leicester Labour Parties (*The Economist* 1995, *The Voice* 1995b). On the one hand, in the years following the 1987 General Election, Larry Whitty congratulated Asian members involved in the recruitment campaigns in Manchester which drew 600 new Asians members to Gorton Labour Party, while, on the other hand, the fear that Asian membership drives might affect the reselection chances of established MPs led the party to conduct a series of inquiries (BBC 2 1995). When mass applications to join the Labour Party were made by Asians in Birmingham, they were accompanied by allegations of entryism and the suspension of three Birmingham constituency parties. In this context, a three-page "code of conduct" issued by the party (*The Observer* 1995) acquired a racial dimension. A solicitor specializing in racial discrimination agreed to take two cases to court: she could find no evidence of people with English-sounding names having their applications delayed, yet knew of 100 applications with Asian names being delayed for up to 18 months. When the party suspended 5,500 black party activists MPs Roy Hattersley, Bernie Grant and Ken Livingstone condemned the disciplinary action (*The Voice* 1995b) while BSS remained silent (*The Voice* 1995c). With New Labour on a mass recruitment drive at the same time as suspending groups of Asian people who wanted to join, allegations of racism were unsurprisingly rife.

The NEC appeared to be concerned about the knock-on effects of successful recruitment drives amongst Asian communities – namely, that they might produce unofficial Asian block votes in the selection of parliamentary candidates. These developments belie a conclusion drawn by Anthony Messina in this volume that the fear of a white backlash is unlikely "to motivate Labour to disown politically its loyal non-white constituency". The deselection of black prospective parliamentary candidates such as Sharon Atkin and Russell Profitt in the 1980s, the imposition of white candidate Kate Hoey to counter a constituency party all-black shortlist, and the suspension of large numbers of black – mainly Asian – members and constituency parties, contradict Messina's conclusion. These leadership interventions signi-fied a repudiation of some of the political claims of Labour's most loyal black constituents.

This is not to suggest that Labour was willing to lose its black support. After all, the party did create BSS. The central point is that black political organization has come to be so wedded to the Labour Party that consecutive leaderships were able to carry out political assaults without fear of losing significant black support. Diane Abbott MP, a member of Labour's NEC, boldly made the point when she stated that Labour took black loyalty for granted. She said, "They feel they don't have to worry about the Black electorate and any time spent on Black issues is wasted" (*The Voice* 1995d).

Even the Labour Party leadership's concession of BSS to its black members and voters appears to offer little opportunity for real influ-ence. From the start, BSS was denied access to the NEC until individual BSS membership reached a target figure of 5,000. This proved extremely difficult for BSS to achieve, so much BSS conference dis-cussion and tensions with the Party leadership focused on seeking easier access to an NEC seat. BSS called for membership through trade union affiliation to be taken into account and for the figure of 5,000 to be reduced and later for all barriers to be taken down. This internal controversy acquired an added twist with arguments over whether MPs should be entitled to stand for the seat (Jandu 1995). At the time of these debates Tony Blair made an interesting statement which criti-cised the BSS struggle for influence within the party but indicated his support for a BSS that would operate as a Labour Party ambassador in black communities:

> I think the danger with such groups is when they concentrate
> on internal politics rather than win support and raise the poli-
> tical awareness of Black people they become unproductive.
> (*The Voice* 1995e).

If "internal politics" is interpreted as BSS' attempts to influence party policy and gain access to decision-making bodies within the party, Blair's statement can be read as an attempt to curb black members' efforts to influence the party leaderships' decision-making, whilst allowing BSS to exist. Furthermore, the settlement finally reached between BSS national committee and party leaders which allowed BSS an NEC seat once BSS membership reached 2,500 did not make a sig-nificant difference to BSS as this figure remained difficult to achieve (*The Voice* 1995f). This adds weight to the argument that, in relation to its black members and voters, the Labour Party since the 1980s operated a delicate balancing act between conceding to the pressures of black claims and the risk of losing white votes. How did black members react to this approach when they began to lose their political clout?

Rather like trade union leaders, black Labour Party members increasingly viewed their allegiance to the party uncritically. John Smith was able to reduce the influence of trade union block votes without affecting their support of trade unionists for the party. Similarly, although the party presented an ambivalent attitude towards black participation within its ranks, black support remained solid. Asian members in Manchester who complained bitterly about the way they were treated, nevertheless remained loyal to the party (BBC 2, 1995). Moreover, when TGWU chief Bill Morris – who was also a key player in the establishment and maintenance of BSS – criticized Tony Blair, BSS distanced itself from his statements. Kingsley Abrams spoke out on behalf of BSS to urge unity behind Blair against the Tories (*The Voice* 1995g). Abrams was formerly associated with the "left" within LPBS, while Morris was identified as on the "right". The tables were turned when Abrams reacted to protect BSS from any fallout in the aftermath of criticisms of Blair's leadership. It was indicative of two developments. First, that the traditional "left"/"right" divisions within the party no longer defined reactions. Secondly, that BSS members were concerned to protect their membership and the position of BSS within the party, even if it meant supporting the Labour leadership against its own members.

This raises the question of why, despite being treated as secondary, black politicians and voters remain loyal to Labour. Saggar and Messina discuss and contribute to the debate surrounding this question in other chapters of this book. I do not wish to reiterate their points here, but rather to emphasize that whatever reasons, causes or influences make one put one's faith in Labour, the very fact of fidelity is an important indicator of a significant change in black political strategy since the 1960s. I wish to illustrate the extent of the alteration by pausing here to compare LPBS/BSS with their 1960s equivalent – Campaign Against Racial Discrimination (CARD).

## THE INSTITUTIONALIZATION OF BLACK POLITICS

CARD was the first substantial post-war attempt by black and white activists to intervene in national British politics on the race question. Hitherto, efforts to access parliament and state organizations were weak and fragmented. The founding of CARD in December 1964 embodied aspirations for a strong, national anti-racist lobby of Asian and African-Caribbean activists with their allies. It existed at a time when membership of the Labour Party was hotly contested, so its relationship with the party, while important, was mainly through intermediaries (Heineman 1972, Shukra 1995b). By contrast, party membership was the lifeblood of LPBS and BSS. It was the key factor which unified their members, despite any difficulties they had with party policy and leadership.

LPBS – BSS's forerunner – shared important formal similarities with CARD. The motivating force behind each project was an attempt to intervene in mainstream British politics. They were coalitions of black people in Britain which intended to act as a lobbying force nationally. As fragile coalitions, they experienced inevitable internal conflicts and tensions. Nevertheless, the founders of both CARD and LPBS wanted to bring Asian and African-Caribbean communities together through claiming a common experience of racism. Given these continuities, why was LPBS more resilient in the face of difficulties? That one attempt made a bigger impact than the other was not a matter of chance but a symptom of what distinguished the two organizations from each other.

There were important ideological differences between the two organizations. CARD had a moderate hue and relatively little influence. It relied on its links with government officials and other intermediaries to influence the British polity. Direct relations with the Labour Party had not been established and the subject was fraught with tensions, because CARD was a coalition of organizations that were mainly independent from the Labour Party. In contrast, LPBS was not dogged by a debate about whether or not members should be within the Labour Party, because electoral support for Labour was taken for granted and, indeed, was the chief unifying factor for LPBS.

The difference between the way that members of CARD and LPBS related to the Labour Party was due to an ideological shift amongst radicals which occurred between the late 1960s and early 1980s to legitimize contact with the Labour Party in pursuit of their objectives. Excluded from mainstream party politics, radicals promoted protest politics until they attempted to break out of its limitations. Radical activists sought to move out of the isolation of working in single-issue campaigns. They found it easier to work with the Labour Party because of a far-left entry into the party and their theoretical re-evaluation of the role of the state (Shukra 1995b: Chapter 5).

Another trait which distinguished LPBS from CARD was its emergence following the urban unrest of 1981. LPBS' demands for black representation through the Labour Party, local authorities and parliament were consistent with the state's post-riot strategy which sought to tie black people more closely to the existing political and economic process (Shukra 1995b: Chapter 1). The result was that LPBS itself became a key intermediary between black community groups and the state. Further, the party political climate was different. The Labour Party was in search of new constituencies of support. LPBS was able to use this, together with Labour's reliance on the inner cities, to manoeuvre within the party, whereas CARD had remained on the fringes of party politics until it collapsed.

Overall the conditions and opportunities to develop a national, black, lobbying organization in mainstream party politics were more favourable in the 1980s than in the 1960s. LPBS and BSS were products of this potential and embodied a change in the pattern of black politics from independent political action to institutionalization. The full extent of the change since the mid-1980s can be seen in the way that Paul Gilroy's analysis needs to be updated. He argued that the growing race relations service and LPBS

> have had only limited success in countering the idea that being political now requires complete dissociation from the corporate structures of formal politics which are in need of drastic re-politicisation
>
> (Gilroy, 1987: 228).

In the early 1980s, many black people stepped into the Labour Party with caution and a critical attitude. Even at the time that Gilroy was writing, LPBS was still on the fringes of the Labour Party and making little headway in gaining recognition. However, a growing conservative climate, together with recruitment campaigns which won increasing numbers of black people to the Labour Party, gradually moderated confidence in the idea that social change might be achieved through independent politics. By the 1990s, loyalty to the Labour Party came to be taken for granted and debates amongst black members focused on access to Labour NEC, internal nominations, committee elections and anti-fascist/anti-racist campaigns.

The situation which Gilroy described in 1987 changed. After the mid-1980s, race politics became incorporated into the mainstream. Both LPBS and the primarily local-government-sponsored machinery of race relations turned the idea that it is necessary to be active in official institutions into received wisdom. When LPBS was set up, the idea of black caucuses was relatively new, but today even the police force and probation officers have formed black groups (*The Guardian* 1995). Gilroy made his point in the context of arguing that the waning of labour conflict was an indicator that the working class was no longer a social force and that the "black movement" was the new dynamic force of change. However, after the late 1980s, the "black movement" also became institutionalized, which by Gilroy's criteria means that the "black movement" is now also in decline. Since black Labour Party members tend to point to their involvement in campaigns to counter this idea, it makes sense to evaluate this next.


## BLACK POLITICAL CAMPAIGNS

Another important area of tension within the Labour Party on the question of "race" centred on anti-fascist/anti-racist campaigns. In the 1970s the Labour Party countered the electoral threat posed by the National Front through anti-fascist activity with Campaign Against Racism and Fascism (CARF) and local anti-fascist initiatives such as All London Campaign Against Racism and Fascism (ALCARAF) supported by the Socialist Workers' Party's Anti-Nazi League (ANL) (Layton-Henry 1984: 155, Shukra 1990a). These campaigns wound down in the early 1980s, with the election of the first Thatcher government. Anti-fascist activity then became the preserve of fringe grouplets such as Anti-Fascist Action and Red Action which made little impact on mainstream politics. It was not until the 1990s that anti-fascist campaigns became significant for the Labour Party again when a series of anti-fascist/anti-racist groupings and regroupings developed (Virdee 1995). The first key groups of the decade were Anti-Racist Alliance (ARA) and a re-established ANL. Both were set up in 1991 and competed for sponsorship, the support of trade unions and Labour Party politicians. Whereas ARA emerged out of the concerns of a dying LPBS and its associated black-led organizations, ANL was historically rooted in the Socialist Workers' Party. Consequently, whilst the agendas of the two organizations often converged, there were frequent differences in emphasis and rivalry for leadership of specific cases and campaigns. The tensions came to a head with the broadcast of Channel 4's *Devil's Advocate* programme (1993) in which families of victims spoke out against both organizations. The response of both ANL and ARA spokespersons when interviewed was to blame each other. The television programme also revealed the extent to which campaigns were under pressure to make their political impulses secondary to the wishes of the victims and their relatives. What developed was a form of moralism in campaigns against racial violence, which limited them to victim-support groups assisting families to take their cases through the judicial system.

The consequences of this were evident when Bernie Grant MP spoke at the rally following a march in South London to protest at the death of Brian Douglas at the hands of the police. In his address Grant appealed to young people to remain peaceful, and called for the police to be brought to account "by the book". There were jeers from the crowd but, with no serious alternative political strategy on offer, they were left to agree. Besides, Grant's authority lay in being able to tell the marchers that these were also the wishes of the bereaved family. This approach deflated the potential mobilizational power of those young people who were angry, and asked them to watch and wait for the state to take some action. The importance of Grant's influence should not be underestimated, as he was able to keep the lid on anger in South London whilst on the same day Bradford burned with the fury of Asian youth.

Public differences within the ARA stimulated the formation of an alternative organization. The National Black Alliance of Asian African Caribbean Organizations, was founded in December 1994 and launched with an "Anti-racist charter for the new millennium", with a high profile National Assembly in February 1995 in the London Borough of Tower Hamlets. The new organization was an attempt by a coalition of black organizations – the Indian Workers Association (GB); the Society of Black Lawyers; the National Black Caucus; and Tower Hamlets Anti-Racist Committee – to lead the anti-fascist/anti-racist agenda. ARA and ANL were included on the platform along with MPs, trade union officials and representatives from other organizations, but the significance of the National Black Alliance was its launch of anti-fascist/anti-racist campaigns behind a realigned black leadership. Keith Vaz's description of these organizations identifies this battle for leadership:

> Activists outside have not got their act together. This constant multiplicity of ARA and Marc Wadsworth faction and Anti-Marc Wadsworth faction, the Black Caucus faction and the 1990 Trust faction and all of this kind of stuff ... I support all of them ... but it would be really nice if they all got together.
> (Vaz 1995)

The view promoted by these anti-fascist/anti-racist groups and alliances throughout the 1990s was that the extreme right was the source of rising levels of racial violence. Campaigns against racist attacks and murders either identified the perpetrators as members of far-right groups or, where it was not British National Party (BNP) members directly involved in attacks, they claimed that BNP activity encouraged popular racism. Anti-fascists also used evidence of the rising influence of the extreme right in other European Union countries to support fears that the BNP's influence might produce a major fascist threat.

However, this anti-fascist perspective was challenged as simplistic by researchers who suggested that, while the BNP and its associated groups were active, their influence was being seen out of all proportion (Miles 1994). Husbands noted that, not only were there no BNP leaders as prominent as Le Pen, but unofficial reports of 2,000 members in the BNP were probably overestimates (Husbands 1994: 575). Moreover, Husbands' 1994 analysis of the electoral performance of the BNP showed that its short-lived success in the Millwall ward in the London Borough of Tower Hamlets was largely due to the local economic and political context, and that the party was not in any position to mount a large-scale election campaign (Husbands 1994: 575). This was supported by Cesarani's (1993) claim that the 1,500 BNP voters in Millwall could not be labelled "neo-Nazis" although they might be described as racists. Their support for the BNP was, in part, the result of local historical factors which turned them into victims of the recession and the development of the Docklands since 1979 (Sivanandan 1994: 64–65, Cesarani 1993, Malik 1993, Husbands 1994: 569–572). Also important in feeding support for the BNP in Tower Hamlets were racialized coding practises deployed by all the local political parties. Michael Keith (1995: 556) noted that "The local political culture had been racialized to the extent that populist bigotry was incidentally generating support for a politics even more overtly nationalistic, that of the extreme right".

Although all the mainstream political parties contributed to an economic and political climate which facilitated the election of a BNP councillor, political activity nevertheless continued to emphasize a fascist threat. The anti-fascist focus enabled the Labour Party to oust BNP councillor Derek Beackon from his seat in May 1994 and formed the basis of black party members' work around four key themes: a) Demands for new legislation to outlaw racial harassment; b) Publicity for specific cases; c) Electoral opposition to the BNP, particularly in East London; d) A campaign to close the BNP Headquarters in Welling, South East London.

The campaigns met with various levels of success in all four areas. The BNP headquarters were closed down in 1995 and it failed to make further electoral gains; cases continued to receive publicity and the lobby for stronger legislation won support within the Labour Party. The problem confronting black organizers and politicians was that, in focusing attention on the extreme right, they played down the role of mainstream parties and the state in the development of British racism. When the government introduced the 1993 Asylum and Immigration

136

Appeals Act, the Labour Party conceded the fundamental idea that immigration constitutes a threat to Britain, but few black organizers drew attention to this. Along with a whole series of immigration controls in Britain since 1962, the Act reinforced the official view that the source of "bad race relations" is the presence of black people in Britain. Arguably, each time parliament relayed this message to the populace, the hand of racists was strengthened and the activities of the extreme right bolstered. From this point of view, the key source of racism would be the state. An Amnesty International report, published in October 1994, which noted official mistreatment of black people detained under the 1993 Asylum and Immigration Appeals Act, reinforced this argument by indicating that international human rights laws and standards were regularly violated through official mistreatment of asylum seekers. In such a context, racial violence on the streets of Britain could be viewed less as an aberration than the expression of establishment-promoted views that black people in Britain have a second-class status (Tompson 1987).

The anti-fascist/anti-racist campaigns virtually ignored the contradiction of their electoral allegiance to a parliamentary party which might be deemed culpable. They also excused Labour's record of broken promises on repealing immigration legislation (Saggar, this volume). Even on a local level, the campaigns bolstered the anti-racist image of the Labour Party rather than challenging the party's ambiguous position on "race". The 1993 Millwall by-election illustrates this point. In that campaign, housing allocation was a key issue, and the Labour and the Liberal Democrats' positions on housing were crucial in creating the conditions in which BNP policy acquired legitimacy. In 1986, the new Liberal-controlled council proposed that Bengali homeless families be removed to a boat moored on the river Thames. When these plans were stopped, the council argued that Bangladeshis who brought their families over to Britain made themselves intentionally homeless under housing legislation and could not therefore be housed by the council (Runnymede Trust 1987: 1–4). When these measures were challenged by the CRE, the council began to give housing priority to the sons and daughters of existing (mainly white) tenants (Sivanandan 1994). The by-election campaigns waged by both Labour and the Liberal Democrats made constant references to "Island homes for islanders" and stressed the rights of "locals", a code word many accepted for white people (Shukra 1993, Husbands 1994: 573). The message which all parties seemed to agree on was that black residents did not deserve council housing. However, when the BNP won a council seat in Millwall, the mainstream politicians condemned BNP policy and portrayed themselves as bearing no responsibility for the outcome. The Labour Party paraded its anti-racist credentials through anti-fascist campaigns and won the seat back at the following local elections.

## MANAGING EQUAL OPPORTUNITY

The ideological retreat of the left within the Labour Party had implications for local authority anti-racism as well as the direction of autonomous organization and anti-fascist/anti-racist consortia. Politicians and key designers of the early 1980s, left-led Labour local authority race relations initiatives made career moves which brought many of them in line first with mainstream organizations and then New Labour. Thus Herman Ouseley who developed early model policies for the Greater London Council in the 1980s became Chief Executive of the CRE and argued that racial equality at work is "good for business" (Van Reenan 1995). On the other hand, some individuals who resisted the ideological shift to the right lost their jobs. Neville Adams who pioneered race relations initiatives in the London Borough of Lewisham was sacked as Principal Race Relations Advisor, when he resisted the authority's transformation of "Race Relations" into a matter of "Equal Opportunities". This reflected a growing gap between acceptable entrepreneurial and managerial methods borrowed from the USA and promoted by Ouseley and the black MPs (Van Reenan 1995: 31, Small 1994: 195) and local authority race relations measures which came to be castigated as "political correctness". New Realist and New Labour politics of the former were in sharp contrast to the Labour-left politics of the latter. The left-led race relations policies were based on the ethos and rhetoric of social need, accountability and community development. By contrast, the USA model was developed on the basis of the more respectable free-market equal opportunities strategy, in which the commercial concerns of the entrepreneur, employer, contractor and service-provider were paramount.

While the two models had quite different theoretical and political biases, the 1990s market-led version of equal opportunities in Britain has its roots in the industrial race relations policies of the 1970s. The first race relations policies in employment were prompted by employer interests at a time when Asian militancy disrupted some of the industries in which Asian workers were concentrated (Duffield 1988). In the early 1970s, employers were offered advice on how to ensure business prosperity:

> No sensible manager would neglect the development of good labour relations at his plant; but race relations – which are an

integral part of industrial relations – are often ignored. For his own sake, an employer should take positive preventative action to avert the danger of latent racial tensions developing into open conflict. The maintenance of industrial peace and the development of racial harmony in Britain demand that the small minority of firms which have adopted equal opportunity programmes be extended to the widest possible area of employment.

(Stewart, 1973: 23)

The measures most commonly promoted under the titles of "positive" or "affirmative action" during this period related to developing policy statements in consultation with trade unions; setting up ethnic monitoring systems; developing recruitment and selection procedures; organizing job and industrial language training; and declaring equal opportunities in promotion and dismissal. All of these measures, however, were developed in the context of management's need to command a greater influence over black workers and establish stability in industrial relations (Shukra 1995b: Chapter 4). These policies and practices were viewed critically by black militants and workers at the time, but through the creation of the left-led municipal race relations service of the 1980s, came to be considered progressive measures in employment. How did this change occur?

The Labour local authority race equality and economic development initiatives of the early 1980s gave ethnic monitoring and equal opportunity policies a radical appearance by emphasising the removal of organizational barriers to the employment and promotion of black people. As the emasculation of local government limited discretionary expenditure, the left in the Labour Party went on the defensive and municipal anti-racism grew increasingly unpopular, culminating in Bernard Crofton's allegations of corrupt employment practices in Hackney Council. Instead it was the entrepreneurial and commercial aspects of equal opportunities which were promoted as the reasonable and sensible manifestation of equal opportunities. The "business brunch" organized by the short-lived Parliamentary Black Caucus testified to the more pragmatic direction adopted by politicians and professionals in the mainstream.

## CONCLUSION

The recent modernization of the Labour Party produced a problem for the Labour leadership. Namely, how could a party which had built its reputation as a proponent of social policies based on state intervention

139

to curb the excesses of the market welcome the market economy without precipitating unmanageable levels of strife within the party? Kinnock initiated the change with a concerted attack on Labour's left wing. Smith pursued an assault on trade union influence and Blair cut deeply into the party constitution and policies, proclaiming the dawn of New Labour.

Black party members who sought to organize on a national basis were significantly affected by these developments. By 1985 LPBS realised that it could not win the support of the Labour leadership, so it allied itself with the Labour left, whose fortunes had risen since 1981. As the left grew weak during the late 1980s, so LPBS lost that particular avenue of influence. At the same time Labour's modernizers were keen to resolve internal party conflicts in a bid to become electable. LPBS was offered the opportunity to distance itself from the left by entering into negotiations for a Black Socialist Society solution to the stalemate. With the Labour left in disarray and the Labour leadership making overtures for the first time, black party members abandoned their original demand for recognition as a section within the party. They also hopped off the fallen left-wing bandwagon and on to New Labour to maintain their other main objective of black representation at all levels of the party. The prize of black party members' work was legitimacy. However, this was conditional on BSS remaining within the framework specified by New Labour politics.

These events were also part of broader developments in black politics. Through LPBS and BSS, black politics in Britain came to focus on the Labour Party, employers and the official institutions of the state. The creation of BSS constituted not just an organizational compromise, but a settlement on a wider dispute about the relevance of the Labour Party as a vehicle for pursuing black concerns. The resolution of this issue can be partly explained by ideological changes within the party, but also by a growing pessimism about the prospects for real social change. The overall result was that the small but lively black political movement of the 1970s became institutionalized.

What were formerly objectionable institutions were presented by black politicians and political organizers in the 1990s as agencies which could be altered to advance black and working-class concerns. In relation to the state, this meant that, rather than public pressure, it was the police, judiciary, parliament and para-statal bodies like the CRE which were called on to arbitrate in cases of racial discrimination, even though the alleged offender might be a state organization. In relation to the Labour Party, black members recognized and tolerated the party's need to balance the black vote against the racist vote, along with the party's ambivalence towards immigration, black representation and even the recruitment of Asian members to the party. Anthony

Messina's contribution to this volume seems to excuse Labour's position. While I agree with his point that "... Labour's leadership will likely become more timid in advertising its previous promises and fulfilling its stated commitments to non-white voters the closer the party progresses toward national power", the evidence presented in this chapter also indicates that Labour has consistently treated its black members cynically. Why, then, should black people maintain their support for Labour?

Saggar (this volume) argues that they do so for "spoils" which may include political positions, jobs and sponsorship for a minority of black people. Crucially, however, these do not stretch to promoting the interests of the majority. That would require a new force for real, rather than cosmetic, social change. Such a movement would need to break free of the restrictive Labour Party and parliamentary political framework. This requires a greater degree of optimism in our ability to forge new political strategies for social change than is currently fashionable. Since most politically-motivated black people today are wedded to old-style mainstream politics, a new youthful leadership may be the most likely source of initiative. It would need to be prepared to address the real social issues of the day without becoming caught up in bureaucracy and questions of representation.

This is not a simplistic call for a return to militant action. Militant protests have the potential to be conservative, as the anti-Rushdie demonstrations in Britain and Million Man March in Washington both showed. Both of these outbreaks of protest revealed the dearth of ideas, vision and leadership in progressive politics. The urgent need to build a broad, inclusive labour and social movement needs to be debated, particularly with young people. Then perhaps new political leaders may emerge to fill the current vacuum in anti-oppressive struggle. Otherwise Britain, like the USA, is liable to become dominated by cultural, religious and bureaucratic methods of dealing with structural social problems.

New Labour has shown how far it is prepared to trample over victims of the political economy in its desperation for parliamentary power. BSS, black-led campaigns and organizations continually prove that the future which they offer is tied to New Labour. An effective force would need to break free of the silence to which New Labour has committed many of its members, and argue about how to build a new movement for real social change.

## NOTE

1. Over the last forty years different words have been used in a variety of

ways to describe those who are termed "black" – that is people of recent "African", "Caribbean" or "Asian" descent. The passing of time has seen the emergence of different, fragmented and even multiple labels and identities. Some of the recent debates about this terminology are discussed later in the chapter. The author does not retain "black" to bestow any authority on it, but because in the context of the organizations under discussion, it is the term most commonly used by those who are the focus of this chapter. Departures from the use of "black" in this chapter occur chiefly when its use might be inappropriate or confusing. In such instances terms such as "ethnic minority" or component group descriptions are given.

## REFERENCES

Abrams, K. 1989. Building for the 1990s. LPBS discussion document.

Amnesty International British Section. *Prisoners Without A Voice*. October 1994.

Carter, B., C. Harris & S. Joshi, 1987. *The 1951–55 Conservative government and the racialisation of black immigration*. Policy Papers in Ethnic Relations no. 11, University of Warwick, Centre for Research in Ethnic Relations.

Cesarani, D. 1993. *The Guardian*, 21 September.

Channel 4 1993. *The Devil's Advocate*, 20 October.

Duffield, M. 1988. *Black Radicalism and the Politics of De-industrialisation*. Aldershot: Avebury.

Geddes, A. 1993. Asian and Afro-Caribbean representation in elected local government in England and Wales. *New Community* 20 (1).

Gilroy, P. 1987. *There 'Ain't No Black In The Union Jack*, London: Macmillan.

Hakim, F. 1995. Labour Party Development Officer (Ethnic Minorities). Interview with the author, May.

Hall, S. 1992. New Ethnicities in *"Race", Culture and Difference*, J. Donald and A. Rattansi (eds), London: Sage.

Heineman, B. 1972. *Politics of the Powerless: A Study of the Campaign Against Racial Discrimination*. Oxford: Claredon (Oxford University) Press.

Husbands, C. 1994. Following the "continental model"?: Implications of the recent electoral performance of the British National Party. In *New Community*, 20(4), July.

Jandu, K. 1995. TGWU Research Officer. Interview with the author, May.

Keith, M. 1995. Making the street visible: Placing racial violence in context. *New Community* (21) 4 October.

Khabra, P. 1995. MP Interview with the author, June.

LPBS 1990. Discussion paper The Next Steps, Priorities for 1990/1.

LPBS 1991. Report of the Chair of the National Committee to AGM.

Layton-Henry, Z. 1984. *The Politics of Race in Britain*. London: Allen and Unwin.

Layton-Henry, Z. 1992. *The Politics of Immigration*. Oxford: Basil Blackwell.

Malik, K. 1993. *The Independent* 23 September.

Miles, R. 1994. A rise of racism and fascism in contemporary Europe?: Some sceptical reflections on its nature and extent. *New Community*, 20 (4) July.

Modood, T. 1988. "Black", racial equality and Asian identity. *New Community* XIV.

Runnymede Trust 1987. *Race and Immigration*, September.

Sewell, T. 1993. *Black Tribunes*. Lawrence and Wishart.

Shukra, K. 1990a. Black Sections in the Labour Party. *Black Politics in Britain*, H. Goulbourne (ed.). Aldershot: Avebury.

Shukra, K. 1990b. Black Sections into the 1990s? Paper presented at the *New Issues in Black Politics Conference*. University of Warwick, May.

Shukra, K. 1993. *The Caribbean Times*, 11 October.

Shukra, K. 1994. Recent Developments in British Anti-Racism. Paper presented at *Migrants in the European Union: Between Integration and Xenophobia* conference in Bonn, Germany, November.

Shukra, K. 1995a. From Black Power to Black Perspectives: the reconstruction of a black political identity. In *Youth and Policy*, Summer, no. 49.

Shukra, K. 1995b. The Changing Patterns of Black Politics in Britain. Unpublished Ph.D thesis, Canterbury: University of Kent.

Shukra, K. 1995c. Managerialism in Community and Youth Work in 1990s Britain. Paper presented at *The Direction of Community Work: analyses, experiences and perspectives in Europe* Conference, Université Paul Valery Montpellier III, France, May.

Sivanandan, A. 1983. Challenging Racism, strategies for the 80s. *Race and Class*, Vol. XXXV.

Sivanandan, A. 1988. Interview with the author, October.

Sivanandan, A. 1994. *Race and Class*, Institute of Race Relations, Jan–March.

Skellington, R., P. Morris & P. Gordon, 1992. *"Race" in Britain Today*. London: Sage.

Small, S. 1994. *Racialised Barriers*. London: Routledge.

Solomos, J. 1989. *Race and Racism in Contemporary Britain*, London: Macmillan.

Solomos, J. & L. Back, 1995. *Race, Politics and Social Change*. London: Routledge.

Stewart, M. 1973. *A Stitch in time – an Employer Guide to equal opportunity in a multi-racial workforce*. Runnymede Trust.

*The Asian Times* 1995. 10 June.

*The Caribbean Times* 1989. 9 June.

*The Guardian* 1990. 20 April.

*The Guardian* 1995. 4 April.

*The Independent* 1990. 30 March.

*The Independent* 1990. 27 April.

*The Voice* 1995a. 17 January.

143

*The Voice* 1995b. 3 October.

*The Voice* 1995c. 10 October.

*The Voice* 1995d. 1 August

*The Voice* 1995e. 14 February.

*The Voice* 1995f. 25 July.

*The Voice* 1995g. 22 August.

Tompson, K. 1987. *Under Siege*. London: Penguin.

Van Reenan, L. 1995. A Black Perspective to British Community and Youth Work. In *Youth and Policy*, Summer, no. 49.

Vaz, K. 1995. MP. Interview with the author, July.

Wongsam, M. 1990. Interview with the author, May.

Virdee, S. 1995. *Racial Violence and Harassment*. London: Policy Studies Institute.

# CHAPTER SEVEN

# Inequality, political opportunity and ethnic minority parliamentary candidacy

## *Andrew Geddes*

## INTRODUCTION

In the mid-1990s there was evidence that political life was held in low esteem by the British public; indeed, politicians inspired about as much trust as estate agents and journalists. How could this opprobrium be counteracted? One set of counter-measures focused on "sleaze" and introduced tighter rules to restrict MPs supplementing their "low" salaries by earning money from outside interests. The House of Commons might also be able to command greater respect if it were more "descriptively" representative of the British people – if it were to reflect more accurately the population's demographic structure. As a result, more "substantive" representation of the interests of constituents could be achieved, although at the risk of representative institutions becoming only "symbolic" rather than substantive (Pitkin 1967, Swain 1993).

This chapter addresses a principle descriptive inadequacy in British representative politics – the effects of parliamentary candidate selection procedures on ethnic minority underrepresentation in the House of Commons. Two questions are addressed: first, what factors contribute to low levels of ethnic minority representation in the House of Commons? Secondly, despite continued underrepresentation, how do we explain recent increases in the level of representation and, also, what constraints may be placed on further increases?

The first question is the more frequently considered, and "resource" models are postulated which point to socio-economic inequalities – such as those in (un)employment and education – as ways of explaining underrepresentation. Underrepresentation is then linked to broader issues of social inequality and racial discrimination in Britain. The second question is less frequently asked, but is likely to become increasingly important. By addressing this second question we extend the analysis to consider resources *and* political opportunity. The analysis of political opportunity draws attention to the ways in which factors such as the level of access to institutional participation and the strength of electoral alignments can affect the "dimensions of the political environment that provide incentives for people to undertake collective action by affecting their expectations of success or failure" (Tarrow, 1995: 85).

## THE FACTORS CONTRIBUTING TO LOW LEVELS OF ETHNIC MINORITY REPRESENTATION

### The political opportunity structure for ethnic minority parliamentary candidates

The notion of the political opportunity structure is more commonly applied to "new social movements", such as the peace campaigns of the 1980s (Kitschelt 1986). However, aspects of these analyses can usefully be applied to analysis of the underrepresentation of Britain's ethnic minorities.

A number of models of political opportunity have been developed by political scientists endeavouring to explain the mobilization of social movements which seek access to the state in order to influence policies. Beckwith (1995: 1) wrote that: "political opportunity structures are conceptualised as a set of independent variables serving to explain social movement mobilisation, strategic choices and success." The political opportunity structure is typically seen as having four main variables: the degree of openness/closure of the formal political process; the degree of stability/instability of political alignments; the availability and strategy of potential alliance partners; and the level of political conflict between elites (Tarrow 1983, 1989). The model was refined by Kreisi (1991) who makes a distinction between three broad sets of properties in a political system: its formal institutional structure (including the electoral system); the informal procedures and strategies with regard to challengers; and the configuration of power in

146

the political system. The first two provide the general setting and act as a constraint on the configuration of power, both between and within political parties (and the state system more generally).

In the context of British parliamentary candidate selection, the opportunity structure is conditioned by the localized nature of the process. This localism provides different contexts for ethnic minority political participation, incorporation or exclusion in different areas; although, of course, national debates and policies also provide important context. These local patterns are dependent on complex historical, political, geographical and socio-economic factors, such as the impact of patterns of settlement on political structures in (mainly) urban areas and the response of those in positions of power and authority to the growth of local ethnic minority communities in a number of British cities. At a more general level it has also been argued that the attempted depoliticization of issues of race and immigration by race relations policy actually marginalized people from ethnic minority communities who became public policy "objects" rather than actors in the political process (Crowley 1993). In more recent times this marginalization has been challenged, and there is some evidence of greater openness in the political system, which has led to increasing numbers of people from ethnic minorities on local councils and in the House of Commons. However, as we shall see, the degree of openness appears to be circumscribed by constraints placed on ethnic minority political participation and representation; these constraints may be both institutional and "cultural".

In the USA, analyses of black political activism link shifts in political opportunity to the structural potential for successful collective action. This is, in turn, linked to organizational capacity, group consciousness and levels of social control (McAdam 1982). In Britain, the strong electoral alignment with the Labour Party means that many of these issues of capacity, consciousness and social control are refracted through the prism of intra-Labour Party debates at local and national level. As we shall see, a range of factors, including the rise of the "new urban left" and black sections in the 1980s, helped provide a degree of openness which facilitated increased ethnic minority participation and representation, albeit not of sufficient magnitude to counter under-representation.

Analysis of political opportunity encourages us to think about the ways in which demands for increased ethnic minority participation and representation interact with inter- and intra-party debates about immigration and race. The analysis of political opportunity structures also provokes consideration of the reaction of those in positions of power (such as party leaders and MPs) to challenges. For instance, at constituency level, incumbent MPs need to consolidate local support

147

and deter challenges. In the Labour Party, the threat of mandatory reselection of MPs has given particular relevance to the politics of recruitment. In recent parliamentary candidate selection contests it is interesting to note the ways patronage-based modes of political action, which sometimes operated in the interests of established (mainly) white politicians, have become racialized – i.e. represented ideologically as involving race – in constituencies where Asian political participation has increased, and (mainly) white, male powerholders have been challenged. Ostensibly, increases in participation would seem to be a positive development and indicative of integration. However, increased Asian participation has, as we shall see, become a "problem" in a number of constituencies.

More recently, analysts of political opportunity have criticized what is seen as an excessive focus on structural and institutional aspects of the political process. These structural factors include the rules of the electoral system which, as Crewe (1983) showed, can act as a strong impediment to ethnic minority representation in Britain. However, Gamson and Meyer (1994) stress the importance of "cultural" and "contextual" factors and indicate their broader focus by referring to political opportunity, rather than political opportunity structures. Gamson and Meyer locate political opportunity along two continua. The first focuses on structural and institutional factors and related levels of stability and volatility. The second makes a distinction between cultural and institutional factors and argues that cultural elements are "crucial factors in political opportunity theorising" (Beckwith 1995: 21). These cultural factors include national belief systems, class consciousness and the prevailing national mood. The role of the media is perceived as being important in identifying meaningful political actors, with the implication that those who are not seen as meaningful are rendered silent. This broadening of the notion of political opportunity shows that constraints on political representation can be both institutional and "cultural". If the "prevailing national mood" is hostile to ethnic minority political participation and representation, this antipathy will place additional constraints on political opportunity. As we shall see later, there is a degree of ambivalence in both the Labour and the Conservative Parties to increased ethnic minority political participation. Such ambivalence can limit the opportunities available to aspiring politicians from ethnic minorities and compound the effects of material inequalities.

### The parliamentary candidate selection process

Candidate selection has been called the "secret garden" of British politics as analysts often focus on MPs' activities once elected, rather than on the important processes governing selection. Yet in many seats MPs are returned with large majorities, meaning that their election is akin to a rubber-stamping of a candidate choice made by party activists. In each of the three main national parties the selection of parliamentary candidates is a local process determined at constituency level. In fact, for Conservative, Labour and Liberal Democrat activists the power to select parliamentary candidates is probably the most significant aspect of local constituency party autonomy.

Parliamentary candidate selection is a jealously guarded local prerogative leading to "centralised parties with decentralised selection" (Denver 1988). The main parties' parliamentary candidate selection procedures can be likened to a market where aspirants seek to sell their services to parliamentary constituencies purchasing the "best" candidate. This market-based analogy has prompted formulation of "supply and demand" models to explain the underrepresentation of women and ethnic minorities (Jewson and Mason 1986a, 1986b, Lovenduski and Norris 1989). These models draw attention to the importance of the resources available to aspirants, as well as to demand-side effects such as low incumbency turnover and prejudice. In the market for political candidates, as in other markets, inequalities pervade the process and result in a "playing field" which is not level for all potential candidates. Early analyses of candidate selection relied on qualitative research techniques – attendance at party meetings and interviews with key actors – to develop an understanding of the formal and informal processes affecting selection (Ranney 1965, Patterson 1966, Rush 1969). In the 1980s, attitudinal data on Labour's selection procedure was gathered (Bochel and Denver 1988). During the selections between 1987 and 1992 a systematic analysis, covering all the main parties, was conducted (Lovenduski and Norris 1994).

The first stage in the selection process sees the parties draw up lists of aspiring candidates. The Conservatives have an Approved List of candidates vetted by Central Office. It contained around 800 names in the 1987–1992 selection round. One estimate suggested that there were between 20 and 30 people from ethnic minorities on the Approved List (Sewell 1993: 71). Norris, Geddes and Lovenduski (1992: 105) put the figure rather lower estimating that 13 (2.3 per cent) were from ethnic minorities. This variance is explained by the fact that the Conservatives do not conduct formal ethnic monitoring of their approved list of candidates.

People are chosen for the Conservative's Approved List after a rigorous process culminating in a weekend-long final selection board. Once on the list, applicants carry the party's seal of approval and are notified of vacancies. Conservative Central Office has a big say in determining the pool of eligibles and could, if it chose, infuse the pool with increased numbers of women or ethnic-minorities, something which, however, gives no guarantee of even being considered by local associations (Lovenduski and Norris 1994: 52).

Labour, too, has its lists of candidates – the A, B, C and W lists. The A list (with around 180 people during the 1987–1992 round) consists of those sponsored by trade unions. Being on the A list is a positive boon for an aspiring candidate because of the financial support offered to a constituency. The B list (around 650 people) is for unsponsored party members who wish to be considered for seats. There are no restrictions on B list membership, although chances of selection are slight when compared to those on the A list. The C list (around 100 people) is for candidates sponsored by the Co-operative Party, with whom Labour has traditional links. The W list (156 names between 1989 and 1992) of women aspirants was introduced in 1989 as a way of promoting women's candidacy.

Liberal Democrat aspirants face a five-stage process which begins with the completion of a standard form, followed by an interview. If successful, the aspirant is placed on a regional approved list from which applications to constituencies can be made. Constituencies seeking a candidate place an advert in *Liberal Democrat News*, although the Liberal Democrats sometimes have difficulty filling vacancies, and are far more likely to present a short-list of one to constituencies with a vacancy than are either Labour or the Conservatives. Constituency Executive Committees draw up shortlists which are then placed before all the local party members, who decide, by one-member-one-vote, on their candidate. The Liberal Democrats fielded six ethnic minority candidates in the 1992 General Election, and a further 19 candidates in the 1997 General Election, none of whom came close to election. Indeed, despite being at national level the most consistently liberal of all the main political parties on "race politics", the Liberal Democrats remain largely peripheral to the issues considered in this chapter, since they attract little support from the ethnic minority electorate, which is of course strongly aligned with Labour. The Conservatives too attract low levels of ethnic minority electoral support, but the Tories have been far more central to the development of "race politics" in Britain than the Liberal Democrats.

After aspiring candidates have got on to the Labour and Conservative lists of candidates they must then search out a seat. In both parties seats are advertised. Aspiring Tory MPs post their *curriculum vitae* (CV) to constituency Conservative associations which have advertised a vacancy. Tory-held seats may attract over 300 applicants. A selection committee is convened to sift through the CVs and whittle them down to between 15 and 25 people for selection committee interview (involving a short speech and a question-and-answer session, something which also occurs at the subsequent stages of the process). Between three and six candidates appear before the constituency association's Executive Committee. Finally, between one and three aspirants appear before a meeting open to all members of the association, who makes the final choice.

In the Labour Party, reflecting its federal structure, aspiring candidates seek nomination from a party branch (for example, a ward, union branch or constituency women's section). Each branch can make one nomination. Labour's selection procedures have evolved through selection by the Constituency Labour Party's (CLP) General Management Committee (GMC), via selection through a complicated electoral college system during the 1987–1992 selection cycle, to acceptance of the one-member-one-vote (OMOV) principle.

During the 1987–1992 selections the Executive Committee of Labour CLPs used the following criteria to determine the composition of the short-list: a) Sitting MPs were included (reselection of MPs was introduced in 1980 (Young 1983); b) If there was no incumbent then, if there were five nominees, there were at least five names on the short list; c) Individuals with over 25 per cent of nominations, including at least one from a party branch, were short-listed; d) A woman was included on the short list if one was nominated (there were no similar provisions for people from ethnic minorities).

Short-listed candidates appeared before a meeting of the CLP which, in the round of selections leading up to the 1992 General Election, used an electoral college with votes split between individual members and affiliates (mainly trade unions). Affiliates were allowed a maximum of 40 per cent of the electoral college, depending upon their size. Many pocket calculators over-heated as Labour activists worked out the composition of the Electoral College and selected, their candidates for the 1992 General Election. Once selected, the candidate has to be endorsed by the NEC. This is usually a formality, but not always. In 1987 the chair of black sections, Sharon Atkin, was not endorsed as candidate for Nottingham East, following an attack on what she saw as Labour Party racism.

It is important to stress that during the selection round prior to the 1997 General Election Labour adopted OMOV for candidate selection. It also established a system of compulsory all-women shortlists in winnable seats as a way of countering underrepresentation of women. It was reported in July 1995 that Labour intended to drop its experiment with all-women shortlists after the 1997 General Election. It had not proved too difficult for Labour members to agree in principle to positive action to promote women's candidacy, but the devil is in the detail. Most Labour members agreed that the underrepresentation of women needed to be tackled, but were sometimes reluctant to see an all-women short-list in their constituency, particularly if there was a "favoured son" lined up for the nomination. The more recent reversal of the women-only short-listing policy has thrown many of these sentiments back into the melting pot, particularly at constituency level.

For Labour and the Conservatives the selection process is controlled locally, although Conservative Central Office can play a role in determining the pool of eligibles on the Approved List. Evidence suggests that Conservatives (party members, candidates and aspirants) are happier with the process than their Labour counterparts (Lovenduski and Norris 1994: 89). Labour's selection process, which is more complicated, has often been a source of controversy, because ideological fault-lines have tended to run deeper and selection has been a battle ground for rival factions (Shaw 1988, Kogan and Kogan 1982). The Conservatives have tended to be less ideological, placing greater emphasis on loyalty. It has been argued, although in perhaps a rather reductionist manner, that Labour's selection process is reflective of an ethos which, despite the recent influx of middle-class members, continues to emphasize a working-class collectivist culture that values local roots. This contrasts with the Conservative ethos of middle-class, meritocratic individualism (Lovenduski and Norris 1994: 54).

### Resource-based models of underrepresentation

Explanations of inequality in formal, elected representative institutions – the House of Commons or local government – often contend that social inequalities based on class, gender and race have a direct effect on underrepresentation. One of the reasons for this is that involvement in the political process is not without cost; it consumes both the time and money of people who seek to participate. It stands to reason that if individuals have severe constraints on their time – such as working shifts, being unemployed, caring for children or for other family members – the chances of participating in politics are reduced. These constraints impact upon parliamentary candidate selection procedures, which are supposed to establish mechanisms within which applicants can be judged alongside others in fair and open competition. The process can be broadly characterized as liberal – it emphasises competition between individuals – and plural – it is supposedly open to people from all social groups. However, the interaction between formal procedures and resource disparities among aspiring candidates prompts the growth of structural inequalities which undermine claims for fairness and lead to an unfortunate homogeneity amongst MPs in terms of, for example, gender, socio-economic status and ethnic origin. Unequal outcomes, especially those that fail to reflect social diversity, are a challenge to the liberal-pluralist selectoral paradigm.

An understanding of how channels of political participation are "differentially available" and "differentially used" was found to be crucial "in understanding the effectiveness of democracy" (Verba, Nie and Kim 1978: 2). Social inequality is very likely to affect levels of political participation by people of lower socio-economic status and formal representative structures will reflect social inequalities. Consequently, we need to take account of who actually participates and recognise that power constraints linked to material and other forms of inequality clearly affect political participation (Schattschneider 1960, Parry, Moyser and Day 1992).

To participate in the parliamentary candidate selection process an aspiring MP needs to be a member of one of the main political parties. However, low levels of party membership amongst certain sections of the population tend to reflect deeper social inequalities which have an effect on parliamentary candidate selection. Research into party membership found only 1 per cent of Conservatives were of Asian origin; moreover, the numbers of Afro-Caribbeans were so small they did not register in the survey (Whiteley, Seyd and Richardson 1994: 38–9). Similar research into Labour's membership found that 3 per cent of its members were from ethnic minorities (Seyd and Whiteley 1992).

Social inequalities, such as higher levels of unemployment, may adversely affect levels of political participation. A survey of the differential experience of the ten major ethnic groups identified by the Labour Force Survey (LFS) in the 1980s found that: "Ethnic minority groups in Great Britain have fared relatively badly in the labour market, tending to be employed in low status and poorly-paid jobs in declining industrial sectors" (Owen and Green 1992: 7). Pakistanis and Bangladeshis, many of whom live in urban areas of industrial decline in the West Midlands and North of England, have fared particularly badly. The economic plight of these groups is compounded by a young age profile and high levels of youth unemployment. The LFS also found poor educational participation, sub-standard housing and patchy social welfare take-up.

On the supply-side of the "market" for parliamentary candidates, it is also relevant to consider representation in elected local government. Evidence suggests that experience derived from being a local councillor is valued highly by parliamentary candidate selectors: around 50 per cent of MPs elected in 1992 had local government experience. A 1992 survey found around 350 local councillors from ethnic minorities serving on elected local authorities in England and Wales (about 1.6 per cent of the total). There is still underrepresentation, but there are now more councillors from ethnic minorities than at any other time

153

and the rate of increase is high. Local activity could, for some people, facilitate participation in parliamentary candidate selection contests and have a positive "supply-side" effect (Geddes 1993).

Evidence from the British Candidate Study of parliamentary selections between 1987 and 1992 suggests that supply-side factors were of particular relevance in the Conservative Party during the 1987–92 selection round (Lovenduski and Norris 1994). The Conservatives have very few voters and party members from ethnic minorities – around 1.5 per cent and 1 per cent respectively. However, Conservatives from ethnic minority groups are relatively successful in getting on the Approved List (2.3 per cent) and selected as parliamentary candidates (1.3 per cent), although only 0.3 per cent are selected for Tory-held seats (Norris, Geddes and Lovenduski 1992: 105).

In the Labour Party there were found to be problems of both supply and demand.

> In absolute terms there are more black candidates and MPs within the Labour Party. But in relative terms, compared with their baseline share of the Labour vote [estimated at 7.9 per cent in 1992], ethnic minorities experience greater under-representation in the Labour Party [estimated at 1.4 per cent of candidates and 1.8 per cent of MPs].
>
> (Norris, Geddes and Lovenduski 1992: 105)

The lifestyle constraints mentioned earlier may explain the relatively low party membership amongst ethnic minorities. In addition, if people from minority ethnic groups do become active in the party, they are disproportionately unsuccessful in securing nomination as parliamentary candidates.

When MPs and parliamentary candidates were asked for their opinions on underrepresentation, we see a difference in opinion between the two main parties which reflects the evidence presented above. As Table 7.1 shows, Conservatives tended to attribute underrepresentation to supply-side deficiencies, Labour MPs and Prospective Parliamentary Candidates to unequal opportunities.

### Demand-side factors

Candidate selection is necessarily a discriminatory process. Local constituency parties have to select between (sometimes) hundreds of applicants and must establish criteria to allow them to do so. The first "sift" through the CVs of the applicants can be rather arbitrary. One selector interviewed by the author said that he identified ten criteria he thought were important and graded each applicant out of ten. He then

154

TABLE 7.1  Explanations for ethnic minority underrepresentation in parliament amongst MPs and parliamentary candidates
Question: "Would you agree or disagree with the following explanations of why there are so few Asian and Afro-Caribbean MPs?"

|  | Con | Lab | Total |
|---|---|---|---|
| Black people are not given opportunities by parties | 0.7 | 4.2 | 2.4 |
| Black people do not come forward to be considered | 3.5 | 0.8 | 2.2 |
| Black people lose votes | 0.9 | −3.8 | −1.3 |
| Black people do not have the confidence | −2.8 | −3.9 | −3.3 |
| Black people do not have the right experience and education | −3.1 | −6.9 | −5.0 |
| Black people do not fit into Parliament | −5.4 | −7.4 | −6.4 |
| Black people are not interested in politics | −5.3 | −8.0 | −6.6 |
| Black people are not suited to the job | −5.3 | −8.1 | −6.7 |
| N | 585 | 543 | 1,128 |

Note: Mean responses were recoded as − agree strong (+10), agree (+5), disagree (−5), disagree strongly (−10).
Source: Norris, Geddes and Lovenduski (1992): 106

had a cut-off point of 60 per cent to identify those he thought should be considered for the list of people to be interviewed. Others may not be so systematic: for example, family snapshots attached to the CV (preferably with cuddly pets) were a positive boon for another (Conservative) selector. Such selection processes obviously depend on perceptions of the qualities necessary in a prospective MP. It is "political abilities" which should be the criteria, but of course this term is amorphous and can conceal a multitude of considerations. Some selectors may feel that ethnic minority candidates would not be accepted locally, and may lose votes, and they may then use this prejudice to exclude ethnic minority aspirants. This prejudice could be fuelled by the events in Cheltenham prior to the 1992 General Election when John Taylor was selected as Conservative candidate. His selection provoked an explicitly racist response as some local Tories spoke of "repelling the invader". There may also be more insidious forms of indirect discrimination where selectors absolve themselves of prejudice and impute prejudice, instead, to the electorate. The end result of both explicit and implicit prejudice is the same: people from ethnic minorities find it hard to get selected. This was summed up by a Conservative Party area agent:

One of the brightest people on the list is an ethnic. He's extremely bright, he's very cultured, he's very educated. I got him an interview but they made it clear to me that they wouldn't select him on the grounds that he wouldn't be accepted locally. Very much a case of we're not prejudiced, but ...

(Lovenduski and Norris 1994: 136).

The potential effects of imputed prejudice are demonstrated in Table 7.2 below which shows that black/Asian candidates were perceived as vote-losers by selectors in both main parties.

Assessments of prejudice in candidate selection, such as that in Table 7.2, have asked selectors not whether they oppose selection of ethnic minority candidates, but whether they feel such candidates are vote-losers. Some selectors could impute their prejudice to the electorate and, by doing so, reveal that racism constrains the demand-side of the "market". However, evidence from the 1992 General Election does not support the assertion that ethnic minority candidates were vote-losers. For Labour, Diane Abbott (+11.1 per cent), Paul Boateng (+7.5 per cent), Bernie Grant (+18.5 per cent) and Keith Vaz (+19.1 per cent) all saw increases in their share of the vote in excess of either regional or national swings to Labour, although Ashok Kumar lost the Langbaurgh seat he won from the Tories in a November 1991 by-election. Conservative candidates fared less well, Taylor was defeated by the Liberal Democrats in Cheltenham with a 10.4 per cent swing against the Tories; whilst Niranjan Deva's share of the vote fell by 10.6 per cent in Brentford. In May 1997, three Labour ethnic minority incumbents (Boateng, Grant and Khabra) all succeeded in outperforming the average regional swing to Labour, suggesting that their

TABLE 7.2 Attitudes of Conservative and Labour party members towards the electoral appeal of candidates Question: "Do you think that for your party in this constituency certain candidates would gain many votes, gain some votes, no difference, lose some votes?"

|  | Conservatives | Labour |
|---|---|---|
| Local candidate | +3.8 | +6.2 |
| White candidate | +3.0 | +2.3 |
| Middle-class candidate | +2.0 | +1.4 |
| Woman candidate | +0.5 | +2.0 |
| Man candidate | +1.9 | +0.9 |
| Working-class candidate | +0.3 | +1.6 |
| Trade Union candidate | −3.0 | +0.5 |
| Black of Asian candidate | −2.6 | −1.8 |

Note: Mean calculated after recoding as − gain many votes (+10), gain some votes (+5), no difference (0), lose some votes (−5), lose many votes (−10).
Source: Norris, Geddes and Lovenduski (1992): 101.

candidacies were now real assets to the party. Other incumbents did not fare so well, and two in notional Labour-held seats (Singh in Bradford West and King in Bethnal Green and Bow) endured very heavy – and surprising – swings to the (Asian) Tory opponents. Of course, a whole range of factors can affect the share of the vote gained by particular candidates, but it is important to recognise that the opinion that ethnic minority candidates automatically lose votes is flawed. Rather, it is the perception that such candidates lose votes which inhibits selectors. The return of Kumar as a Labour MP in Middlesbrough and Cleveland South in 1997 illustrates this point, as well as the candidate's determination to re-test the potential prejudice of this particular local electorate.

## RECENT INCREASES IN THE LEVEL OF REPRESENTATION

### Labour's opportunity structure

We now move on to the second question raised in the introduction to this chapter and analyze how constraints on political opportunity can compound resource disparities and further exacerbate inequalities in the formal structures of representative politics. For instance, in the early 1980s the links made between Labour's black sections activists and the so-called "loony left" ran the risk of delegitimizing ethnic minority political activity more generally. More recently, increased Asian participation in the Labour Party has been rendered problematic by being portrayed in some quarters as ethnically-motivated (and hence undesirable) and prone to corruption.

The historical context of Labour's opportunity structure can be assessed during four overlapping periods. First, during the 1970s when ethnic minority registration and turnout increased. Secondly, intra-Labour Party debates in the late-1970s and 1980s about more effective representation, culminating with the black sections debate. Thirdly, the tough "disciplinarity" and shift to the right during Neil Kinnock's party leadership in the 1980s and early 1990s which marginalized black sections which had aligned themselves with the party's left-wing (Knowles 1992: 142–145). Fourthly, the response, particularly since the 1992 General Election (although also before it) to increased Asian political participation in a number of selection contests for the 1997 election.

Intra-party pressure was exerted after the 1979 General Election defeat by the Labour Party Race Action Group (LPRAG 1979) and by a National Executive Committee report on *Labour and the Black Elec-*

*torate* (Labour Party 1980) urging increased ethnic minority partici-pation. These documents did not assuage growing numbers of Labour Party members from ethnic minorities who began to seek more authoritative structures of representation and participation. This occurred at a time when the Labour Party moved to the left and some Labour-led local authorities, particularly the GLC, sought to become more responsive to the needs of ethnic minority residents. One result was pressure for black sections, modelled on women's sections and based on the principle of self-organisation with rights of representa-tion and, amongst other things, nomination rights in parliamentary candidate-selection contests. Black sections pressed for greater recognition of the interests of the black electorate and increased repre-sentation both within the party and, by operating through the party, within elected institutions at local and national level (Black Sections 1988). In the run-up to the 1987 General Election, Paul Boateng (who contested Stevenage in 1983) was selected from an all-black short-list in Brent South. Diane Abbott and Bernie Grant, who had local gov-ernment experience in London, were selected for Hackney North and Stoke Newington and Tottenham respectively. In Leicester East, Keith Vaz was selected following substantial Asian abstention in the 1983 General Election, which was linked to the selection of a white London-based lawyer to contest the seat (Shukra 1990: 182).

It would be wrong to suggest that the selection and election of Diane Abbott, Paul Boateng, Bernie Grant and Keith Vaz was deter-mined by their ethnic origin or that they were selected because of the colour of their skin. They all had other skills which are highly valued by selectors. Importantly, within the context of Labour's selection process, most were "local" in the sense that they were prominent activists, or had strong connections, either in the seat for which they were selected or in surrounding areas. They also had political experi-ence derived from previous parliamentary candidacy or from local government: for example, Bernie Grant was leader of Haringey Council, a position in which he had attracted substantial controversy in 1985 following the Broadwater Farm estate disorders. In addition they had to satisfy the local "selectorate" on a wide range of political issues – ranging from management of the economy to nuclear weapons – and thus relate to important intra-party debates between the left- and right-wings.

The four candidates selected for the 1987 General Election were all on Labour's left wing. Indeed, sections of the tabloid press were quick to make links between ethnic minority candidates and the "loony left". This so-called London effect was seen as contributing to Labour's 1987 defeat. During the 1987 campaign Ken Livingstone and Bernie Grant appeared more times in the press than any other Labour

158

politicians except for Neil Kinnock, Roy Hattersley and Denis Healey (Sewell 1993: 128). Even though the four candidates were successful in the seats for which they stood, the links made between their ethnic origin and supposed extremism could fuel the imputation of prejudice we noted earlier, i.e. the idea that candidates from ethnic minorities are vote-losers. As Sewell (1993: 25) notes:

> Race was inscribed in the use of phrases like "loony left" and the "London effect". These terms were popularized by the media, who created controversy by giving a somewhat partisan account of the supposed extremism of some Labour-controlled authorities.

All four MPs elected in 1987 were returned in constituencies with relatively large ethnic minority populations, but, even though they were prominent within black sections and their ethnic origin was a potential resource (alongside others) in parliamentary candidate selection contests, they also had to satisfy the party selectors – and ultimately the electorate – across a wide range of other issues, on many of which there is little difference between black and white voters in the seats for they were elected.

In addition to the complexities of intra-party debates and the ways in which ethnicity may have potential as a selectoral resource in some constituencies, it is also useful to bear in mind the small number of seats that become available at each election. For example, at the 1992 General Election only 25 per cent of seats were not retained by the incumbent. Taken together, these factors help to explain why the number of Labour MPs from ethnic minorities increased during the 1980s and 1990s, but also why the rate of increase was slow. If the rate of increase is to be speeded up, more positive steps could be taken. Labour, albeit temporarily, decided to take such steps for women candidates in order to counter another glaring inequality in the House of Commons. They have, though, run into problems in a number of selections where local CLPs have not been willing to respond to what are construed as edicts from Walworth Road which interfere in one of the few areas of local party autonomy.

It could be asked whether such positive action has implications for other underrepresented groups. Should there, for example, be all-Asian shortlists in seats with large Asian communities? For example, in Bradford West, where around 28 per cent of the population are Muslims, or in Birmingham Sparkbrook, where around one-third of the local electorate are from Mirpur? This may be less likely, given Labour's decision not to repeat this particular form of positive action. Also, there are problems with the prioritization of equality issues in the context of a single-member-based electoral system. Given that each constituency can make only one choice for its candidates, as opposed to multi-member constituencies in proportional representation systems, some aspects of political equality may take precedence over others. This may prove to be the case for people from ethnic minorities aspiring to elected office.

### Constraints on ethnic minority participation and representation

An analysis of the opportunity structure for ethnic minority political activists seeking to challenge power holders can be instructive. It draws our attention to the context given to participatory issues by intra-party debates. In recent Labour Party parliamentary candidate selection contests prior to the 1997 General Election, the "problem" of increased Asian political participation has arisen. Racialized assumptions have sometimes underpinned explanations for increased activism and its effects.

The nature of the disputes seems also to demonstrate a change in the participatory underpinnings of the race relations paradigm which, it could be argued, "bureaucratized" the response to "problems" of immigration and race based on:

> ... a mutual relationship between the community leaders, the council and the Labour party. The community leaders delivered the vote, the councils delivered the money and the Labour party won a new layer of support.
> (*New Statesman and Society* 1995: 18)

This relationship was challenged in the 1980s and 1990s in a number of selection contests in areas with large ethnic minority populations. Four reasons can be adduced for the change from "bureaucratized" politics to more "participatory" modes of action. First, the role of Labour's "new urban left" has been analysed by Gyford (1985). He notes that issues of race played a prominent part in the urban left's political agenda, particularly in London in the early 1980s. Secondly, participation within the Labour Party increased in the 1970s and 1980s. On top of that, urban disorder in 1980/81 and 1985 prompted debate about the incorporation of minority communities within the formal political process. Thirdly, the race relations framework militated against participation. It was construed by some as neo-colonial and paternalistic and rendered members of minority communities public policy "problems" and *objects of* policy rather than *actors in* decision-making processes (Crowley 1993). Finally, the unrepresentativeness of Labour Party structures was apparent to members from minority communities who, in the 1980s and 1990s, have been prepared to challenge people in positions of power, such as local councillors and sitting MPs.

In parliamentary candidate selection contests MPs and local CLP office holders, such as membership secretaries, play vital roles; indeed, the post of membership secretary is a particularly important job. Some constituencies, in Birmingham for example, were notorious for pre-empting challenges by keeping membership very low. It is also important to bear in mind that the Labour Party has not been a bastion of democracy and openness where procedures are only now being challenged by new and "alien" forms of political participation. Forms of patronage politics have been, and will presumably continue to be, important in internal Labour Party politics. This does not mean that Labour's internal politics can be characterized as variations on a theme of patronage politics; but there is evidence in some constituencies of the development of networks of dependence and support between people in positions of power and authority and their supporters. The traditional beneficiaries of these forms of patronage politics sought to keep tight control of party membership and cultivate support, for example, amongst powerful trade unions and ethnic minority communities. In the late 1970s and early 1980s there were challenges to these forms of patronage politics. In particular mandatory reselection of sitting MPs placed great emphasis on the politics of recruitment. The move to OMOV has only intensified this emphasis. Some selection contests have been bedevilled with allegations of membership irregularities and other accusations. These disputes have been particularly controversial and well publicised in areas with large Asian populations and has led to claims of "Asian entryism".

At the heart of the issue of increased Asian participation in the Labour Party is whether the response to it is racist or whether the form of participation and the ends linked to it are not in accord with Labour's aims, values and rules. The politics of party membership have often been controversial in the Labour Party. We can identify some reasons why increased Asian party membership may rightly or wrongly be viewed with suspicion by other Labour members.

First, Labour is increasingly emphasizing individual party membership and moving away from collective mechanisms for representation and expression of interests through, for example, trade unions' bloc votes at party conferences and in candidate selection contests. Secondly, Labour has had long experience of attempted "entryism" by left-wing groups which have sought to influence Labour's policies in a way not seen by party leaders and many members as corresponding with Labour's aims and values. This was particularly the case during the party leadership's battle against the Militant Tendency. Thirdly, there have been other instances of suspicion of party membership that is construed as ethnically motivated. For example, after the First World War, Irish voters were "one of the most consistently pro-Labour elements within the working class" (Fielding 1993: 105); but increased Irish participation within the Labour Party was not universally welcomed. In Manchester and Liverpool, for example, there was hostility towards increased Irish membership of the party. In 1935 a former secretary of Manchester Trades Council declared that "The man who was a Catholic first, an Irishman second and a Labour man last ought to be given his marching orders" (Fielding 1993: 106). Irish party members were seen as pursuing aims with which many other Labour members were not in sympathy. For example, many Labour members were intensely hostile to church schooling, but many Irish Catholics were strongly in favour. Also, many feminist Labour supporters favoured increased access to birth control as a way of improving women's living standards, but numerous Irish Catholics were opposed.

For these reasons, even when Labour is riding high in the opinion polls and trying to cultivate mass membership, new members may not always be welcomed. The particular issue we now move on to consider is the response to increased Asian participation. Allegations and counter-allegations have bedevilled a number of selection contests.

In Manchester Gorton the sitting MP, Gerald Kaufman, stood down from his position as Shadow Foreign Secretary after the 1992 General Election. This led to rumours that he would retire from Parliament at the next general election. Fifteen per cent of the population in the Gorton constituency is of Asian origin, mainly Mirpuri Pakistanis. In 1993 more than 600 Asians applied to join the Labour Party from the Gorton constituency. The number of applications made was extraordinarily high, given that Labour had just experienced a general election defeat and the prevailing mood seemed to be one of apathy rather than participatory zeal. It was claimed that many of the applicants were recruited by London-based Ahmed Shazzad, who intended to challenge Kaufman in the reselection contest. A local party official alleged that:

Recruitment was clearly orchestrated, a canvassing process in the Asian community. We learned they were knocking on doors, telling people that Gerald was retiring and that there ought to be a Muslim MP for Gorton. We believe people were asked to join the party not to become involved in the Labour Party, but to get someone elected.

(*Independent on Sunday*, 1994: 3)

A number of allegations were made concerning membership irregularities: a) In some cases the subscription was paid by just one person. Is this because of vote manipulation or because it was easier to collect cash and pay with one cheque? b) Some applicants were not on the constituencies electoral register, which is a condition for CLP membership; c) Some applicants gave false addresses.

Of the first batch of 376 applications from Asian people, 62 were rejected. The second batch contained 249 names, of which 116 were rejected. Overall, 28 per cent of applications were rejected. The suspicion was that votes were being bought to manipulate the outcome of the selection contest.

The processing of some Asian people's valid applications were delayed as they were subject to close scrutiny. It was also alleged on BBC's *East* programme that party members of Asian origin were excluded from the branch meetings which made the nominations for the candidate selection process. The result was that Kaufman secured the two-thirds of nominations necessary to prevent a challenge. Three Asian members took the Labour Party to court, alleging discrimination under the Race Relations Act. Kaufman also claimed that "ethnic minority voters are only too open to manipulation" (*New Statesman and Society* 1995: 18).

In Birmingham the City Council has, until relatively recently, been controlled by Labour's right wing. Even though the city has a large ethnic minority population, black section groupings, which were aligned with Labour's left, made little impact. However, in recent years there has been increasing tension surrounding selection contests in a number of inner city constituencies. Solomos and Back (1995 Ch. 5) have shown how minority political participation has been resisted by people who have traditionally been in positions of power and who have often invoked racialized assumptions about the inferiority of minority political participation to justify their dominance. It was claimed, for example, by one interviewee in Solomos and Back's study that there was some kind of evolutionary scale of political development and that native Brummies were higher on that scale than ethnic minority groups. The racially-charged assumptions that underpin such a statement, redolent of nineteenth-century pseudo-scientific racism, are only too clear.

Parliamentary selection contests in Birmingham have been controversial. In Ladywood, which has a large Asian population, the sitting MP, Clare Short, saw off a challenge from Sardul Marwa amidst allegations that the right-wing electricians union had created "phantom" branches in order to boost its pro-Marwa vote in the constituency. The NEC found the allegations to be substantiated, suspended the contest and cut the electrician union's delegation from 17 to 10. Short narrowly won the reconvened selection contest. In Small Heath, where there is also a large Asian population, there were allegations that Roger Godsiff manipulated the trade union vote to secure victory in the selection contest and see off three Asian challengers, although the NEC endorsed his candidacy. Similar allegations to those made in the Ladywood contest about "phantom" branches were levelled, though Labour's Director of Organization, Joyce Gould, ruled that the protestors had "no right" to challenge the number of delegates from trade union branches (Back and Solomos 1993).

The boundary changes made after the 1992 General Election altered the electoral geography of Birmingham's inner-city areas and produced a number of contentious selection contests. In February 1995, four constituencies – Sparkbrook, Ladywood, Perry Barr and Small Heath – were suspended following accusations that candidates in the Sparkbrook constituency, angling to replace Roy Hattersley, were targeting housing renovation grants towards Labour Party members as a way of building support for the forthcoming selection contest. Roger Godsiff and city councillor Raghib Ahsan were amongst those named. However, the allegations were dismissed by the local government ombudsman and the district auditor. There were suspicions that the allegations were made to prevent Ahsan securing the Sparkbrook seat, whilst Ladywood and Perry Barr were suspended to prevent challenges from Asian candidates to sitting MPs, Short and Jeff Rooker.

In Bradford, the University and Toller wards in the Bradford West constituency were suspended. The former's suspension occurred in October 1994 after a fight broke out between rival Asian factions at a party meeting, the latter's after an unexpected Tory victory in the May 1995 local elections. Membership and financial irregularities were alleged. It was also claimed that some local Labour members helped the Tory campaign. Both wards remained suspended until the parliamentary selection was completed.

In East London, a Tower Hamlets councillor, Rajan Jalal, was suspended from the Labour Party for two months for writing a document that was highly critical of council policies. The *London Evening Standard* also published accusations that Jalal was recruiting *en masse* amongst the Asian community to influence the Bethnal Green and Stepney selection contest. Jalal denied the allegations and claimed that the suspension, which was not invoked until four months after he wrote the document, was a way of keeping him out of the selection contest.

On top of these disputes there has also been strife in other areas with large Asian populations, such as parts of Glasgow, Leicester, Hounslow and Nottingham. The events in Manchester, Birmingham, Bradford, London and elsewhere seem to render overly simplistic explanations for the reaction to increased Asian participation in the Labour Party, which rely on a blanket condemnation of "racism". There is evidence that racism may have played a part, particularly in the way in which Asian political participation has in some instances been characterized as ethnically motivated and rendered less legitimate as a consequence. However, a number of other factors may be relevant. For example, the Labour Party is bound by its own rules, as well as expectations of proper behaviour, and is entitled to exclude members who do not adhere to imposed standards. It may be rather difficult to condone fights at party meetings and support for Conservative candidates. However, it could also be maintained that these standards are not applied across the board, and that people from ethnic minorities who challenge the people in positions of power and authority have more often fallen foul of the party rulebook than white transgressors.

A fear on the part of some people in positions of power in the Labour Party is that increased Asian participation may be "alien" to traditional party norms. Clearly, increased Asian participation threatens the position of, mainly white and male, powerholders in a number of Labour's inner city strongholds. Responses to the challenge have sometimes invoked racialized assumptions to question the legitimacy of increased minority participation and portray it as "criminal" and "alien".

Solomos and Back's (1995) study of the local politics of race in Birmingham uses discourse analysis to assess the effect of racialized thinking in local politics in Birmingham. In particular, they were interested in the ways supposed racial attributes are given social and political meaning and how these meanings are then translated into political action. It could be argued that this technique runs the risk of "reading" Birmingham's politics solely from the perspective of race and that, for example, a specialist on Labour's internal politics may postulate other explanations for some actions.

Back and Solomos' study reveals the ways in which racialized modes of thinking have been utilized to characterize minority political participation. Asian people, for example, are assumed to participate *en bloc* and not as individuals. They are also seen as more likely to be corrupt, as the following quote from a Labour Party official in Birmingham makes clear:

> Once it gets round that Asian politics is corrupt and that Asians vote not as individuals according to political choice, but *en bloc* according to family or clan affiliation, then the right of many Asians to be party members is open to question.
> (Solomos and Back 1995: 184)

165

This statement seems to construe Asian political participation as a lower form of political activity. It does not see Asian people as individuals capable of making choices, but as a bloc of easily-manipulated voters swayed by "old-fashioned" affiliations such as kinship and religion. It even goes so far as to suggest that Asian Britons' participatory rights be revoked unless they learn to conform to the traditions of the Labour Party (whatever they may be). It is interesting to note some cross-party cultural tensions in addressing South Asian political participation. Labour has its difficulties, whilst at the other end of the political spectrum some on the "new right" have argued that cultural differences militate against social and political integration, and thus lessen the sense of national consciousness upon which the "new right" often likes to lay great emphasis (Casey 1982).

The view of minority political participation as "problematic" in a number of CLPs shows that we should not make simple connections between the apparent openness afforded to Labour's participatory structure by debates in the 1970s and 1980s, and the party's responsiveness to increased participation. Those who seek to challenge people in positions of power and authority must have a number of obstacles to overcome. These include the procedural aspects of the politics of patronage, the way in which local networks of support can be cultivated, and in which minority political participation can be viewed as illegitimate and alien and thus as a "problem", even though participation in politics is often viewed as indicative of integration.

### The Conservative's opportunity structure

The Conservatives are handicapped by their reputation as an anti-immigration party. There has, however, been a modest increase in ethnic minority electoral support for the party and an uplift (albeit very small) in membership. The Conservatives dilemma is that:

> There is a real tension between the pervasive belief among ethnic-minority activists that the Conservative Party will offer opportunities based on merit irrespective of colour and the racially circumscribed realities that black Conservatives are positioned within.
>
> (Solomos and Back 1995: 216)

In the 1992 General Election the Conservatives fielded seven ethnic minority candidates, five of whom contested Labour-held seats. The Conservatives have tended to select ethnic minority parliamentary (and local election) candidates in areas with large ethnic minority populations. For example, Qayumm Chaudhary challenged Roger

Godsiff in Birmingham Small Heath and Mohammed Khamisa stood against Roy Hattersley in Birmingham Sparkbrook. Both of these areas have large Asian populations, but it has been noted that Asian Tories are not as good at getting the vote out as Asian Labour Party members (Solomos and Back 1995).

The experience of John Taylor in Cheltenham could have a chastening effect. The pool of aspiring Conservative MPs from ethnic minorities is small and, even if people did decide to come forward to seek selection, they are likely to encounter party members at the grassroots who have yet to reconcile themselves to multi-ethnic Britain. This reality may prove to be less of an isolated attitude than many aspirants had originally anticipated.

The 1992 cases of Taylor in Cheltenham, and Niranjan Deva in Brentford and Isleworth, are worth examining in more detail. Objectively, Taylor seemed an ideal Tory candidate. He is a trained barrister, was a Conservative councillor in Solihull, a parliamentary-candidate for the Birmingham Perry Barr constituency in the 1987 general election and a senior ministerial advisor in the Home Office. In addition to these qualifications, Taylor performed well in the early stages of the Cheltenham selection contest. He faced stiff competition from over 250 applicants, including former MPs. However, the constituency's executive committee was so impressed by him that he received over 50 per cent of the votes at this stage of the process. According to the party's rules this meant that Taylor was the only candidate who needed to be presented to the general meeting, open to all members of the association. At the general meeting there was strong opposition to Taylor's candidacy, demonstrated by the relatively narrow 111 to 83 vote in favour of adopting him as prospective parliamentary candidate. Discontent quickly bubbled to the surface. Some of it was openly racist:

> I don't think we want a bloody nigger to represent us in Parliament . . . . There are plenty of niggers in London but would you vote for a black man in the country town of Cheltenham?
> (*Sunday Times* 9 December 1990)

Other opponents were more subtle in their opposition to Taylor on the grounds that he was not "local". Of course, Taylor was not local in the sense that he was from Birmingham and had gained political experience in both his home city and London, not in Cheltenham. However, many Tory MPs are not from the constituencies for which they are selected. For example, John Major was selected for Huntingdon in Cambridgeshire, but was from South London. The existence of a centrally approved list of Tory talent and the meritocratic ethos that pervades Tory selections means that the local emphasis is not as great as in the Labour Party. It is hoped that, even if a candidate is not from the constituency, she or he will aspire to "localness" by moving in to it. It might, therefore, not be too extreme to suggest that the degree of opposition to Taylor's candidacy could have had something to do with the colour of his skin.

Additionally, one needs to consider some features of the Cheltenham selection contest. There would seem to be evidence of failings within the local Conservative association. The presentation of only one candidate to the association's general meeting could be seen as undemocratic; whilst the inability of the executive committee, which seems to have been enthusiastic about Taylor, to "sell" him to other association members could be construed as a failure of local party management. It could also be the case that some activists in the Cheltenham constituency just did not hit it off with Taylor on a personal level, irrespective of his and their own ethnic origin and, as a result, felt less inclined to campaign for him in what was always going to be a very close contest. There were also claims that Taylor had been foisted on to the local association by Conservative Central Office. Central Office may indeed move in strange and mysterious ways, but there is no evidence of it intervening directly to affect the Cheltenham selection. Perhaps the "cock-up" theory holds more water than the conspiracy theory.

Not surprisingly, given the divisions within the local association, the Tories lost Cheltenham, although, in truth, they would have been under strong pressure from the Liberal Democrats, had candidate selection been problem-free. In contrast, Nirj Deva's selection in Brentford and Isleworth was far less difficult. He too had many of the qualities regarded highly by party selectors: he had, for example, stood as Conservative candidate in nearby Hammersmith in the 1987 general election. He was also selected for a seat where around 15 per cent of the population was of Asian origin, compared to Cheltenham where only 2 per cent of the population are from ethnic minorities. Finally, when comparing party management in Cheltenham and Brentford, it should be noted that Deva was not the only candidate presented to the constituency association's general meeting. The Brentford and Isleworth Tories were far more supportive of Deva than Cheltenham's were of Taylor. Deva was comfortably elected to the House of Commons in 1992 with an anti-Tory swing no greater than that in neighbouring constituencies. To that extent, it would have been reasonable to think that his chances of survival were, presumably, only helped by the supportive relationship with local Tory activists which his original adoption had initiated. The electorate in Brentford in 1997 thought otherwise, however. Indeed, the activists may also assist in what analysts of congressional representation in the United States describe as the movement from "expansionist" to "protectionist" stages of constituency incumbency (Fenno 1978).

It is important to take into account the particularities of selection contests and to note that a broad generalization of Tory selection procedures would not enable us to identify key differences between the selection and election of Deva and the selection and defeat of Taylor. There are chinks of opportunity within the Conservative Party for ethnic minority parliamentary candidacy, although very low levels of electoral support, small numbers of party members and anti-immigration/"immigrant" sentiment mean that the Conservatives have been less successful than Labour in selecting candidates from ethnic minorities who stand a good chance of election.

## CONCLUSION

Inter-party debates on race and immigration in the 1970s repoliticized the issues with seemingly positive participatory effect on the Labour Party, which became more concerned to cultivate its strong support within ethnic minority communities. The participatory consequences of repoliticization for the Conservatives were largely negative in that it seemed to confirm the party's anti-immigration status.

One of the effects of repoliticization for the Labour Party was that "bureaucratized" modes of political action were replaced by a more participatory framework, within which ethnic minority activists challenged the paternalistic relationship between (mainly) white, male powerholders and "community leaders". However, these increases in participation and political activity, which could be construed positively as indicative of integration, have sometimes been viewed negatively as a challenge, not only to the people in positions of power, but to the basic principles of internal party democracy. In the 1980s, links were made between black sections activists and the "loony left". In the 1990s there were a number of allegations made about irregularities in the recruitment of Asian members and manipulation of parliamentary candidate selection contests. The effect of both these developments has been the racialization of ethnic minority political participation.

Relatively new forms of political participation, such as that by ethnic minorities, seem to be causing particular problems for Labour. In particular, increased Asian participation has become a fiercely-disputed issue in a number of constituencies and illustrates tensions within the Labour Party which are far from resolved. It also highlights the importance of considering resources *and* political opportunity because the material inequalities which help generate unrepresentative political institutions also compound with the political opportunity structure to exacerbate the effects of these inequalities. There did seem to be greater openness and receptiveness within the Labour Party to ethnic minority interests in the 1980s, and there was an increase in ethnic minority representation at local and national level. However, this openness has not necessarily prompted fuller particpation in the party and more "descriptive" representation in the House of Commons, because the negative effects of the racialization of ethnic minority political participation mean that it can be dismissed as an inferior type of political activity, and one with a tendency towards corruption and based on ethnic allegiance rather than individual conviction. As a result racialized forms of political participation are rendered less legitimate.

These issues illustrate the potential for tension between perceptions of ethnically-motivated political allegiance and questions of political (il)legitimacy. In turn, these considerations lead to a broader debate about "race politics" in Britain, covering both political processes and systemic outcomes that cut across the political parties. This chapter has focused on unequal access to the political process and has sought to show that it is not just the question of "resources" (or the lack of them) that affects the scope for political action, although resource disparities are significant. It is also important to consider the ways in which institutional/structural and "cultural" factors place additional constraints on political opportunity. Gains that have so far been made to counteract ethnic minority underrepresentation have tended to be small and hard-won. The prospects seem gloomy for substantial increases leading to a more representative House of Commons. It could, however, also be the case that opportunity will beget further opportunity and the evident increases in representation at local and national level of recent years may have the effect of reinforcement. This, in turn, could help diminish the mistrust which compounds the impact of material inequalities and reduces the chances for people from ethnic minorities of participating more fully in political parties and in the political life of the country.

## REFERENCES

Back, L. & J. Solomos 1992. *Who Represents Us? Racialized Politics and Candidate Selection.* Research Paper No. 4, Department of Politics and Sociology, Birkbeck College, University of London.

Beckwith, K. 1995. *The Opportunity in Political Opportunity Theory: A Review of the Social Movements Literature.* Unpublished Paper.

Black Sections 1988. *The Black Agenda*, London: Hansib.

Bochel, J. & D. Denver 1988. Candidate selection in the Labour Party: what the selectors seek. *British Journal of Political Science*, Vol. 13, 45–59.

Casey, J. 1982. One nation: the politics of race. *The Salisbury Review*, Autumn, 23–8.

Crewe, I. 1983. Representation and the ethnic minorities in Britain. In *Ethnic Pluralism and Public Policy*, N. Glazer & K. Young (eds). London: Heinemann.

Crowley, J. 1993. Paradoxes in the politicization of race: a comparison of the UK and France. *New Community*, Vol. 19, No. 4, 627–43.

Denver, D. 1988. Britain: centralized parties with decentralized selection. In *Candidate Selection in Comparative Perspective*, M. Gallagher & M. Marsh (eds). London: Sage.

Fenno, R. 1982. *Home Style: House Members in their Districts.* Glenview (Illinois): Scott, Foresman.

Fielding, S. 1993. *Class and Ethnicity. Irish Catholics in England 1880–1939.* Buckingham: Open University Press.

Gamson, W. & D. Meyer 1994. Framing political opportunity. In *Opportunities, Mobilizing Structures and Framing: Comparative Applications of Contemporary Movement Theory.* D. McAdam, J. McCarthy & M. Zald (eds). New York: Cambridge University Press.

Geddes, A. 1993. Asian and Afro-Caribbean representation in elected local government in England and Wales. *New Community*, Vol. 20, 43–57.

Gyford, J. 1985. *The Politics of Local Socialism*, London: George, Allen & Unwin.

*Independent on Sunday* 1994. Entryism or racism? 25 September, 3.

Jewson, N. & D. Mason 1986a. The theory and practice of equal opportunities: liberal and radical approaches. *Sociological Review*, Vol. 34, 307–34.

Jewson, N. & D. Mason 1986b. Modes of discrimination in the recruitment process: formalization, fairness and efficiency. *Sociology*, Vol. 20, 307–34.

Kitschelt, H. 1986. Political opportunity structures and political protest: anti-nuclear movements in four democracies. *British Journal of Political Science*, Vol. 16, 57–85.

Knowles, C. 1992. *Race, Discourse and Labourism.* London: Routledge.

Kogan, D. & M. Kogan 1982. *The Battle for the Labour Party.* London: Fontana.

Kreisi, H. 1991. *The Political Opportunity Structure of New Social Movements: Its Impact on their Mobilization.* Berlin: WZB.

Labour Party 1980. *Labour and the Black Electorate.* London: Labour Party.

Labour Party Race Action Group 1979. *Don't Take Black Votes for Granted.* London: LPRAG.

Lovenduski, J. & P. Norris, P 1989. Selecting women candidates: obstacles to the feminization of the House of Commons. *European Journal of Political Research*, Vol. 17, 533–62.

Lovenduski, J. & P. Norris, P 1994. *Political Recruitment: Gender, Race and*

171

*Class in the British Parliament*. Cambridge: Cambridge University Press.

McAdam, D. 1982. *Political Process and the Development of Black Insurgency*. Chicago: Chicago University Press.

*New Statesman and Society* 1995. Party colours, 14 July, 18–19.

Norris, P., A. Geddes & J. Lovenduski 1992. Race and parliamentary representation. In *The British Elections and Parties Yearbook 1992*. D. Broughton, I. Crewe, D. Denver & P. Norris (eds). Hemel Hempstead: Harvester Wheatsheaf.

Owen, D. & A. Green (1992). Labour market experience and occupational change amongst ethnic groups in Britain. *New Community*, Vol. 19, 1–29.

Parry, G., G. Moyser & N. Day 1992. *Political Participation and Democracy in Britain*. Cambridge: Cambridge University Press.

Patterson, P. 1966. *The Selectorate*. London: Macmillan.

Pitkin, H. 1967. *The Concept of Representation*. Berkeley: University of California Press.

Ranney, A. 1965. *Pathways to Parliament: Candidate Selection in Britain*. London: Macmillan.

Rush, M. 1969. *The Selection of Parliamentary Candidates*, London: Nelson.

Schattschneider, E. E. 1960. *The Semisovereign People*. New York: Holt, Rinehart & Winston.

Sewell, T. 1993. *Black Tribunes: Black Political Participation in Britain*. London: Lawrence & Wishart.

Seyd, P. & P. Whiteley 1992. *Labour's Grassroots: The Politics of Party Membership*. Oxford: Oxford University Press.

Shaw, E. 1988. *Discipline and Discord in the Labour Party*. Manchester: Manchester University Press.

Shukra, K. 1990. Black sections in the Labour Party. In *Black Politics in Britain*, H. Goulbourne (ed.). Aldershot: Avebury.

Solomos, J. & L. Back 1995. *Race, Politics and Social Change*. London: Routledge.

Swain, C. 1993. *Black Faces, Black Interests: The Representation of African Americans in Congress*. Cambridge (Mass.): Harvard University Press.

Tarrow, S. 1983. *Struggling To Reform: Social Movements and Policy Change During Cycles of Protest*. Cornell University: Western Societies Program Occasional Paper No. 21.

Tarrow, S. 1989. *Democracy and Disorder, Protest and Politics in Italy 1965–1975*. Oxford: Clarendon Press.

Tarrow, S. 1995. The Europeanization of conflict: reflections from a social movement perspective. *West European Politics*, Vol. 18, No. 2, 223–51.

Verba, S., N. Nie & J. Kim 1978. *Participation and Political Equality: A Seven Nation Comparison*. Cambridge: Cambridge University Press.

Whiteley, P., P. Seyd & J. Richardson 1994. *True Blues: The Politics of Conservative Party Membership*, Oxford: Oxford University Press.

Young, A. 1983. *The Reselection of MPs*. London: Heinemann.

PART THREE

# Levels of participation and policy influence

# CHAPTER EIGHT

# Integration within the British political parties: perceptions of ethnic minority councillors

*Jessica R. Adolino*

## INTRODUCTION

Historically, British society has been relatively homogeneous, but in the post-war era substantial migration has converted it into a multicultural and multiracial society. The political representation of ethnic minorities[1] is an important new development in British politics. A transition has been taking place among ethnic minorities from a primarily protest mode of participation to one of engagement in mainstream politics and institutions (Goulbourne 1990: 1). For the first time since the early 1900s, several members of ethnic minority groups were elected to Parliament in the 1987 General Elections, and their numbers increased in 1992 and in 1997. In addition, the number of ethnic minority local councillors rose slowly over the course of the 1980s. Following the May 1990 local elections, at least 328 members of ethnic minority groups were serving on local councils throughout Britain, many for the first time. These newly-elected councillors supply the data for my research.[2]

Participation in parties, elections and representative institutions are all important means for promoting political integration in democratic societies. This is the case because

such processes and institutions tend to reinforce identification with the rules, procedures and values of the polity, they

175

enable the articulation of demands, they facilitate consent, and they strengthen acceptance of the legitimacy of the political system

Solomos and Back 1991: 216.

The process of increasing ethnic minority political representation may thus have important ramifications for ethnic minority politics and the British representative system overall. As Studlar and Welch (1990: 1) note: "the quality and quantity of minority group representation in government, especially those chosen by popular vote, is one test of how well racially or ethnically integrated an advanced industrial society is".

The term *integration*, when used in the context of relations between majority and minority populations, is typically defined as follows:

> Integration is a situation in which groups of different cultural backgrounds and different beliefs can participate in society on equal footing without losing their essential distinctiveness as individuals. People retain their cultural identity but are accepted as equal if total integration is attained.
>
> (Cashmore and Troyna 1982: 61)

The political integration of ethnic minority elites in Britain would be evidenced by a broad consensus among them as to the perceived legitimacy of the regime and its agents, to the need for and the value of institutional participation, and to the effectiveness of the system's outputs for their communities (Benyon and Solomos 1988: 416). Such political integration might also be defined by their incorporation "into the political system not as nominal but as effective members who participate actively in the decision-making process" (Anwar 1980: 56). Broadly speaking, ethnic minority elite political integration might thus be evidenced by these individuals:

a) Articulation of a desire for incorporation and acceptance into the political process.
b) Assertion of the value of ethnic minority participation in political parties, elections and pressure groups.
c) Belief in the possibility of effective ethnic minority participation in and influence over policy formulation and decision-making.
d) Perceptions that the regime's outputs are beneficial to ethnic minorities, responsive to their demands and wants, and effective in their implementation.
e) Affirmation of the value of increased ethnic minority representation on local councils and central government.

176

f) Positive identification with the polity, the political system, and pre-vailing values.

The perceptions and evaluations of ethnic minority councillors of political participation will reveal the extent to which they subscribe to the democratic myth: "that ordinary citizens ought to participate in politics and that they are in fact influential" (Almond and Verba 1965: 352). Were ethnic minority councillors to offer opinions that suggested a failure to believe that this "myth" held true for ethnic minorities in Britain, this would have negative implications for their political integration. That is, it would imply that ethnic minority councillors doubt the efficacy of political participation for ethnic minorities and, following on this, are unlikely to see potential for their political integration.

Of course, integration is only one of the ways in which ethnic minorities may be associated with the wider political system. Alternatively, ethnic minority councillors' perceptions may imply future minority–majority relationships characterised by:

- Ethnic minority unity arising from the development of a racial and ethnic consciousness.
- The dilution of ethnic minority politics as a result of political institutions' creation of buffer mechanisms intended to sidetrack and patronise ethnic minority activists under the guise of providing special help.
- Growing ethnic minority disenchantment, alienation and withdrawal from the political process, which might result either in alternative forms of communal organisation, such as religion, or more disruptive, violent expressions of individual alienation, such as the periodic eruption of violence in the inner cities.

(Jeffers 1991: 78).

In this chapter I focus on ethnic minority councillors' attitudes towards political participation and forms of political organization and assess the extent to which councillors feel they have equal access to power and influence in political parties. Specifically, I consider whether these perceptions imply an unfolding pattern of political integration.[3]

I first consider the types of participation ethnic minority councillors endorse as likely to be most effective in achieving their goals. Consideration is given to their assessments of both conventional and unconventional political activities. I further explore whether they view the major political parties as the most effective channels for making progress toward ethnic minority political goals, and the degree to which they support the creation of alternative political organizations for ethnic minorities. I finally evaluate councillors' views of the responsiveness of political parties to ethnic minorities and their ability to influence these institutions.

It is important to note the distinction between officeholders' *actual* and *perceived* integration. The nature of my data restricts my discussion to the realm of perception. All the findings discussed here involved these councillors' own perceptions of their integration into partisan institutions, rather than more objective indicators, such as voting records or policy outputs. For example, voting records would indicate whether these councillors went their own way in their policy-making behaviour or pursued more integrationist strategies (that is, adhered to party discipline). Additionally, the attitudes of white local councillors concerning the issues addressed here would also provide useful insights into ethnic minority councillors' political integration.

Obtaining such information, however, was beyond the scope of my study. My research relies on reconstructing the political world of these elites as it appears through their eyes. Such a strategy will be sufficient "since it is assumed that what and how people think and what and how they believe about the world in which they live influences greatly the way they as leaders will act, behave and decide" (Eldersveld et al. 1981: 2).

## THE INSTITUTIONAL SETTING

The British local governmental system is an important facet of the wider democratic system. Local authorities provide a voice for the local community, act as a buffer to the central government, supply local services, recruit people into the political process, and relieve some of the pressure on central administration (Byrne 1990: 55). In addition, the political function of local government also contains a representational, or democratic, dimension which has been particularly significant for ethnic minorities, since this is the setting in which they have had the greatest electoral success. Further, the local environment has also been the most productive governmental stage for addressing ethnic minority concerns.

The most important debates over the construction of ethnic minority-related political agendas and the introduction of initiatives promoting racial equality have taken place within the confines of local government. In the 1980s, the rise of local authorities controlled by the left in the Labour Party had important implications for ethnic minority politics. These Labour-controlled local authorities, especially in London, became (and remain) the primary vehicle for advancing anti-racist programmes by those concerned with the struggle for racial equality.

For a variety of reasons, the pursuit of racial equality at the local council level did not meet with universal success. These included poor implementation of policies, unrealistic expectations, the effects of Conservative local government reforms and Conservative attacks on reform efforts. As a result, anti-racist, race-equality and multicultural programmes were frequently "marginal, symbolic and cosmetic" (Butcher et al. 1990: 134). Nonetheless, some limited gains were achieved, albeit slowly and not as comprehensively as might have been hoped: the number of ethnic minority staff in town halls has increased, access to services is more fairly provided, race monitoring is a fairly widespread practice, and race issues have been firmly placed on the local political agenda. Even in the aftermath of the defeat of the urban left in the 1990s, local government appears to remain the best hope for pursuing ethnic minorities' goals. Following on this, the experiences of ethnic minority elected representatives within local political institutions will be particularly instructive.


## THE QUESTION OF AN ETHNIC MINORITY AGENDA

An important area of debate discussed elsewhere in this volume surrounds the question of the existence of a specifically ethnic minority political agenda. Scholars differ in the extent to which they believe there is such an agenda and whether, to the degree it exists, it is accepted by ethnic minorities as a whole (Messina, this volume; Saggar, this volume). Implicit in my discussions of ethnic minority councillors' experiences and aspirations is an assumption that such an agenda does indeed exist. In particular, my consideration of councillors' evaluations of political institutions specifically relies on their assessment of these institutions' responsiveness to "ethnic minority concerns".

Evidence of a shared ethnic minority political agenda was supported by both survey and interview data. Over two-thirds of survey respondents (67.5 per cent) identified discrimination as the most important problem facing ethnic minorities, with unemployment ranking second (28.9 per cent) and crime identified as the third most important (4.7 per cent).[4] Councillors also mentioned restrictive immigration laws, the dilution of cultural values and a lack of political

179

representation as being other important problems facing ethnic minorities. Such responses clearly indicated councillors' recognition of a range of issues that were of specific importance to ethnic minorities and that were distinct from the concerns of the general population.

Interviews with ethnic minority councillors further revealed the primacy of discrimination or racism[5] issues. All councillors interviewed mentioned racism or discrimination in their response to a question regarding the most important problems facing ethnic minorities in the country, for example:

> The biggest problem is racism. It doesn't matter what you do, it is just there (Labour councillor).

> Racism is probably the worst problem in our society ... I think that until we begin to accept that all people of all races, of all colours, of all creeds are equal, we haven't really started to live as human beings together and so it must be the greatest problem (Conservative councillor).

Further, there was a clear consensus among those interviewed that, while other problems, such as unemployment, housing, education and the poor quality of social services were shared with the white working class, these problems were further compounded for ethnic minorities by the effects of discrimination. The following comments illustrate their positions:

> Racism, that is the major problem. Then, the other general problems that the society as a whole faces – housing, education, social services ... whatever the general public faces, we face with the extra dimension of the racism of the society (Labour councillor).

> Most of the issues facing blacks today are also issues facing white working class people – housing, unemployment. But within these issues there is a differentiation, because there is discrimination (Labour councillor).

In short, ethnic minority councillors clearly identified discrimination and racism as the most significant problems confronting ethnic minorities. Such findings suggest a shared set of public policy concerns. Beyond this, the persistent use of language such as "ethnic minority issues", "ethnic minority concerns", and "black issues" suggested that a common theme, or agenda, was present in the consciousness of councillors interviewed. Such issues and concerns included, specifically, the pursuit of anti-racist policies, immigration control reform,

180

increasing political representation and policing issues. Councillors further noted that problems that ethnic minorities face that also pertained society-wide were issues not only in and of themselves, but were compounded by the effects of racism and discrimination, thereby making them even more difficult to solve for ethnic minorities.

I would argue, therefore, that it is possible to talk about such things as an "ethnic minority agenda" and "ethnic minority issues" and the perceived responsiveness of political institutions to these concerns. The perceptions of ethnic minority councillors clearly indicated that, while many of ethnic minorities' expectations and demands are similar to those of white citizens, these were supplemented by concerns that clearly placed questions of discrimination and racism at the top of a distinctive ethnic minority political agenda.

## FORMS OF PARTICIPATION

The degree to which ethnic minority councillors attest to the effectiveness of traditional democratic activities[6] will be an important indicator of their political integration. Were ethnic minority councillors to give strong endorsement to unconventional political activities[7] and alternative forms of political organization arranged along racial and ethnic lines,[8] this could be interpreted as evidence of a lack of political integration.

In the literature on ethnic minority political participation in Britain, there has been considerable discussion about the effectiveness of conventional political activities for ethnic minorities. Participation in political parties and elections is often seen as a hallmark of political integration and support for democratic politics (Layton-Henry and Studlar 1985: 307). As Solomos (1989: 141) further notes, such participation tends to reinforce identification with the rules, procedures and values of the polity, while enabling the articulation of demands, facilitating consent and strengthening acceptance of the legitimacy of the political system.

However, political participation need not be limited to formal institutional channels and may indeed fall into categories that are not commonly acknowledged as being legitimate. It is often argued that, for groups lacking in organizational and economic resources, collective action in the form of protest is the most effective type of political action (see Gamson 1968, Piven and Cloward 1974, 1977). According to Piven and Cloward (1974: 265), "the ability of an outcast minority to advance in the face of majority prejudices partly depends upon its ability to develop countervailing power". They argue that such power is to be developed through disruptive political strategies which create crises to which political leaders must respond. In their view, electoral-representative systems can never be responsive to the powerless in society, and protest is the only effective form of political action for members of powerless groups.

In the British case, "the absence of opportunities for institutional participation by local people" in local government (and national politics as well) has been frequently discussed (Benyon and Solomos 1988: 416–18). This lack of effective channels and opportunities for participation for inner-city residents (large numbers of whom are ethnic minorities) is argued to have important implications for the maintenance of political order (Benyon and Solomos 1988: 417):

> Participation is important not only to legitimise the regime and to aid the effectiveness of its performance, but also to enhance identification with the polity. Institutional participation facilitates integration and lowers the probability of dramatic non-institutional participation, or voice, in the form of violent protest. The lack of opportunities for participation in inner city areas may result in low levels of citizen consent and may adversely affect citizens views of the political system's legitimacy.

In keeping with this perspective, Benyon and Solomos (1988: 418) argue that the root cause for the resort to non-traditional forms of participation observed among ethnic minorities in the early 1980s, particularly violent protest, was

> the exclusion of specific groups from the processes of political, social and cultural incorporation ... as this exclusion operates systematically over a long period, it produces a deep sense of injustice in the excluded groups which can flare into a violent form of protest.

Thus, they pursue a line of argument similar to that of Piven and Cloward, envisioning a future of increasing disaffection among ethnic minorities and a consequent turn to unconventional political behaviour.

Other scholars have argued, however, that protest politics, particularly violent protest, will be the exception rather than the rule among Britain's ethnic minorities. For example, Studlar (1986: 181) notes the following:

Asians, who are by several indicators the most isolated group, are peaceful, fearful of violent repercussions and wedded to leaders who are reasonably adept at the politics of bureaucracy . . . . [Afro-Caribbeans] are individualistic, lack organization and are probably too sceptical to mount an effective concerted attempt at political violence.

Studlar (1986: 182) further argues that rather than sustained unconventional political behaviour, what is more likely is sporadic, undisciplined street protest that is "not likely to yield substantial political benefit unless it can be utilised by non-white leaders as a threat to elicit political concessions". Solomos (1990) also argues that any wholesale withdrawal from conventional political activities on the part of ethnic minorities is unlikely.

The data indicated that ethnic minority councillors generally supported the use of conventional political activities. The most traditional forms of democratic participation (running for office, voting, joining political parties and community associations) were rated as "effective when ethnic minorities use them in pressing for change" (see Table 8.1). Indeed, a majority of ethnic minority councillors rated these activities as *very* effective.

A variety of other conventional, but less institutionalized participatory activities (attending city meetings, contacting elected officials, joining single issue groups, signing a petition, and initiating court actions or legislation), also received majority endorsement as being effective, although they were more likely to be described as being only *somewhat* effective (Table 8.1). Overall, there was a general tendency to consider all conventional forms of political participation to be useful when ethnic minorities use them in pressing for change.

These high approval ratings are not surprising given these councillors' status as active participants in the formal political system. One would not expect those individuals who comprise the formal political system to describe its most fundamental participatory activities as illegitimate or ineffective.

Two less conventional methods of expressing political voice, attending mass demonstrations and joining in boycotts, were also considered to be effective by a majority of ethnic minority councillors. Mass demonstrations received significantly greater support, with 41.8 per cent of councillors rating this activity as *very* effective and 49.3 per cent as somewhat effective. However, only 17.8 per cent of councillors endorsed boycotts as being *very* effective, with an additional 40.4 per cent viewing them as only somewhat effective.

Beyond these two activities, non-traditional forms of participation did not receive majority endorsement as practical by ethnic minority

TABLE 8.1  Effectiveness of various forms of participation

| Activity | Percentage identifying these as very or somewhat effective | | |
|---|---|---|---|
| | Very effective | Somewhat effective | Combined effectiveness |
| Traditional | | | |
| Running for elective office | 74.7 | 23.4 | 98.1 |
| Voting | 77.3 | 19.5 | 96.8 |
| Joining political parties | 74.8 | 21.9 | 96.7 |
| Joining/working in community associations | 61.3 | 33.6 | 94.9 |
| Writing/calling elected officials | 48.4 | 40.0 | 88.4 |
| Attending city meetings | 40.6 | 42.7 | |
| Initiating court actions and legislation | 34.9 | 36.9 | 71.8 |
| Joining single issue groups | 22.6 | 46.7 | 69.3 |
| Signing a petition | 23.9 | 40.0 | 63.9 |
| Non-traditional | | | |
| Attending mass demonstrations | 41.8 | 49.4 | 91.2 |
| Joining in boycotts | 17.8 | 40.5 | 58.3 |
| Occupying buildings or factories (sit-ins) | 9.0 | 21.4 | 30.4 |
| Joining in wildcat strikes | 8.5 | 17.6 | 26.1 |
| Using group or violent protest | 8.3 | 11.7 | 20.0 |
| Refusing to pay taxes or rent | 6.8 | 11.0 | 17.8 |

Source: Author's survey, 1990.

councillors. Less than one-third of councillors rated sit-ins as effective and just over one-quarter considered wildcat strikes to be useful in pressing for change. Additionally, only a small minority of councillors viewed any of these alternative forms of participation (with the exception of mass demonstrations as being *very* effective). Further supporting these findings, only one-third of ethnic minority councillors agreed with the statement that the only way ethnic minorities can get the government's attention is to go outside normal political channels. An equal number of councillors *strongly* disagreed with this notion, thus indicating a general feeling among these councillors that traditional political methods work reasonably satisfactorily for ethnic minorities.

## ALTERNATIVE POLITICAL ORGANIZATIONS

As demonstrated in the previous section, ethnic minority councillors endorsed the use of conventional political activities over more traditional methods. The question remains, however, whether they believe there is a need to seek alternatives to the "established politics" of the Labour, Conservative and Liberal Democratic Parties. Such alternatives might take the form of the creation of a separate ethnic minority party or parties, or of their own sections of the major parties (as in the Black Sections movement within the Labour Party), or of a non-partisan pressure group. These attitudes may in particular be of central importance insofar as elite attitudes influence mass behaviour.

Scholars differ as to the degree to which ethnic minorities are interested in, or see a need for, breaking away from established political institutions, especially the political parties. Jacobs (1988: 174), for example, notes:

> The demand for an independent black political party which would stand against Labour and which would seek to aggressively defend black interests has had some appeal to those who regard the political system as racist and who see the established political parties in the same light.

Jacobs argues that those ethnic minorities who support the notion of an independent ethnic minority political party go far beyond the notion of ethnic minority sections within the existing parties, because they see ethnic minorities "as having their own interests, which are quite distinct from those of whites". He further claims that the independent party idea is connected "with the idea of black nationalism, which seeks to promote black demands as part of a defence of black culture and nationhood" (1988: 174).

By contrast, other scholars argue that ethnic minorities generally feel a need to be involved in these institutions in order to have direct access to political power. For example, Fitzgerald (1988: 259) argues that what the "evidence suggests is not a general spurning of British politics [by ethnic minorities], but rather an aspiration to greater involvement. Moreover, there is little sign of support ... for increasing black involvement on a racially separate basis". With reference to an ethnic minority pressure group, Studlar (1986: 176) also notes that while "there is always the possibility that a broad, effective umbrella group of nonwhites may be formed with a leadership that can command mass support, ... it is highly unlikely".

Evidence at the mass level does not suggest an intention to reject mainstream politics on the part of ethnic minorities.[9] One might argue that, given the nature of the British party system, ethnic minority voters have been given no credible alternatives to the mainstream parties. However, in the 1990 local elections the Islamic Party of Great Britain contested a number of local council seats throughout the country. The Islamic Party won none of the seats contested at that election, even in areas with large ethnic minority populations.[10] Such results indicate that at the mass level there is little interest among ethnic minorities in turning away from the mainstream parties.

The data indicated that ethnic minority councillors were strongly committed to their communities working through established partisan institutions. Over 90 per cent of councillors surveyed believed that this was very or fairly important. Widespread support was also demonstrated among councillors in the interviews:

> I think that to be a full member of the system in the future you should be among them [whites] ... I think that ethnic minorities would be better off getting involved in the party ... then they can be effective ... What we should be doing is supporting how the [party] system works, making sure enough blacks are joining the party (Labour councillor).

> Working through the [party] system is the way to achieve things for ethnic minorities. It is knowing the system, knowing how to use it, and knowing the limits of the system ... We can succeed within the party system, in spite of the imponderables, in spite of the blockages and so on which are put in our way (Labour councillor).

In keeping with these findings, only 13.1 per cent of survey respondents supported the formation of an independent all-ethnic minority party and less than 10 per cent asserted the importance of forming either independent all-Asian or Afro-Caribbean parties. This lack of support was also echoed among those councillors interviewed. Opposition to separate ethnic minority parties was often expressed not in terms of loyalty to existing partisan structures, but of a belief that the political system was structured in such a way as to make new alternative parties impotent. The following views are representative of this perspective:

> At the moment there is no way we could hope of ever having any sort of strength to build our own political party. It would never get off the ground. We have to fight within the Labour Party to acquire power and responsiveness (Labour councillor).

> As for a political party representing a particular community, I don't think they'd have a hope in hell of winning anything. Simply because people get elected to office in a party set-up ... and one sole voice, even if they get into the council or Parliament, will have no prestige or influence or rights, other than

occasionally standing up and speaking. Whereas a member of a party group has at least access to the leaders and has a potential for obtaining office within the party and I think that is the way forward (Conservative councillor).

Majority support was expressed, however, for the creation of ethnic minority sections in the established political parties among those councillors surveyed. Over 60 per cent of surveyed councillors believed the creation of such sections was important. Of those councillors interviewed who had an opinion on the formation of a Black Section in the Labour Party, there was also general support for such sections (59 per cent). Support for the formation of a Black Section was primarily based on a perceived need for the increased representation and articulation of ethnic minority interests, while at the same time continuing to work within established political structures:

I'm in the Black Section and we've always argued that you need to organize within the party and that's the main benefit we see in having that organizational strength ... . We believe we've had a major impact as a black organization within a mainstream party and the only black organization in a national party (Labour councillor).

I think the whole idea of Black Sections is to actually get the party to take on board some of the fundamental issues that affect the black community ... part of the whole notion of Black Sections was in fact to get the party to take us seriously (Labour councillor).

We don't want to be apart from the Labour Party movement, we want it to be within the structure, but be recognised that our concerns are legitimate and we want them to be addressed (Labour councillor).

Nearly all of those councillors interviewed who opposed the creation of separate ethnic minority sections felt that such sections represented separatism or exclusionism. Others went on to describe such sections on grounds similar to those used to reject policies of positive discrimination. Thus, they were objected to on the grounds that they involved a form of "special treatment" that would ultimately produce white resentment.

I myself am opposing it ... because I feel that if we make a separate organization or grouping, then whatever we want to achieve, we won't be able to achieve without the help of the section .... We must cooperate with majority, not separate sections .... We can succeed not by confrontation, but cooperation (Labour councillor).

The fighting for the Black Sections movement has created animosity between Asians and blacks, and that I don't want to see because that weakens [the ethnic minorities]. I opposed Black Sections early on. I said to the Labour movement, if we have to have a separate organization of blacks inside the Labour Party what we have is Labour Party apartheid (Labour councillor).

I am personally dead against it still. I don't want them to provide us with special consideration .... If we are speaking on behalf of the [ethnic minority] community, they should activate, they should be represented on first a local basis, and then we ask for these things. If people don't want to come, then we should have individual ability so that everybody recognises this person is okay, he should be there (Labour councillor).

Those councillors interviewed were also asked about the utility of ethnic minorities forming a non-partisan pressure group to represent ethnic minority interests. Overall, there was little endorsement of such a strategy. Those opposing such a group were most likely to do so out of party loyalty, feelings that such groups could not be effective, or that they were too often or too easily used for others' purposes. Such groups were often further described as isolationist and counterproductive.

## THE RESPONSIVENESS OF POLITICAL PARTIES

As we have seen, among ethnic minority councillors the existing parties were by and large the political organizations of choice. Such findings lead us to consider ethnic minority councillors' views about the responsiveness of these institutions once ethnic minorities have turned to them.

The perceived responsiveness of political parties will be an indicator of political integration to the extent that parties are important for demand articulation and for generating positive identification with the political system. As Anwar (1986: 150) notes, "because political decisions lead to political loyalties, the policies and attitudes of a particular party ... towards ethnic minorities in particular, are important".

188

As Benyon and Solomos (1988: 416) further note, "feelings of responsiveness are integral to individuals' political integration insofar as such integration is evidenced by a belief in the effectiveness of a political system's outputs for a particular community". Further, the policies and initiatives of political parties are very important in encouraging citizens, and particularly ethnic minorities, to participate in the political process. As Layton-Henry and Studlar (1985: 308) argue,

> The integration of black and Asian voters into mainstream politics not only requires increasing participation on their part but also a willingness by the parties ... to accept, even encourage, such involvement. Party members will have to welcome black and Asian people as full members, adopt them as candidates and persuade their supporters to vote for them in local and national elections. The parties will also need to respond to the particular interests of the ethnic minorities and allow them to influence party policy.

Rather than meeting such requirements, however, the parties in Britain are generally agreed to be doing just the opposite. It is a commonly-held belief that the major British political parties' central concern is with ensuring that ethnic minority issues remain *off* the political agenda. Further, many claim that "the black communities increasingly believe that Labour sees them largely in terms of electoral gain" (*New Statesman and Society* 15 July 1988: 13).

Additionally, participation in political parties and elections need not translate into issues achieving agenda status or increased policy responsiveness. In fact, it has been argued that in Britain "electoral politics has hitherto not been an effective vehicle for non-white demands" (Studlar 1986: 177). Studlar (1986: 178) further maintains that,

> Participation in elections and parties will not necessarily lead to race-related issues reaching the formal agenda, much less result in outcomes preferred by non-whites. At best such participation may help to legitimise non-whites' participation as full citizens in British society and thereby improve their potential access to central decision-makers.

Hence, if councillors perceive that political parties are not responsive to ethnic minorities in terms of the issues they address or the opportunities for participation they offer to ethnic minorities, then they are not likely to be institutions that are facilitating political integration. If, conversely, councillors believe that political parties are responsive to ethnic minority demands and open to ethnic minorities' full and effective participation, then these institutions may function as important channels for political integration. The responsiveness of political parties can be measured relative to ethnic minorities' role in partisan decision-making, their ability to increase their levels of representation, and the parties' willingness to address issues deemed important to ethnic minorities.

## ETHNIC MINORITIES' DECISION-MAKING ROLE

Ethnic minority councillors were generally dissatisfied with their ability to influence their parties' policies and actions. A large majority of those councillors surveyed (80.9 per cent) agreed with the statement that "the political parties were more interested in ethnic minorities' votes than their opinions". Half of this majority *strongly* agreed with this characterization of the intentions of the major political parties.

Councillors, when interviewed, commonly believed that the Labour Party paid attention to ethnic minority demands only insofar as they needed the votes of the ethnic minority community in a particular area. Nearly all Labour councillors interviewed believed that their party primarily used ethnic minorities as "voting fodder" and was unwilling to allow them to have a greater say in party decision-making. Such views were characterized by the following statements:

> There is a tendency for Labour to use blacks as voting fodder. And, too bad that is something we have to fight against. And the ethnic minorities are now actually getting wiser to that and they are actually saying to the Labour Party we are not going to be your voting fodder. You've got to give us power as well (Labour councillor).

> Unfortunately, ethnic minorities do not get much from the Labour Party. One always hears that the Labour Party is the natural party for ethnic minorities, but it isn't and it is very sad really. Because the Labour Party is looking more towards the middle class and attracting that particular section of the community. It feels that the ethnic minority will have no choice but to support them, whether they like it or not. Because if they don't support the party, then they are the ones who are losers. We are left out to fend for ourselves within the political arena if we don't cooperate with the Labour Party (Labour councillor).

## WILLINGNESS TO INCREASE ETHNIC MINORITY
## REPRESENTATION

One issue that focused particular attention on the Labour Party's responsiveness to its ethnic minority constituents was the creation of a Black Section representing ethnic minorities within the party. A majority of interviewees viewed this issue as a prime example of the Labour Party's lack of responsiveness to ethnic minority demands for representation *within* party structures. For example,

> A large part of it has to do with their reluctance to allow black people voice, an independent voice ... at the end of the day it is about votes and elections, a fear of white backlash if the party seems to be giving power to blacks (Labour councillor).

> They [the Labour Party] are moving towards the centre, and because they are moving towards the centre, they have to appease the electorate at the centre. And the electorate at the centre couldn't give a damn about black people. So, you don't want to start setting up organizations that are going to put off your white liberal voters, it will frighten them off (Labour councillor).

Related to the issue of recognition for a Labour Party Black Section is the willingness of the political parties to nominate additional ethnic minority candidates for political office. Survey data indicated that 97.2 per cent of councillors considered more ethnic minority elected officials to be very or fairly important for ethnic minority progress. Evidence from the interviews further supported this perspective, with nearly all councillors aspiring to increased levels of representation for ethnic minority citizens, at the local and, in particular, at the national level. For example,

> I think ethnic minorities need far more councillors and MPs, to get their voice heard in the system. If you do not have faces in the system, you cannot survive. The representation of blacks is now at a minimum level and it must improve (Labour councillor).

> I think that we are miles behind real representation. But the local representation will not make much difference unless you have the national level representation as well. Because actual decisions are made at the national level rather than the local (Labour councillor).

191

Most ethnic minority councillors were pessimistic about the likelihood of increasing representation, at least within the Labour Party. For example, two-thirds of surveyed councillors stated that they had no influence over their party's selection of ethnic minority candidates. Interviewed councillors overwhelmingly echoed this perspective:

> I feel that there will no doubt be an increase in black represen-tation in Parliament. I feel that if you as a local candidate worked with your community, with your local government, party, wards, whatever, and let them see what you are made of, then no head office can stop that at all, in actual fact if they did it would cause a great outcry .... They [the party] have to be very careful, because if a chap's work is known locally and he's worked very hard, then he's going to fight all the way (Labour councillor).

> The Labour Party has got to put black and ethnic minorities into winnable seats ... in many areas we [blacks and ethnic minorities] have a majority – or we have a decisive say in who wins. I guess we are seen as a liability in such a situation .... Black and ethnic minorities have been for years ... voting for white candidates in the Labour Party ... and now the question of our voting for a black candidate seems to be a great problem (Labour councillor).

> You're talking about power. If you have more black MPs, there are fewer white MPs. And for all the talk about equality of opportunity, nobody is prepared to give up their seat for a woman or black. They are threatened by the increasing number of blacks. Insignificant, maybe, but if you have 30 black MPs, you're talking about ten per cent of the parliamen-tary Labour Party (Labour councillor).

Such pessimism was borne out at the 1992 General Election, where fewer ethnic minority candidates ran for Parliament than in 1987 (24, compared to 29 in 1987), though the aggregate total across the three major parties rose substantially in 1997 to 44 candidates. In 1992, only the Conservatives *increased* their number of ethnic minority candi-dates (although only two were selected in potentially winnable seats) and the number of candidates selected by the Labour Party decreased. The 1997 boost in numbers was chiefly the result of many more Liberal Democrats being selected.

## ISSUE RESPONSIVENESS

Previous research at the mass level has indicated that ethnic minority voters were generally satisfied with the Labour Party's policies on race and immigration and that they were dissatisfied with the Conservative government's record on these issues. As Layton-Henry (1990: 59) notes,

> On racial discrimination, Labour's policies are endorsed much more strongly than those of the Conservatives. Satisfaction with Labour's policies on race and immigration is particularly high among Asians, (60 per cent satisfied to 13 per cent dissatisfied) and dissatisfaction with the government's record is very high among Afro-Caribbeans (76 per cent dissatisfied to 8 per cent satisfied).

However, similar sentiments were not echoed by ethnic minority councillors. Labour Party councillors interviewed in particular believed that their party had very limited objectives with respect to ethnic minority issues, namely racism, discrimination and immigration. There was a general consensus among interviewed councillors that the Labour Party was reluctant to put ethnic minority issues prominently on the party's agenda out of a fear of alienating white voters. Shukra (1990: 189) has argued that

> The Labour leadership has shown that it controls the Labour Party's direction. For black people that means they may participate and pursue anti-racist policies only on the terms acceptable to the Labour leadership. These terms are highly influenced by the potential vote-losing effects of many (of their) demands.

Ethnic minority councillors interviewed generally supported this argument:

> It's gone some way, but I think the party has a long way to go still in meeting the satisfaction of the black and ethnic minority electorate .... . Some have a fear of alienating the white voters if they come out [on ethnic minority issues] and I suppose that is where the major frustration with the party is (Labour councillor).

> The Labour Party in my view feels that if they were to focus on black issues, that they might lose white vote (Labour councillor).

There was a general belief among these councillors that, while the Labour Party has made some progress in addressing ethnic minority issues, the pace of such progress is much too slow.

> I think the party has a long way to go still in meeting the satisfaction of the black and ethnic minority electorate .... There are a number of issues, starting with immigration policy – the party hasn't yet got a policy on it or it doesn't spell out what the alternative to [the Conservative's] laws would be .... There is some fear of alienating the white voters if they come out and that I suppose is where the major frustration is with the party (Labour councillor).

In general, Conservative councillors did not even recognise a need to address "ethnic minority" issues by their party:

> They are as responsive to the needs of blacks as much as they are responsive to the needs of everyone. Because having said that, if their policies cater for the needs of everybody in this country, we must never forget that being black is only one part of this (Conservative councillor).

> There are very few issues of national politics which primarily concern only the ethnic minorities and as long as we are responsive to an issue and in that response we also take into account the extent of benefit or disbenefit for ethnic minorities or a particular community group (Conservative councillor).

## CONCLUSIONS

The attitudes of ethnic minority councillors about political participation and organization suggest a pattern of political incorporation that involves integration within British political institutions. In keeping with their status as active participants in Britain's formal political processes, ethnic minority councillors widely endorsed traditional political activities as effective when ethnic minorities use them in pressing for change. A variety of non-violent, non-disruptive participatory activities also received majority ratings as effective among these councillors, although they were viewed as being less effective than more traditional institutional forms of participation. Only a minority of councillors endorsed as effective expressions of political voice that involved disruptive or violent tactics or dramatic "non-institutional" participation.

Ethnic minority councillors also exhibited a strong belief in the need to work through established political organizations to achieve ethnic minority goals. Support for existing partisan structures was widely demonstrated in both the survey data and among those councillors interviewed. Reinforcing this evidence was the widespread lack of interest in alternative partisan organizations or pressure groups among all councillors. Support for existing forms of political organization was largely based on recognition that any alternative political groupings would be impotent in the British political system as currently configured. The only new form of political organization that received endorsement from these councillors was the creation of ethnic minority sections within the existing parties (particularly the Labour Party). Support for such sections may still be interpreted as an expression of an interest in working through established political structures, given that such sections would operate within existing parties.

In short, councillors clearly articulated a desire for incorporation and acceptance into the British political system. They asserted the value of ethnic minority participation in existing mainstream political institutions and sought to become involved in a manner that could provide direct access to political power. The evidence with respect to forms of political participation and organization thus does not suggest an intention to reject mainstream politics by ethnic minorities – and, therefore, a path of alienation – but rather an aspiration to increased participation and integration.

The findings with respect to councillors' views of the responsiveness of partisan institutions, however, clearly had more negative implications for ethnic minority political integration. Ethnic minority councillors were generally dissatisfied with the degree to which the British political parties were open to ethnic minorities' full participation and receptive to ethnic minorities' demands. As is commonly agreed to be the case, the parties, particularly the Labour Party, were regarded by ethnic minority councillors as "using" ethnic minorities for electoral gain, denying them full and equal participation in partisan activities and avoiding ethnic minority issues. Overall, councillors demonstrated little faith in ethnic minorities' ability to participate effectively in and influence party decision-making and policy formulation, suggesting a developing pattern of alienation rather than integration.

One important indicator of this general level of dissatisfaction was to be found in the pattern of support for a separate ethnic minority section within the Labour Party. Ethnic minority councillors' frustrations with their party's "colour-blind" policy positions and its perceived determination to keep ethnic minority issues off the party's agenda were manifested in widespread support for the formation of a Black Section. As suggested above, support for such a section can be interpreted positively in that it implies a desire to participate within mainstream political organizations. However, this support for section-alism also clearly reflects a general level of frustration with ethnic minorities' ability to compel the Labour Party to respond to their interests and demands in the absence of an officially recognized entity.

Ethnic minority councillors were especially unhappy with the responsiveness of political parties regarding the nomination and elec-tion to office of ethnic minorities. Councillors' impressions (especially Labour councillors') suggested that candidate selection was primarily a function of electoral considerations and was a manifestation of par-tisan competition. As such, candidates were chosen primarily on the basis of whether a particular individual was likely to win (or not lose) a seat, rather than as a concession to ethnic minority pressure, in response to feelings of responsibility to ethnic minority constituents, or as a reflection of a commitment to increase the political representa-tion and participation of ethnic minorities. The nomination and elec-tion of ethnic minority candidates, therefore, was not indicative of any significant change in the nature of party politics or a devolution of power to ethnic minorities, particularly within the Labour Party. Rather, such selections were interpreted as partisan politics "as usual". Such findings are troublesome for ethnic minority political integration. Higher levels of ethnic minority institutional participation via elective office clearly require the commitment and co-operation of the major parties. To the extent that these parties, especially the Labour Party, ignore such obligations, an increasing rate of political integration for Britain's ethnic minorities may not be a given.

These findings are illustrative of the degree to which the political fortunes of ethnic minorities are related to Labour Party politics in Britain. As Messina argues elsewhere in this volume, ethnic minorities' dependence on the Labour Party results from the logic of Britain's two-party system and its electoral mechanisms, as well as the fact that the Labour Party remains the natural choice for promoting ethnic minority interests. Thus, as a result of ethnic minorities' overwhelm-ing membership in the Labour Party, what happens in a political sense to ethnic minorities continues to be strongly dependent upon Labour partisan factors.

This reliance on the Labour Party may ultimately serve as a limi-tation on ethnic minorities' political integration, for several reasons. As we have just discussed, it will depend on the degree to which such integration is related to increased electoral representation and the extent to which the party continues to restrict ethnic minorities' opportunities for such representation. Additionally, the Labour Party was described by councillors as prepared to tolerate the participation of ethnic minorities in its ranks only within the limited parameters defined by the party leadership. For example, councillors commonly characterized the ethnic minorities' role in the Labour Party as "voting fodder" and viewed the party as unwilling to allow ethnic minorities to play any significant part in party decision-making. Councillors further described the Labour Party as reluctant to address ethnic minority concerns directly, especially racism and discrimination, and, in fact, believed the party leadership had made a point of removing such issues from its agenda. Hence, to the extent to which the quantity and quality of their participation is conditioned by terms set by the Labour Party, and to the degree to which these terms continue to be restrictive and non-responsive, the political integration of ethnic minorities may be circumscribed. In short, ethnic minorities' dependence on the Labour Party, and the past performance of this party regarding ethnic minorities' concerns, does not appear to bode well for ethnic minorities' future political integration.

Overall, the findings indicated a strong commitment among ethnic minority councillors to democratic political institutions and a desire to participate actively in mainstream political life. As previously noted, such findings have positive implications for the political integration of ethnic minorities. At the same time, however, the experiences of ethnic minority councillors within one such institution – the party system – suggest a need for caution before being too optimistic about the pace of this political integration. Ethnic minorities clearly desire and expect such integration. Yet their experiences within partisan bodies, especially the Labour Party, suggest a rising level of frustration that over the long-term could produce a situation of political alienation. Such alienation would not necessarily be manifested in violent opposition to the political system (nor would it be likely, given the predispositions of ethnic minority councillors discussed earlier). However, it is possible that the continuation of such negative experiences within political institutions will produce ethnic minority apathy and perhaps even their withdrawal from active political life. This would clearly be an undesirable and unacceptable condition for citizens in a democratic society.

Preventing such alienation and achieving the full participation and integration of ethnic minority citizens in British politics will be dependent in part on the efforts of the political parties. Ethnic minorities' full participation in the political system demands that the political parties afford them the opportunity to increase their level of representation. The parties must be willing to cede some of their power (particularly in terms of whites' control of electoral seats) to their ethnic minority members who desire participation on equal footing with whites. Ethnic minorities must be granted increased say in the selection of their party's candidates, as well as full representation

197

within party structures. Further, the political parties need to be responsive to the concerns of their ethnic minority members and to allow their participation in party agenda-setting and decision-making.

At present, it is difficult to predict the likelihood of such changes in partisan behaviour and intentions, particularly those of the Labour Party. Prior to the 1992 General Election, ethnic minority councillors were hopeful that the Labour Party would return to power and they expected this to increase the party's willingness to address their concerns. Obviously this never happened. The 1992 election result served to dampen further the ethnic minorities' enthusiasm for the Labour Party as the likelihood of the party's ever being re-elected, and, with it, the anticipated recognition of ethnic minority concerns, seemed more remote than ever. A similar expectation prior to 1997, on this occasion, however, fully justified, will arguably create a rather new context for such enthusiasm.

Recent changes in Labour's leadership and its election to office present an opportunity for speculation about a political context that gradually may become more conducive to the articulation and representation of ethnic minority interests. Tony Blair's efforts to reduce the role of trades unions in party decision-making, presumably creating a more open political atmosphere within the party, may present new opportunities for ethnic minorities to make their voices heard. Additionally, Blair's personal appeal and the party's enhanced electoral position may open the party up to address ethnic minority areas that previously had been considered too costly in political, especially electoral, terms. Clearly, these are potentially important developments that have yet to fully unfold. The future trajectory of the relationship between ethnic minorities and the political parties, especially the Labour Party, still remains unclear. However, the truth is that, if the perceived absence of a real commitment to ethnic minority concerns by these institutions persists, the full integration of ethnic minorities into democratic political institutions will be seriously hindered.

## NOTES

1. The ethic origins of Britain's non-white population basically divide along Afro-Caribbean (or West Indian) and Asian lines. The Asian category primarily includes Indians, Pakistanis and Bangladeshi. A smaller percentage of the non-white population derives from Southeast Asia, the Meditterranean and other parts of the New Commonwealth. Scholars have referred to these ethnic groups in a varity of ways: the entire racial population has been referred to as "black" or "non-white", West Indians

have been termed "blacks" and Asians "browns"; or each group has been identified by its country of origin. I have chosen to avoid the term "black" because of its imprecision; I will refer to Britain's non-white population as its ethnic minority population and to this population's leaders as ethnic minority leaders. The exceptions to this will be instances where reference to specific ethnic groups is more appropriate.

2. The data used in the study derive from a survey conducted in autumn 1990 consisting of 46 in-depth, semi-structured interviews with a sample of sitting ethnic minority councillors. The data are also the product of a mail survey of all ethnic minority councillors (N = 347), incumbent (N = 295) and retired (N = 52), also conducted in autumn 1990, with a response rate of 49.5 per cent (146) and 39.5 per cent (18), respectively.

3. Ethnic minority councillors are overwhelmingly representatives of the Labour Party (92.4 per cent). Reflecting this, the partisan composition of the interview sample was 41 Labour Party members, 4 Conservative, and 1 Liberal Democrat. Mail survey respondents' partisan affiliations were 91.5 per cent (150) Labour, 4.9 per cent (8) Conservative, 2.4 per cent (4) Liberal Democrat, and 1.2 per cent (2) Independent. When drawing conclusions about ethnic minorities and the British party system, it is important to note that the number of non-Labour respondents was small, but was nonetheless reflective of the population of ethnic minority councillors overall.

4. These responses were provided to a question asking councillors to rank relative to each other these three problems.

5. When councillors used the term racism they were generally speaking about discrimination issues.

6. Traditional or conventional forms of participation include the following: running for elective office; joining political parties, community associations, single-issue groups; contacting elected officials; attending city meetings; signing a petition; and initiating court actions or legislation.

7. Such alternative forms of participation include attending mass demonstrations, boycotts, sit-ins or wildcat strikes; using group or violent protest; or refusing to pay taxes or rent.

8. Such groupings include a separate all-ethnic minority party, distinct Asian or Afro-Caribbean parties, ethnic minority sections in the established parties, or a non-partisan ethnic minority pressure group.

9. Data from the 1987 General Election indicated that the Labour Party remained the overwhelmingly popular choice among ethnic minority voters, with 72 per cent of those polled indicating an intention to vote Labour, 18 per cent Conservative and 10 per cent Alliance. Actual voting patterns at the 1987 General Election indicated that 61 per cent of Asians and 92 per cent of Afro-Caribbeans voted for Labour, compared with 31 per cent of whites (Anwar 1990: 43). The ethnic minority population remained a bulwark of Labour Party support (Layton-Henry 1990: 59). Such patterns persisted at the 1992 elections, with 77 per cent of Asians and 85 per cent of Afro-Caribbeans expressing a preference for Labour (Ali and Percival 1993). Preliminary polling figures from 1997 indicate a 70/25/4 split among Asians for the Labour Party, the Conservative Party

199

and the Liberal Democratic Party respectively, and an 86/8/4 split among blacks (MORI 1997).

10. For example, in Bolton, an area with a large Asian population, even in the ward where the Islamic Party performed best their candidate needed seven times as many votes to beat Labour's winning vote. In other wards, the Islamic Party candidates needed nine times, 13 times, and 18 times as many votes (Le Lohé 1990: 109–10).

## REFERENCES

Ali, A. & G. Percival 1993. Race and representation: Ethnic minorities and the 1992 elections. London: Commission for Racial Equality.

Anwar, M. 1980. *Votes and Policies: Ethnic minorities and the General Election 1979*. London: Commission for Racial Equality.

Anwar, M. 1986. *Race and Politics: Ethnic minorities and the British political system*, London: Tavistock Publications.

Anwar, M. 1990. Ethnic Minorities and the Electoral Process: Some recent developments. In *Black Politics in Britain*, H. Goulbourne (ed.). Aldershot: Gower.

Almond, G. & S. Verba 1965. *The Civic Culture*. Boston: Little, Brown.

Back, L. & J. Solomos 1994. Labour and racism: Trade unions and the selection of parliamentary candidates. *The Sociological Review* vol. 42, 165–201.

Benyon, J. & J. Solomos 1988. The simmering cities: Urban unrest during the Thatcher years. *Parliamentary Affairs*, vol. 41, 401–22.

Butcher, H., I. Law, R. Leach & M. Mullard 1990. *Local Government and Thatcherism*. London: Routledge.

Byrne, T. 1990. *Local Government in Britain*. London: Penguin.

Cashmore, E. & B. Troyna 1982. *Black Youth in Crisis*. London. George, Allen and Unwin.

Crewe, I. 1983. Representation and the ethnic minorities in Britain. In *Ethnic Pluralism and Public Policy*, Glazer, N. and K. Young (eds). London: Heinemann.

Eldersveld, S., J. Kooiman & T. Tak 1981. *Elite Images of Dutch Politics*, Ann Arbor: University of Michigan Press.

Fitzgerald, M. 1984. *Political Parties and Black People: Participation, representation and exploitation*. Nottingham: Runnymede Trust Publications.

Fitzgerald, M. 1988. Afro-Caribbean involvement in British politics. In *Lost Illusions: Caribbean minorities in Britain and the Netherlands*, H. Entzinger (ed.). London: Routledge.

Fitzgerald, M. 1990. The emergence of black councillors and MPs in Britain: Some underlying questions. In *Black Politics in Britain*, H. Goulbourne (ed.). Aldershot: Gower Publishing.

Gamson, W. 1968. *Power and Discontent*. Homewood, IL: Dorsey.

Goulbourne, H. 1990. Some Introductory Remarks. In *Black Politics in Britain*, H. Goulbourne (ed.). Aldershot: Gower Publishing.

Jacobs, B. 1988. *Racism in Britain*. London: Christopher Helm.

Jeffers, S. 1991. Black Sections in the Labour Party: The end of ethnicity and godfather politics? In *Black and Ethnic Leaderships in Britain: The Cultural Dimensions of Political Action*, M. Anwar & P. Werbner (eds). London: Routledge.

Knowles, C. 1992. *Race, Discourse and Labourism*. London: Routledge.

Layton-Henry, Z. 1990. Black electoral participation: An analysis of recent trends. In *Black Politics in Britain*, H. Goulbourne (ed.). Aldershot: Gower Publishing.

Layton-Henry, Z. & D. Studlar 1985. The electoral participation of black and Asian Britons: Integration or alienation? *Parliamentary Affairs*, vol. 38, 307–18.

Le Lohé, M. J. 1990. Political issues. *New Community*, vol. 17, 105–13.

Messina, A. 1987. Ethnic minority representation and party competition in Britain: the case of Ealing borough. *Political Studies*, vol. 35, 224–38.

MORI 1997. Asian voting: preliminary results. Unpublished briefing notes, February 1997.

Paige, J. 1971. Political orientation and riot participation. *American Sociological Review*, vol. 36, 810–20.

Piven, F. & R. Cloward 1974. *The Politics of Turmoil*. New York: Pantheon.

Piven, F. & R. Cloward 1977. *Poor People's Movements*. New York: Pantheon.

Shukra, K. 1990. Black Sections in the Labour party. In *Black Politics in Britain*, H. Gouldbourne (ed.). Aldershot: Gower Publishing.

Solomos, J. 1989. *Race and Racism in Contemporary Britain*, London: Macmillan.

Solomos, J. 1990. In *Black Politics in Britain*, H. Gouldbourne (ed.). Aldershot: Gower Publishing.

Solomos, J. & L. Back. 1991. Black political mobilization and the struggle for equality. *The Sociological Review*, vol. 39, 215–37.

Studlar, D. 1986. Nonwhite policy preferences, political participation and the policy agenda in Britain. In *Race, Government and Politics in Britain*, Z. Layton-Henry & P. Rich (eds). London: Macmillan.

Studlar, D. & S. Welch. 1990. Voting for Minority Candidates in Local British and American Elections. In *Ethnic and Racial Minorities in Advanced Industrial Democracies*, A. Messina (ed.). Westport, CT: Greenwood Press.

Weil, P. & J. Crowley. 1994. Integration in theory and practice: a comparison of France and Britain. *Western European Politics*, vol. 17, 110–26.

Werbner, P. 1991. Black and ethnic leaderships in Britain. In *Black and Ethnic Leaderships in Britain: The cultural dimensions of political action*, M. Anwar & P. Werbner (eds). London: Routledge.

# CHAPTER NINE

# The role of black and Asian MPs at Westminister

*Jaqi Nixon*

## INTRODUCTION

There has been much detailed research and considerabale debate about the role of black politicians at local authority level. However, there has been little systematic scrutiny of the work of black and Asian[1] Members of Parliament. Prior to the general election of 1987, when four black candidates were elected to Parliament, there were, unsurprisingly, arguments supporting the urgent need for the presence of black politicians in mainstream politics. After the election of two additional Asian MPs in 1992 there was further speculation about what role they would play and what influence they would have at Westminister. The debate will only intensify with the election of nine (all Labour) in 1997. It seems appropriate, therefore, that after a decade of having a small group of black and Asian Members of Parliament, we should now begin to examine in more detail the part they play and the effect they have had, or appear to be having, on British politics at the centre.

This chapter considers the views of the six MPs in the 1992 cohort in respect of their Parliamentary role. It concentrates specifically upon the question of whether they regard themselves as generalist politicians at Westminster, or whether they prefer to accept the mantle of black or minority politician as their particular responsibility. It goes on to consider whether or not the presence of black and Asian MPs has made any difference to parliamentary politics by ensuring that issues of race do feature regularly in mainstream politics at the national level. Finally it attempts to assess the extent to which the contribution of black and Asian MPs at the centre could be further enhanced.

## BLACK REPRESENTATION AT THE CENTRE

It is important to note at the outset the significance of having some representation, however small, from black and Asian communities at Westminster. A number of commentators have argued that only when black and minority issues are represented in mainstream politics is it possible to avoid a continuing marginalization of these issues. Anwar (1986: 97) has noted, for example, that

> It is by incorporating ethnic minorities into the political system, not as nominal, but as effective members who participate actively in the decision-making process, that their alienation can be prevented.

As regards central government specifically, Studlar noted in 1986 (178) that

> However discomforting it may be for theorists of democracy, electoral politics on the Parliamentary level offers few benefits for non-whites, at least in their current situation.

Not least because of the absence of black representation at the centre prior to 1987, Bulpitt (1986) has also argued how successive governments have always managed to off-load important policy decisions on race to the periphery, but, now, with the election of black and Asian politicians to the House of Commons since 1987 it may be suggested that the days of marginalization and off-loading of race issues on to the periphery are over. Certainly Le Lohé (1989: 159–70) described the events of 1987 as "a watershed in the history of black and Asian political involvement".

Having succeeded in securing membership of the parliamentary elite, how might black and Asian MPs be expected to demonstrate political credibility? Are they expected to deal primarily with issues of race in order to ensure that these surface regularly on the political agenda? Or do their constituents, the Party Whips and their parliamentary colleagues expect them to demonstrate an ability to address a wider range of issues, and to move beyond the boundaries of race and the specific interests of black people? Are they expected to speak with

203

one voice on matters of race, or is diversity of opinion viewed as a better indicator of political maturity? All these different perspectives have support, not least among the MPs themselves, and it is appropriate that the arguments for each are briefly considered.

Having a small coterie of black and Asian MPs finally break into the predominently white parliamentary system may well give rise to the expectation that, collectively, they should give priority to race and minority issues. Using the architectural metaphor employed by Cerny (1986), black and Asian MPs are well placed to seek out and to put pressure on the "interstitial gaps and tensions" which exist in current political and policy structures. By applying pressure to these fissures, they are able to test out the relative strength or weaknesses of existing structures and, in so doing, may help to reshape them more in the interests of black or minority communities. This is not to suggest that black and Asian MPs have a monopoly of interest in race or minority community matters, but rather that they are more likely to be identified as a legitimate proxy for the politics of all the black dispossessed (Reed 1986, Lovenduski and Norris 1994). Moreover, as Messina's data (Chapter 3 this volume, Table 3.5) suggest, there are particular issues which have greater political salience for ethnic minority voters than for the white electorate. Thus, black and Asian Members of Parliament may be expected to carry specific responsibility for these issues both in Westminster and elsewhere.

Alternatively, it can be argued that political credibility at Westminster should be judged according to whether black representatives are able to move beyond race-specific issues, depending upon their personal interests, knowledge and experience. As a number of studies have demonstrated, issues which are of concern to black people are also those which are shared with the white electorate. In his study of local politics, for example, Eade (1989: 189) has noted:

> Local interest groups dealt with a variety of demands which *cut across* Bangladeshi/white distinctions, and local political competition depended upon appeals to *numerous social categories which were not directly related to constituencies of anti-racism and socialism.* [emphasis added]

Studlar (1986: 176) goes further, in fact, and suggests that "there is no such thing as a distinctive non-white political agenda". Thus, from this perspective and in the context of national politics, black and Asian politicians would be expected to represent a wide range of policy interests. Some of these may overlap directly with race or minority issues, but others are of concern to the electorate as a whole. Indeed, as Saggar (Chapter 2 this volume) makes clear, the scope for developing race-specific agendas depends upon the existence of a complex web of interrelated factors. Since the six 1992 Members of Parliament represent a wide range of ethnic and racial interests, it seems unlikely that the combination of factors required to generate specific race agendas would be present for much of the time. Moreover, as Goulbourne (1990: 104) has argued

> Irrespective of their intentions, black Members of Parliament will not be able to respond to issues which affect non-white groups scattered throughout several constituencies.

Many commentators in the past have reported in pessimistic terms the inability of black groups or their representatives to present a single view on race or minority issues for any length of time (Studlar 1986, Fitzgerald 1988, Ben Tovim, Gabriel, Law 1986). Currently, by virtue of their very small number, black and Asian MPs may be able to adopt a unified view on particular race issues, and some may feel it is imperative that they do so. An alternative perspective is that different viewpoints on race, as on other matters, reflects a democratic system in good health. The interests and abilities of black and Asian MPs are as diverse as amongst any other group of politicians and hence, apart from the discipline imposed on all Members by the party Whips, a diversity of opinion is to be both expected and preferred. As a policy universe (Wright 1988) race covers an extensive territory and within it there are many sub-areas, or "packs" of separate policies about which there are bound to be different perspectives and points of view. Certainly, at more general levels of analysis, as Lovenduski and Norris's research has revealed (1994), there is a very low (or non-existent) correlation between race and key social values held by black MPs.

Whether one believes that black and Asian MPs should be primarily single-issue politicians, or adopt a generalist role in the House, and whether they should share similar or differing views on issues pertaining to race, the key question remaining is whether their presence in Parliament makes any difference at all to the shape or content of political agendas at the centre. Are they able to exert any influence on input, processes or outcomes which are of direct concern to black and minority interests?

What follows is an exploratory analysis of the role of the six black and Asian Members of Parliament. It does not offer a detailed or comprehensive account of all their political activities and interests, nor does it attempt to evaluate their overall performance or effectiveness as MPs. Rather, it seeks to illustrate the extent to which there is both common purpose and diversity in the roles and perspectives adopted by this group of MPs. By drawing on both empirical data and the

TABLE 9.1  Six MPs and their constituencies (1992–7) with share of vote (percentages)

| MP | Constituency | Vote | Increase since 1987 | Ethnic minority vote* |
|---|---|---|---|---|
| Abbott | Hackney North/ Stoke Newington | 57.8 | 9.1 | 39.3 |
| Boateng | Brent South | 57.5 | 5.6 | 55.6 |
| Deva | Brentford & Isleworth | 45.8 | −1.9 | 16.5 |
| Grant | Tottenham | 56.5 | 12.9 | 45.3 |
| Khabra | Ealing/Southall | 47.4 | −3.3 | 53.2 |
| Vaz | Leicester East | 56.5 | 10.4 | 31.7 |

Source: *The Runnymede Bulletin* May 1992
* Anwar, M. (1986) *Race and Politics* Estimates

views of the MPs themselves, it is hoped that we may move beyond speculation or any unrealistic expectations of what black and Asian MPs can or should deliver.

Table 9.1 provides brief information about the constituencies which the six MPs represented between 1992 and 1997.

## MPs' PERSPECTIVES

It has to be said at the outset that the influence of individual back-bench MPs, and particularly of Opposition backbenchers, is generally slight. What influence they do have is more likely to be constituency-based, rather than to do with major issues of wider significance. As a number of commentators have suggested (Austin 1994, Norton 1994), the increasing burden of work generated by constituency responsibilities threatens to overwhelm members' ability to contribute, on a personal basis, to matters of national concern. Moreover, within the precincts of Westminster itself, backbencher influence is more likely to be covert, rather than in the public arena, taking place "in the day-to-day interaction of MPs and Ministers, for example in party committees and in tea-rooms and bars" (Drewry 1984: 91). Thus when the subject matter for investigation is so elusive, of necessity one has to draw primarily upon what is on public record and, in this instance, on the views and information provided by the MPs them-selves.

As to whether black and Asian MPs identify themselves as gener-alists or as single-issue MPs, it is worth noting the stance which members seek to adopt. Bernie Grant and Piara Khabra provide useful points at polar ends of what may be regarded as a possible continuum. Grant (Interview 1995) makes clear his position:

> I'm interested in general issues but general issues affect black people. I'm not a generalist MP. I'm not a black African MP. I'm an African MP. I'm quite happy working on race issues.

Grant (Interview 1995) compares his stance on race issues with that of his Labour colleagues:

> The other MPs are generalists, although black. They'll raise issues in an immigration debate, something like that, but by and large, they wouldn't stick to it. They've all got their own thing to do so they don't bring up the black dimension into what they do.

Khabra's position does indeed suggest an alternative approach. In support of Studlar's view, he explains (Interview 1995):

> I do not want to reduce my ability just to being a representative of ethnic minorities. No, that's not what I was elected for. I was elected as a member of the Labour Party ... We want to be part of the community, we don't want to be different. ... There isn't any issue which isn't common to all votes, to all races–unemployment, housing etc ... except for racial discrimination.

Boateng's position, though veering towards the latter, is more representative of an intermediate position (Interview 1995):

> I am an MP who is black. I am not a black MP. I am an MP with a wide variety of interests and who has had portfolios which are not race-specific but who has a commitment and a responsibility to the struggle for racial justice.

It is reasonable to suggest that Abbott also adopts this perspective. Her endeavours to raise awareness about gender as well as race issues, and to speak for women's interests (*The Guardian* 1989), are indicative of this:

> The agenda I bring to politics concerning low pay, benefits and so-called social issues like health and education, is one a man might not see as a priority.

Likewise, Vaz carried in Opposition a special brief for the inner cities within the Labour Party and in this capacity tended to make reference to constituency-specific, rather than race, issues. This approach was reflected in his contribution to the 1994 Housing and Urban Policies Debate (*Hansard* 1994) in which he cited a number of inner-city constituencies in need of greater central government funding or as having examples of appropriate urban projects. No reference was made to the race dimension of this particular policy area.

An additional check on MPs' own views about their role in the House is whether their party leaders and backbench colleagues also regard them as representatives primarily of minority interests. Boateng (Interview 1995) is adamant that they do not:

> My experience has been that the respective leaders of our party have always sought to utilise my talents whether as an economics spokesperson or as a legal spokesperson in a way which has no regard at all to the fact that I happen to be a person who draws upon African as well as British ancestral roots ... I don't think I have been treated any differently as a result of the colour of my skin.

Similarly Khabra does not believe his backbench colleagues single him out because of his Asian origins. In contrast Grant is of the view that he is expected to raise race issues (Interview 1995):

> The other MPs are generalists – they'll raise a black issue in an immigration debate, something like that, but by and large they wouldn't stick to it (i.e. to offering a race dimension) ... So I think a lot of backbenchers and some Front Bench Members, too, would come to me for specific help.

Some commentators have suggested that these different approaches are primarily shaped by party concerns over electoral sensitivities to candidates who might present race and immigration as priority issues. Solomos (1993: 246), for example, refers to the Labour Party "fearing that it would pay an electoral penalty" if it adopted a clearer policy on immigration. But as far as the black and Asian MPs are concerned, the results of the 1992 and 1997 General Elections do not support a simple interpretation of a high negative correlation between a race specialist approach and electoral success. It is the case, as Table 9.1 shows, that Grant achieved a 12.9 percentage increase in the number of votes for the Labour Party in 1992 (the second largest swing for Labour), with further advancement for Labour in 1997. Thus with ethnic minority groups accounting for over 30 per cent of the electorate in some of the other constituencies, it could be argued that black and Asian MPs who adopt a more specialist stance would fare better. However, the evidence would not support such a proposition. Vaz and Abbott, for example, who project a considerably more generalist approach than Grant, were not far behind him in increasing the Labour vote in 1992 (10.45 per cent and 9.15 per cent respectively). Neither performed especially well in 1997. Moreover, as a percentage of the total constituency vote, Abbott and Boateng both achieved over 57 per cent and Grant and Vaz both secured 56.5 per cent in 1992. For reasons which have nothing to do with personal perspectives on generalist or race issues, but have a great deal to do with party machinations at constituency level, Khabra returned 3.3 per cent fewer votes for the Labour Party and achieved 47.8 per cent of the total vote in 1992. His 1997 result more than made up for any disappointment, however. It should also be noted that the percentage of minority ethnic voters in Boateng's and Khabra's constituencies is over 50 compared to about 45 in Grant's constituency.

## MPs' CONTRIBUTION

In considering the extent to which different personal perspectives affect political activity or shape in any way the type of contribution made to policy debates once MPs are elected to Westminster, it is necessary to explore what sources of empirical evidence are available to us. Broadly, it is possible to identify three areas of activity in which MPs have the opportunity to contribute to policy development or political agendas. First, on the floor of the House they are able to engage in debates on legislation or adjournment debates, and ask questions of Ministers, either as Questions for Written Answers or for Oral Answers. Secondly, they contribute to other parliamentary work away from the Chamber which may include being a member of a Standing Committee, a parliamentary Select Committee, an All-Party Committee or other parliamentary working groups. Thirdly, away from the House, MPs may be involved in a range of activities which include working with particular interest groups within their own party, with peak organizations at national or international level, or with other groups or organizations with whose work they wish to be identified.

All these activities inevitably cover a wide range of interests. For the purpose of this chapter it is useful to classify them into three broad categories: first, issues which may be regarded as specifically or primarily concerned with race; secondly, areas which may be classified as primarily constituency matters; and thirdly, those which are of a general nature and which appear not to be directly associated with either race or constituency issues. Starting on the floor of the House, where backbencher performance is at its most public, it is possible to give a breakdown of contributions made by the six black and Asian MPs over a period of time (Table 9.2). Here, contributions to debates are combined with Oral and Written Answers, though in fact the majority are Written Answers. According to Richards (1974: 107) these are "less popular [than Oral Answers] as being unlikely to capture public attention or stimulate executive action". On the other hand, Written Answers are seen as a more effective means of obtaining information that would otherwise be difficult to acquire (Norton 1993).

It is important to note some of the limitations of these data. As we have noted, the energies of all MPs are increasingly consumed by the growing demands made upon them by their constituency work, much of which will not be reflected in their contributions on the floor of the House. Indeed, as Norton (1993: 159) suggests, this increasing work-load may "reduce their capacity to attend to parliamentary duties". In respect of the specific figures provided in Table 9.2, it should also be noted that both Deva and Khabra only entered the House in 1992 and so may have required some time to acclimatize themselves to the culture and procedures of the House before making a more weighty contribution.

TABLE 9.2   Contributions of black and Asian MPs on the floor of the House

|  | Abbott | Boateng | Deva | Grant | Khabra | Vaz | Total Race |
|---|---|---|---|---|---|---|---|
| April–Nov 199 |  |  |  |  |  |  |  |
| General | 31 | 13 | 12 | 9 | 2 | 86 |  |
| Constituency | 4 | 4 | 5 | 3 | — | 7 |  |
| Race | 9 | 4 | 1 | 7 | 2 | 32 | 55 |
| Total | 44 | 21 | 18 | 19 | 4 | 125 |  |
| April–Nov 1993 |  |  |  |  |  |  |  |
| General | 15 | 29 | 16 | 2 | 5 | 151 |  |
| Constituency | 3 | — | 3 | 2 | — | 5 |  |
| Race | 8 | 5 | 1 | 4 | 3 | 16 | 37 |
| Total | 26 | 34 | 20 | 8 | 8 | 122 |  |
| April–Nov 1994 |  |  |  |  |  |  |  |
| General | 4 | 75 | 18 | 3 | 7 | 90 |  |
| Constituency | — | 3 | — | — | 2 | 1 |  |
| Race | 2 | 5 | — | — | — | 12 | 19 |
| Total | 6 | 83 | 18 | 3 | 9 | 103 | 111 |

Contributions include Debates, Written Answers and Oral Answers.
Where both general and race issues, or both constituency and race issues were raised, race was given priority in enumerating the type of contribution.
Sources: Official Report, Parliamentary Debates, Commons, Vols. 207–241 (Hansard).
Fortnightly Index to the House of Commons Parliamentary Debates (Hansard).

With these limitations in mind, the figures are nevertheless indicative of the scale and type of activity engaged in by the six MPs. The data suggest the following: a) in quantitative terms Vaz has consistently made the largest contribution on the floor of the House both in respect of general issues and on race; b) that overall, general issues are raised more than race-specific or constituency issues; c) to date the MPs have helped to ensure that race-specific issues are raised on a regular basis, if not frequently, in the House; d) though it may be inappropriate to extrapolate an emerging trend from these figures, for the periods covered there has been a decline in the number of race-specific issues raised by the MPs on the floor of the House;

To add some qualitative data to these bare figures it may be noted that they include contributions, sometimes substantial, made by the six MPs to debates which helped to make public their concern about race and related issues. For example, both Khabra and Deva used their 'maiden' speech to draw attention to their philosophy and constituency interests. Khabra (Hansard 1992):

My constituents will not tolerate racism of any kind ... [They are] united in their determination not to let the NF or any other racists enter the constituency. We have the strength to resist racism; my constituency is proud of being multi-racial. I stand for secularism and democracy.

Deva (Hansard 1992):

Mine is a multi-racial and cosmopolitan constituency in which all communities live side by side in harmony. We are an example to the rest of the country. We must work to build a sustainable partnership that will last for generations to come ... based on talent, merit and opportunity and in which class, colour and religion will have no part to play.

Also, all but Deva made some contribution to the Asylum and Immigration Appeals Bill debate in 1992, Abbott and Boateng raised issues in the Ethnic Minorities debate, also in 1992, and Abbott and Vaz contributed to a debate on Immigration Regulations in 1993. Abbott and Boateng also made substantial contributions to the Criminal Justice and Public Order Bill debate in 1994 in respect of supporting the introduction of a new clause concerning racial attacks.

The totality of the MPs' contributions on the floor of the House, covering a range of subjects, thus demonstrates a readiness on the part of all of them to participate in policy areas other than race. At the same time, however, they are not neglecting race or minority issues. Indeed, a cursory comparison with the contribution made by white

211

MPs who might be viewed as sympathetic to black and minority interests, would suggest that, numerically, this contribution from black and Asian MPs is essential in securing a race perspective in the Chamber.

From the evidence available it is also apparent that Grant is not alone in carrying responsibility for race matters on to the floor of the House. Vaz and Boateng appear to have contributed most, as this may be judged quantitatively, and Abbott and Boateng have offered rather more, in qualitative terms, in their contributions to debates.

Away from the floor of the House, the work of backbenchers involved in Select Committeees is probably the next most public activity. Appointment to Select Committees is in the hands of Party Whips, though members themselves do have the opportunity to express their preference. From 1987 until 1992 Vaz was a member of the Home Affairs Committee. During this time he made use of a number of opportunities to raise race-related matters. Other MPs have been selected for backbench committees which have no direct interest in matters of race. Since 1987 and until his appointment in 1992 as Labour spokesperson for Legal Affairs in 1992, Boateng served on the Environment Committee. Since May 1990, Abbott has served on the prestigious Treasury and Civil Service Committee. More recently Khabra was appointed to the Members' Interests committee. These last three give very limited scope for introducing a race or black perspective, and certainly no-one did so during the period under study. Grant, meanwhile, has made clear his wish to serve on either the Home Affairs Select Committee or the National Heritage Committee, both of which provide opportunities for race or minority subjects to be scrutinized. Khabra, too, has an interest in the former.

Less accessible to public view, though available to the public, are the records of debates of Standing Committees. Early in 1993 Khabra served on the Standing Committee for Trade Union reform and Employment Rights Bill and the European Standing Committee on Overseas Aid. During 1994 Grant served on the European Documents Standing Committee and Boateng served on the Police and Magistrates, Judicial Pensions Standing Committee. None of these provided opportunities for introducing race-related issues. In contrast, in serving on the Standing Committee for the Asylum and Immigration Appeals Bill, Grant was able to argue for an amendment which would retain the right of appeal. Among other things he argued (Standing Committee 1992)

> Immigration Officers and westerners generally fail to understand the enormous significance of the institution of the family in other parts of the world, especially for black and other minority ethnic people.

Deva, also serving on this committee and supporting the government, argued against the amendment but indicated his wish that the new proposals should be implemented with sensitivity. Thus, at a distance from work which takes place in the Chamber, Grant's activities would appear to be more in keeping with his own perception of himself as the MP who has a specialist interest in race.

Whether or not black and Asian MPs speak with one voice on race matters probably depends upon the existence of formal structures and processes as much as upon personal intent, to enable this to happen. The existence of a Black Caucus of MPs within the Labour Party collapsed before the 1992 election after the then four MPs failed to agree that this was an appropriate way forward for the future. Already, in 1987, they had demonstrated disagreement on the issue of Black Sections in the party and, after their election to Parliament, none of them was greatly enthusiastic about actively supporting the Black Sections campaign (Sewell 1993). The addition of two Asian MPs in 1992 has only confirmed a general antipathy towards adopting separatist tactics for race issues. Khabra, for example, argues that these are already dealt with effectively elsewhere, "on the whole, race relations issues are properly debated in Party Policy groups and in the Party's Forum, and the Party Conference" (Interview 1995).

After the election of the first Asian Conservative MP in 1992, albeit for a single term, it was inevitable that party politics and discipline would also cut a swath through most collective endeavours on race issues which sought to include all six backbenchers between 1992 and 1997. What does exist, however, is the All-Party group on Race and Community Relations on which four of the Members serve. In 1994 the All-Party group invited an academic to prepare a discussion paper on racial violence (Parekh 1994). During the 1992–97 parliament, there appears to have been one issue on which all black and Asian MPs were united, namely their opposition early in 1994 to the government's plans for changes in Section 11 funding. Although it made no difference to government policy it was significant that Deva shared a platform with Labour colleagues on this issue. As Boateng has explained "One is able to have common cause from time to time, but it's much more difficult to do it in our system [of government] with a much more ideologically-driven Parliament" (Interview 1995).

He confirmed that this was an unusual example of black and Asian members from Government and the Opposition being able to demonstrate a united front.

Moving away from the precincts of Westminster altogether, the interests of black and Asian MPs in race and minority issues appears not to diminish. Indeed, in some respects their association with race-related matters seems more apparent. All MPs have been, and continue to be, associated with a number of national organizations which are directly concerned with race issues. Boateng, for example, is a member of Black Lines, a group which gives advice to black gay people with HIV or AIDS, and is also a member of the Sickle Cell Society. Khabra is a member of the Joint Council for the Welfare of Immigrants, the Anti-Racist Alliance, and is an active contributor to the Indian Workers Association. Grant is a member of the Commission for Racial Equality's Standing Conference on Racism in Europe.

## INTERNATIONAL NETWORKS

This collection of personal, as opposed to specifically political, interests of Members does suggest that race and minority issues begin to cohere around broader general themes or policy domains, namely those of citizenship and human rights. Moreover, if we go on to examine their interests even further afield, and in particular their involvement in international networks, the link between race-specific problems and broader issues of minority and human rights becomes even more apparent. All black and Asian MPs have ample opportunity to make connections or alliances with black or minority interests abroad, and there is no shortage of invitations to attend conferences or other gatherings which seek to address issues of international concern. Indeed, Grant, who claims to have become increasingly disillusioned with opportunities presented at Westminster to highlight race issues, is clear nevertheless that he is prepared to be involved specifically with these matters "because it also involves . . . foreign affairs" (Interview 1995). For Grant this encompasses mainly, though not exclusively, many contacts with, and visits to, the Caribbean states and with the Anglophone African states. He is involved in the UN Group for Parliamentarian Global Action and the São Paulo Forum for Caribbean Labour Party groups seeking to obtain a better deal for the region. Within this wider context it is clear that he is able to inject a race-specific dimension into international or Third World issues such as overseas aid. A question he raised in the House helps to illustrate this point (House of Commons 1995):

> To ask the Secretary of State for Foreign and Commonwealth Affairs what has been the result of ethnic monitoring of the ownership of British firms that have received contracts from the Overseas Development Agency for Work in the field of information technology in South Africa.

Similarly, Boateng has expressed his belief (Interview 1995) that

> It is very important to ensure that in a European context the dimension of racial justice is taken on board and I do that ... I have addressed meetings on racial justice issues all over Europe. I regard these networks as being very important and one has a responsibility to make a contribution to them.

For his part Khabra visited Strasbourg during 1995 to raise the issue of minority representation with the Chair of the European Union Social Affairs Migrants Forum. Vaz has also been involved, as an individual, with political leaders or parties in South Africa and in India, and takes an active interest in immigration procedures in respect of the latter.

In this wider international context Abbott's generalist interest in financial matters also takes on a different perspective. Her concerns are often associated with race and minority rights as these relate to overseas aid and to problems of debt for low income countries.

Thus, from this very truncated list of examples of visits and commitments overseas, it would appear that within an international framework there is considerable scope for black and Asian MPs to play a key role in representing and furthering the interests of black and minority communities, and certainly all of the Labour MPs do so. It may be suggested, also, that the further removed black MPs are from Westminster and from the constraints of party politics, the more they appear willing to adopt a shared perspective on the importance of race and minority interests. As Sewell (1993) makes clear in her preface, race plays a key role in the international arena where:

> The universality of the 'race problem' – that common experience of racial discrimination, prejudice, hatred and exploitation ... binds together people of colour all around the world.

That concerns about race issues in an international context are to some extent obscured by policy areas such as overseas debt or the global environment, makes the need for expertise at highlighting the race dimensions embedded within them all the more important. In other respects, as Solomos makes clear (1993 218), the current debates taking place in a European context about "who belongs and who doesn't" make a transparent connection between citizens' rights, religious and cultural identity and issues of race and racism. These are the "new" agendas for race, and they have become a proxy for age-old concerns in domestic politics about discrimination, social segregation and racial justice.

215

## MPs' INFLUENCE

Finally, there remains the key question of whether the presence of six black and Asian MPs between 1992 and 1997 made any difference to the politics of race at Westminster. There can be no simple answer to this question, primarily because of the host of methodological problems one encounters in seeking to identify and measure outcomes from political processes, and in trying to establish unitary causes. The views of political commentators, constituency activists and ordinary voters, not to mention those of the backbenchers themselves, and their colleagues, all tend to look in quite different directions in order to assess difference or impact. Moreover, problems of definition and measurement are not merely academic if one is engaged in making judgements or public statements about people's performance. Solomos (1993 247), for example, argued after the 1992 election that

> on current evidence their influence is likely to remain marginal and limited. In the longer term increasing black political involvement and political representation, and alliances with other political forces, may help to fundamentally transform the terms of political debate about racial inequality in British society.

Here no definitions are offered of key terms such as "influence", "marginal", "increasing" or "other political forces", so it would be difficult to reach a conclusion one way or the other. What Solomos appears to be suggesting is that more of a critical mass of black MPs is a necessary condition for there to be any impact. The MPs interviewed would certainly agree that there are considerable limitations in having such a small group of politicians operating at the centre. In addition, as Vaz makes clear, "We have to be realistic about how much ... black MPs can really do to change the lot of all blacks; our hands are tied by the same bureaucracy that impedes others" (Sewell, 1993: 158).

However, all black and Asian MPs would want some recognition for the difference, as they perceive it, that their presence has made in Parliament. Khabra (Interview 1995):

> It does have an impact first within the party political system. Second on the media – they know there are representative of the ethnic communities who can raise race issues in the highest political institution of the country.

Grant (Interview 1995):

216

Yes. It's quite clear that black and Asian MPs have been able to add an expertise – a sort of local touch – to issues involved in race that wouldn't otherwise be there. But also ... we have brought in issues to do with race that people didn't think there was any need for.

Boateng (Interview 1995):

> The presence of black MPs has ensured that the debate (on race) takes place in a context which is no longer an ethnic monoculture, so at least MPs are aware in the House and in the Chamber, of a multi-racial, multi-cultural society ... Not an unimportant symbol that the cockpit of democracy should reflect in part this racial diversity.

All six members from the 1992–97 cohort would also argue that they are hard-working constituency MPs, each with a large proportion of ethnic minority voters. At this level, in addition to their ability to secure a majority at the last election, their impact or effectiveness would have to be judged in terms of, for example, the number of letters they respond to, the number of surgeries they attend, the number of delegations they receive, whether they encourage casework, and so on (Norris, Vallance, Lovenduski 1992).

One area of constituency work in which all black and Asian MPs do contribute a great deal is that concerned with immigration and nationality cases. Vaz, for example, informed the House that he deals with 60 new immigration cases a week (Hansard 1992). Grant, in a personal interview, also singled out the immigration casework he has done in Tottenham, where he works in collaboration with the local police and the local authority.

## ALTERNATIVE STRATEGIES

We have noted already that, in Parliament, Opposition backbenchers (as five of our six cohort were up to 1997) have little scope for making an impact, and that a small number of black and Asian MPs could only ever have a limited collective influence in policy and political debate. Nevertheless there is a range of views about how matters might be improved to ensure race and minority interests receive more attention at Westminster.

Fitzgerald (1990), for instance, has suggested that the Party Whips have played a part in constraining opportunities for black MPs to raise race issues. However, the assumption that this is an intentional party strategy is not borne out by the evidence. Although Grant does support the view that the Whips could help to improve matters, he sees the problem in terms of a colour-blind approach, not one of omission by design. Even so, this ethnocentric tendency remains a stumbling block to raising the awareness of politicians at Westminster to race and minority perspectives.

Grant also believes that if black and Asian MPs were better organized, they would make much more headway. Of the four MPs concerned, he was clearly the most disappointed about the demise of the Black Caucus within the party. However, his preferred model for securing collective political action is more akin to one promoted by Jesse Jackson, with whom he keeps in regular contact. This model proposes a National Rainbow Alliance, which garners support both inside and outside government from a range of groups lobbying to enhance opportunities for the disadvantaged. Prior to the 1992 election, Grant (Interview 1991) was optimistic that such an alliance would emerge in Britain and it was clear that he saw himself as playing a central role in its promotion. By 1995 he could only report that this strategy had not found favour with the wide variety of groups who, potentially, could have become involved.

Boateng also casts an eye across the Atlantic to find alternatives. Unlike Grant he would prefer to see a strengthening of the existing structures of Parliament rather than the creation of new strategies. Specifically he argues for a stronger Select Committee system with greater powers and more resources. This would "enable the spotlight to be targetted more effectively on failings in the system" (Interview 1995).

Select Committees are already capable of addressing specific "issues" as well as government policies, and, as such, are an essential antidote to a legislative assembly which is dominated by "getting Government business through the House and which doesn't enable enough debate and scrutiny of some Bills" (Boateng Interview, 1995).

More controversial than the alternatives proposed so far would be any attempt to increase the number of black MPs by introducing arrangements for the selection of candidates comparable to those adopted – then dropped – for women in the Labour Party. Since some inner-city constituencies with a high proportion of ethnic minority voters have already succeeded in returning a black or Asian Member of Parliament, the case for black-only selection lists may at best seem flimsy. Extending the measure to marginal seats is unlikely to secure political acceptance, not least because these constituencies do not include a high proportion of black or minority voters. As it is, the clouds of controversy have already gathered over the decision to impose women-only selection lists, leading, in turn, to the decision being revoked by the party prior to the 1997 election.


## CONCLUSION

In terms of domestic politics at Westminster the task of a black or Asian MP remains part of a long struggle, effectively on two fronts – as a backbencher who may be given responsibility for general policy areas, and one who, at the same time, remains conscientious about keeping the House alert to race and minority agendas. Boateng (Interview 1995) describes this situation as "Janus-like".

The evidence presented here suggests that the collective effort of the six MPs analysed has indeed ensured that race issues have not been neglected at Westminster. We have noted, for example, that on at least 37 occasions during April–November 1993 the MPs used the opportunity to introduce, or contribute to, a race-specific topic on the floor of the House. Whether the situation would have been better if black and Asian politicians had not been available to take up the mantle of minority responsibity cannot be proved, but it seems improbable. It follows, therefore, that the larger the number of black MPs, the proportionately larger their overall contribution within the Chamber is likely to be.

Perhaps rather more significant is the range of parliamentary Committee work in which the six MPs engage. It is here that their specialist knowledge and personal experiences help to ensure a closer scrutiny is undertaken of policies specifically concerned with race, such as immigration or racial attacks. There is less evidence, to date, that all demonstrate a willingness to inject a race dimension into debates on general policy areas.

Although MPs may differ about the appropriate means for achieving greater input on race issues in national politics, there is nevertheless a common view amongst the Labour Members (in opposition) that once their party is in government, more effective use will then be made of their specialist skills and knowledge. Grant is of the view that he is currently under-used, especially in international affairs where his contacts are extensive and well placed. He believed in 1995, however, that he would be more useful in a Labour Government, though no appointment to its junior ranks has been forthcoming since May 1997. Similarly, Khabra, who claims to have existing good relations with the Shadow Cabinet, hoped to be able to contribute rather more following Labour's victory.

Yet black and Asian MPs, no less than others, are realists as much as idealists. They have to work for what is achievable rather than for what is always the most desirable. Moreover, a number of the group are politically ambitious and would seek promotion beyond the back benches. It is possible to suggest that the more elevated a black or Asian Member becomes, the more likely that they will be required to hold a brief which does not fall within the policy domain of race. This appears to be the case following Boateng's appointment to the Government's health team after May 1997. In addition, except when party discipline requires otherwise, greater seniority for some Members may also encourage division, rather than unity, between backbenchers and individual Ministers on strategies or policies for race.

However, in the context of European and international politics, as we have noted, links between wider policy agendas and race issues are already more overt. Indeed, it can be argued that race itself moves centre-stage, rather than remaining as a peripheral theme. In addition there is evidence to suggest that in respect of global issues, black and Asian MPs have more of a common purpose and a shared view about the means required to achieve desired ends. At present in this international arena, the MPs are working more on their own initiative, rather than with the support of the party leaders. Yet it is here, where national credibility is at stake, and where there is a need in Europe to check the increasing influence of extreme right-wing parties (Baimbridge, Burkitt, Macey 1995), that the potential for extending the contribution of black and Asians is at its greatest.

## NOTE

1. There has been considerable debate about racial and ethnic classification. Modood (1988), for example, has argued for a separate "Asian" identity rather than for the use of the generic term "black". In contrast, and in the context of a culture of integration, rather than one of resistance, Anwar (1990) believes "black" is the more appropriate. However, since MPs themselves differ in the way they wish to be described, the use of "black and Asian" is preferred here.

## REFERENCES

Anwar, M. 1990. Debates in *New Community* 16(4) 607–615.

Anwar, M. 1986. *Race and Politics*. London and New York: Tavistock.

Austin, M. 1994. Backbench Influence: A Personal View. In *Parliamentary Affairs* 47(4) 686–704.

Baimbridge, M., B. Burkitt and M. Macey 1995. The European Parliamentary Election of 1994 and racism in Europe. In *Ethnic and Racial Studies* 18(1) 128–30.

Ben-Tovim, G., J. Gabriel and I. Law 1986. *The Local Politics of Race*, Basingstoke and London: Macmillan.

Bulpitt, J. 1986. Continuity, Autonomy and Peripheralisation: The Anatomy of the Centre's Race Statecraft in England. In *Race, Government and Politics in Britain*, Z. Layton-Henry & P. B. Rich (eds). London: Macmillan.

Cerny, P. G. 1986. *The Changing Architecture of Politics*. London: Sage.

Drewry, G. 1984. Legislation. In *The Commons Today*, S. A. Walkland & M. Ryle (eds). Glasgow: Fontana.

Eade, J. 1989. *The Politics of Community*. Aldershot: Gower/Avebury.

Fitzgerald, M. 1988. Different Roads? The development of Afro-Caribbean and Asian political organisations in London. In *New Community* XIV (3) Spring 385–96.

Fitzgerald, M. 1990. The Emergence of Black Councillors and MPs in Britain: Some underlying questions. In *Black Politics in Britain*, H. Goulbourne (ed.). Aldershot: Avebury.

*The Guardian* 1989 Tuesday Women. Interview by Louisa Saunders, 10 October, 21.

Goulbourne, H. (ed.). 1990. *Black Politics in Britain*. Aldershot: Avebury.

Hansard 1992 (Khabra). *Official Report. Parliamentary Debates. Commons* Vol. 207, cols. 335–6.

Hansard 1992 Deva. *Official Report. Parliamentary Debates. Commons* Vol. 210, cols.446–8.

Hansard 1992 (Vaz). *Official report. Parliamentary Debates. Commons* Vol. 213, col. 83.

House of Commons 1992. *Standing Committee A. Asylums and Immigration Appeals Bill*. 8 December, col. 612.

House of Commons 1995. *Order Paper* No. 34, Friday 20th January.

Le Lohé, M. J. 1989 The performance of Asian and black candidates in the British General Election of 1987 in *New Community* 15 (3), Spring 159–70.

Lovenduski, J. and P. Norris 1993 *Gender and Party Politics*. London: Sage.

Lovenduski, J. and P. Norris 1995. *Political Recruitment: gender, race and class in the British Parliament*. Cambridge: Cambridge University Press.

Modood, T. 1988. "Black" Racial Equality and Asian Identity. In *New Community* XIV (3) Spring, 397–404.

Norris, P., E. Vallence and J. Lovenduski 1992. Do Candidates make a difference? Gender, Race, Ideology and Incumbency. In *Parliamentary Affairs* 45(4) 496–517.

Norton, P. 1993. *Does Parliament Matter?* Hemel Hempstead: Harvester Wheatsheaf.

Norton, P. 1994. The Growth of the Constituency Role of the MP. In *Parliamentary Affairs* 47(4) 705–20.

Parekh, B. 1994. *Racial Violence: A separate offence? A Discussion Paper*. The All-Party Parliamentary group on Race and Community, Houses of Parliament, Session 1993/4.

Reed, A. L. 1986. *The Jesse Jackson Phenomenon*. Yale: Yale University Press.

Richards, P. G. 1974. *The Backbenchers*. London: Faber.

Runnymede Trust 1992. *The Runnymede Bulletin*. May.

Sewell, T. 1993. *Black Tribunes. Black Participation in Britain.* London: Lawrence and Wishart.

Solomos, J. 1993 *Race and Racism in Britain.* 2nd edn. London: Macmillan.

Studlar, D. T. 1986. Non-white policy preferences. Political participation and the political agenda in Britain. In *Race, Government and Politics in Britain* Z. Layton-Henry & P. Rich (eds.). Basingstoke and London: Macmillan.

Wright, M. 1988 Policy community, policy network and comparative industrial policies. In *Political Studies* XXXVI (4) 593–612.

# CHAPTER TEN

# Community politics and the problems of partnership: ethnic minority participation in urban regeneration networks

## *Philip Nanton*

This chapter examines one aspect of the politics of race which is conducted beyond the ballot box and political party politics. This form of politics is often identified as "community politics". The term "community politics" implies a political process which is parallel to the mainstream of national and local electoral politics. It is a politics of pressure and influence using the resources available to the group at a particular time. These resources may be based on notions of separate identity and may range from political agitation, marches, and civil unrest, to negotiation and compromise. Mobilization is often developed through community associations. Beyond these general features the notion of community politics can be manifest in a variety of ways, many of which may operate in a locality simultaneously.

One manifestation of community politics involves political agitation among migrant communities concerned with developments in their homeland. Alternatively, it may involve internal competition within an ethnic minority institution – for example a temple, mosque or church – for leadership by electoral and other strategies. A third form encompasses a focus on political competition or tensions between different ethnic minority groups in a locality. This form of political activity, like "temple politics", has in the past often been ignored by political analysts, although James (1993) has examined inter-community rivalries arising between the Asian and Afro-Caribbean communities and he has attempted to identify the foundations on which these rivalries are based.

One aspect of community politics which has received considerable critical attention is the negotiation for resources between community associations and central and local government. On the "community side", two schools of thought are influential. One view has increasingly come to identify racialized division as central to the way that community politics has developed in Britain. Many analysts have adopted this perspective. Early proponents were Rex and Moore (1967). Their argument, developed later by Rex and Tomlinson (1978) suggests that, in the context of race and ethnicity in Britain, the exclusion of West Indians and Asians from the labour market produced racialized class divisions. These divisions, they claim, have resulted in the pursuit of different strategies by West Indian and Asian communities. The former were identified for the most part as withdrawing from competition into a focus on issues of identity. The latter, they argue, focus on capital accumulation, social mobility and negotiation with the host society. (For a detailed review and critique of these and other racialized perspectives on community politics see Solomos and Back 1994.) In contrast, more recent analysis by Werbner suggests that ethnic minority groups have the potential for unity through their organizations. This may be achieved by formulating joint discourses and creating broader associational networks or alliances. In doing so, she argues, "they draw on a growing realization of common predicaments and experiences which unite them as communities of suffering. The move is from narrow associational loyalties to encompassing unities" (Werbner 1992: 33). Goldbourne (1990) suggests that West Indian perspectives are less racialized than they appear, because their focus of concern is an all-encompassing one – that is, to obtain justice.

Where analysts have examined the relationship between ethnic minority community associations and government, a common theme of the analysis identifies various ways in which government acts to marginalize or exclude attempts by associations to influence policies or distributive justice (BenTovim et al. 1989, Qaiyoom 1993).

This chapter seeks to develop the debate around the feature of community politics, which is concerned with negotiations between community associations and central and local government. It offers a perspective on the involvement of black and ethnic minority organizations in urban regeneration and illustrates that in the new competitive context of urban regeneration a strategy of developing partnerships between community associations and government has been developed. For the most part, the strategy has not been successful in increasing resource distribution towards ethnic minority communities nor in building their confidence in the new regimen for urban development. The evidence suggests that an important reason for this failure in the strategy of involvement is the underlying tension which exists between an area perspective and an ethnic-specific perspective on urban regeneration. An area perspective has been adopted by central and local government and other official agencies at both national and local levels. In contrast, an ethnic-specific perspective on urban regeneration has been adopted by black and ethnic minority community associations.

Evidence is also adduced to demonstrate that a strategy pursued by black and ethnic minority groups intended to boost their capability to negotiate resources has been wrongly labelled as "networking". However, where the notion has developed between community associations and government it has served as an effective state mechanism to incorporate particular community associations.

"Community politics" is defined here, then, as a continuous process of negotiation for resources between black and ethnic minority community associations and government around policy and distributive justice, the aim of which is to combat racism, discrimination and disadvantage. The chapter examines ethnic minority community associations and their involvement in urban regeneration networks to illustrate one of the ways in which community politics has developed. Evidence is provided of a form of politics comprising both racial exclusion and incorporation into policy networks.

The first part of the chapter examines the preconditions for community politics in the urban environment. It outlines the basis on which they have developed and the shape and mobilization of such politics through community associations in Britain. The second part illustrates the circumstances in which some new features of community politics are developing. The third section analyses the implications of the evidence presented in the case study, and suggests the need for the analysis of community politics to be developed beyond the more usual focus on notions of exclusion.

## CHARACTERISTICS OF THE COMMUNITY POLITICS OF RACE

### Political demography

One influential feature of the way that the community politics of race has developed arises out of the demographic characteristics of ethnic minority communities. The total non-white population constitutes only about 5.5 per cent of the British population as a whole. There are few members of non-white minorities in Scotland and Wales and the distribution in England is very skewed, with concentrations in urban areas and in particular areas within these. Over twice as many of the Afro-Caribbean and Bangladeshi populations live in metropolitan areas compared with the white population. All minority groups are more likely than whites to live in metropolitan areas, with as few as one-fifth of the total of ethnic minority groups living in non-metropolitan areas. London exhibits the most substantial non-white population concentration as shown in Table 10.1.

Brown (1984) suggests that this concentration reflected earlier patterns of settlement by the immigrant generation. There was much less indication of dispersal of West Indian and Asian communities than might have been expected from the patterns of migration of other groups in the past. Although some movement has taken place, it has tended to consist in spreading within the boundaries of the same local authorities. However, it is important to note that different minorities are concentrated in slightly different areas. Two implications of these social and demographic features – a population concentrated in a relatively small number of electoral wards and which diminishes at constituency and at local authority level because of their limited weight of numbers – are that, first, ethnic minority communities or those who are conscious of themselves as such are politically powerless in terms of electoral politics. Secondly, to exercise some influence to change or enhance their circumstances, other methods of representation and lobbying beyond conventional party politics need to be deployed to enhance political influence. Since the high profile attempts in the late

TABLE 10.1  Distribution of GB population 1991 by region and ethnic origin

| | W % | BC % | BA % | BO % | I % | P % | B % | C % | OA % | O % |
|---|---|---|---|---|---|---|---|---|---|---|
| England | 85.1 | 99.1 | 97.4 | 96.6 | 98.0 | 94.4 | 97.0 | 90.3 | 95.8 | 94.3 |
| Greater London | 10.3 | 58.2 | 77.1 | 45.2 | 41.3 | 18.4 | 52.7 | 36.1 | 57.1 | 41.7 |
| West Midlands | 9.1 | 15.6 | 2.5 | 10.5 | 18.9 | 20.7 | 11.9 | 6.1 | 5.8 | 8.4 |
| West Yorks | 3.6 | 3.0 | 1.2 | 3.7 | 4.1 | 16.9 | 3.7 | 2.5 | 2.3 | 3.6 |
| Greater Manchester | 4.5 | 3.4 | 2.5 | 5.2 | 3.5 | 10.4 | 7.0 | 5.3 | 2.5 | 4.4 |
| Wales | 5.4 | 0.7 | 1.3 | 1.9 | 0.8 | 1.2 | 2.3 | 3.1 | 1.9 | 2.6 |
| Scotland | 9.5 | 0.2 | 1.3 | 1.5 | 1.2 | 4.4 | 0.7 | 6.7 | 2.3 | 3.0 |
| All Metropolitan | 39.9 | 86.3 | 88.7 | 73.4 | 75.6 | 77.5 | 84.0 | 64.6 | 78.7 | 70.1 |
| All Metropolitan Non-London | 29.6 | 28.1 | 11.7 | 28.2 | 34.3 | 59.1 | 31.4 | 28.5 | 21.6 | 28.5 |
| All Non-Metropolitan | 60.1 | 13.7 | 11.3 | 26.6 | 24.4 | 22.5 | 16.0 | 25.4 | 21.3 | 29.9 |

W: White, BC: Black Caribbean, BA: Black African, BO: Black Other, I: Indian, P: Pakistani, B: Bangladeshi, C: Chinese, OA: Other Asian, O: Other
Source: 1991 Census

TABLE 10.2  Age distribution by ethnic group, 1988–90

| | All origins | White | Total Ethnic Minority | Afro-Caribbean | African Asian | Indian | Pakistani | Bangladeshi | Chinese | African | Other/Mixed |
|---|---|---|---|---|---|---|---|---|---|---|---|
| Under 16 | 20 | 19 | 34 | 28 | 33 | 29 | 45 | 46 | 26 | 34 | 39 |
| 16–24 | 14 | 14 | 17 | 19 | 15 | 17 | 17 | 20 | 16 | 16 | 16 |
| 25–44 | 29 | 29 | 31 | 28 | 41 | 29 | 26 | 21 | 42 | 37 | 32 |
| 45–59/64 | 19 | 19 | 14 | 20 | 10 | 18 | 11 | 13 | 13 | 12 | 9 |
| Post-retirement | 18 | 19 | 4 | 5 | 1 | 6 | 1 | 1 | 3 | 2 | 3 |

Source: 1988, 1989, 1990 Labour Force Surveys (GB).

1970s and early 1980s by mainstream parties to win over the black and Asian urban electorate, it has come to be recognized that electoral calculations offer no benefit to any of the parties in making race-specific overtures in their national campaigns (Messina; Le Lohé; Saggar (this volume)). It is arguable that in the eyes of the majority of voters, non-whites' greatest national political impact may be seen in terms of their association with civil disturbances, and other episodes such as the *The Satanic Verses* affair. The parties would only stand to gain from such disturbances in elections precisely by taking a stand against those responsible for them.

One demographic feature which should not be overlooked is the disproportionate youth of the non-white population. It has been sug-gested that part of the reason for the non-white population's limited political power is that a large proportion was below voting age. This position is changing fast. Table 10.2 indicates potentially a much greater proportion of non-whites than whites among new voters. Not only is this position likely to continue, but the effects will be much starker in inner-city areas where whites who remain are older than average and where there is a disproportionate concentration of ethnic minority growth. Another electoral side effect, the result simply of age structure, is that white versus non-white voting allegiances could be widened, since older groups are usually farther to the right than younger ones. However, given the limited total numbers of this popu-lation and assuming substantial levels of continued electoral non-registration, a dramatic change in the established patterns is unlikely. Overall, the demographic features of a population, concentrated in small numbers in metropolitan areas and in a relatively small number of electoral wards, and declining at constituency and local authority level, suggest that methods of representation and lobbying over and above mainstream political party participation will be needed for these communities to be able to voice their concerns properly.

Many areas of above-average ethnic minority settlement are also those with the most severe problems of long-term economic and social decline. The Department of the Environment's 1991 Index of Local Conditions ranks local authorities according to the estimated severity of deprivation. Of the ten local authorities ranked highest in depriva-tion, nine have a higher than average ethnic minority population, ranging from between 2.5 and 7 times as high as the national average. Five of these top ten authorities (Newham, Hackney, Tower Hamlets, Lambeth and Haringey) contain particularly high concentrations of black Caribbean and Bangladeshi groups who are most likely to be concentrated in such areas (Table 10.3). These findings are reinforced by evidence of disproportionate growth of the ethnic minority popu-lation within these communities due to a) natural increase b) "white

TABLE 10.3    10 districts with largest minority populations 1991

| | Selected ethnic groups and indication of deprivation | | | | |
|---|---|---|---|---|---|
| | As % of total pop. | Deprivation ranking | | As % of total pop. | Deprivation ranking |
| **Black** | | | **Pakistani** | | |
| Hackney | 22.0 | 3 | Bradford | 9.9 | 23 |
| Lambeth | 21.8 | 8 | Pendle | 9.4 | — |
| Southwark | 17.7 | 2 | Slough | 9.1 | 95 |
| Haringey | 17.1 | 10 | Birmingham | 6.9 | 5 |
| Brent | 16.5 | 29 | Waltham Forest | 6.3 | 20 |
| Lewisham | 16.3 | 11 | Luton | 6.2 | — |
| Newham | 14.4 | 1 | Blackburn | 5.9 | 31 |
| Waltham Forest | 11.3 | 20 | Newham | 5.9 | 1 |
| Wandsworth | 10.7 | 21 | Rochdale | 5.5 | 89 |
| Islington | 10.6 | 4 | Hyndburn | 4.8 | 89 |
| **Indian** | | | **Bangladeshi** | | |
| Leicester | 22.3 | 36 | Tower Hamlets | 22.3 | 7 |
| Brent | 17.2 | 29 | Newham | 3.8 | 1 |
| Ealing | 16.1 | 37 | Camden | 3.5 | 15 |
| Harrow | 16.1 | — | Luton | 2.7 | — |
| Hounslow | 14.3 | — | Oldham | 2.4 | 38 |
| Newham | 13.0 | 1 | Westminster | 2.3 | 26 |
| Slough | 12.5 | 95 | Hackney | 1.8 | 3 |
| Wolverhampton | 11.4 | 27 | Islington | 1.6 | 4 |
| Redbridge | 10.2 | — | Haringey | 1.5 | 10 |
| Sandwell | 7.9 | 9 | Birmingham | 1.3 | 5 |

Note: The Black group is not disaggregated since the distribution of the three Black groups across the top ten districts is similar. The ranking of the districts varies slightly
Source: Department of the Environment (1991) Index of Local Conditions (extract from top 100 districts).

flight", i.e. long-term white migration out of inner city areas and c) a younger minority-group age structure than the white population which has remained behind.

In addition to these features, the black population is likely to be deterred from outward mobility by a fear of hostility should they move to areas where they are few in number, together with a relatively high dependence on council housing or owner occupancy of properties with low commercial values. A further potential restraint is the cohesiveness and accessibility of cultural and community facilities, e.g. churches, mosques or temples. However, census-based data do reveal some out-migration. This migration is characterized by movement over shorter distances than whites (Champion 1996). However, the pattern of black and ethnic minority concentration, characterized by both inter- and intra-urban concentration, with different groups located in different localities, continues to be the dominant one, and is particularly identifiable at the local ward level (Owen 1994). These characteristics suggest that future mobility will be limited and concentration will continue in identifiable inner-city localities.

### The shape and mobilization of community politics

Community-group politics has its origins in the early years following immigration. In the 1980s it was given a major boost with positive action by many local authorities (following the models of Lambeth Borough Council and the Greater London Council) to encourage and support non-white community associations with funding. These associations are not-for-profit organizations which were developed within ethnic minority communities in the wake of the migration of the 1950s and 1960s. Their precise number is difficult to estimate. An official funding register for such organizations which was prepared in 1992 has listed 1,547 catering for the non-white population, of which 488 were run by people of Caribbean origin. By 1994 "Sia", the National Development Agency for the Black and Ethnic Minority Voluntary Sector, had established a database of 2,500 organizations.

The original purpose of these organizations was to respond to the local conditions experienced by these communities in the host society. Their interventions give shape to the day-to-day community politics of the locality. Small has described the origin and key features of these associations. She writes:

> Black organizations emerged in response to specific needs such as discrimination, poor housing and indifferent education. Many have remained local. Most do not have a specific policy to exclude white people, but at the same time they do not actively go out of their way to encourage them.
>
> (Small 1993: 10)

This focus for their activities of necessity has brought them into direct contact with local government.

A number of the issues which were taken up at the local level were in time reflected in national campaigns: those especially concerned with policing were taken up by Afro-Caribbean communities, while those concerned with immigration were predominantly adopted by Asians. Non-whites have also organized caucuses on their own behalf within, for example, professions and trade unions, and this has been mirrored in the campaign for "black sections" within the Labour Party which began in the early 1980s.

However, the interface with the local political establishment has become much tighter in two ways. Through various co-options and consultative mechanisms, the local authority system has sought to bring non-whites into regular dialogue. This has also developed through special posts and units created by local government. Through these measures many local authorities have considerably increased employment among the ethnic minority population.

There has been a significant overlap of personnel between these various types of activity. Thus, many local councillors have come from a background of ethnically or racially-based political activism, including community-group involvement. A considerable number of such councillors appear to have held local government posts – often at senior levels – in the "race" structures of other authorities before they were affected by the restrictions of the 1988 Local Government Act, which stopped elected members in one authority holding senior or politically sensitive posts in another.

Throughout all of these developments it should be noted that, despite initiatives to set up organizations and campaigns which were open to Afro-Caribbean and Asian membership, the reality has been that most of the political activity described here has taken place on an Afro-Caribbean or Asian basis rather than on a collective "black" one. The most recent and dramatic example of this has been the Muslim protest over *The Satanic Verses*. Not only have "black" initiatives tended to become dominated by one or other of the two main groups, but many Asian initiatives are also fragmented between different Asian groups. In many cases there has been friction resulting from competition for resources or other forms of recognition (James 1993).

The relationship between urban regeneration networks and black and Asian community politics provides a good example of the way in which community politics have developed. The link between marginal groups and the state needs to be established in such a way that the analysis can take account of the marginalization which characterizes the experience of black and Asian community associations on one hand (Hausner and Associates 1992, Medas 1994), and, on the other, the dominant policy-making environment of "partnership" through which perceptions and beliefs about urban regeneration are implemented.


## ETHNIC MINORITY GROUPS AND URBAN REGENERATION NETWORKS

### The climate for urban regeneration partnership

In the context of urban regeneration the state and its agencies are important actors in the shaping of the "network" relationship.

Networking implies a complex series of relationships through which power and influence are distributed in order to give effectiveness to a policy. This activity has increasingly been exercised in a self-conscious manner. Three features which have been influential in this process are the dominant belief systems or ideology of "privatism" and competition, the incentives which are provided for participation, and, lastly, the common bond created, through the manipulative practice of the state or its agencies, in pursuing the policy of regeneration.

In the past fifteen years, government ideological assumptions have moved to embrace public-choice theory in its approach to urban regeneration. The dominance of these notions has resulted in the encouragement of competition in the public sector. As part of this approach, local government has been perceived by central government as a monopoly producer which operates policies, including those of urban regeneration, insufficiently targeted to meet the needs of its consumers and citizens. This perspective provides an explanation for a number of central government policies towards local urban regeneration. After 1987, central government discontinued the Urban Programme, imposed controls over total local government expenditure and introduced a series of programmes in deprived areas to perform specific tasks in a limited time. These institutions included Urban Development Corporations (created first in 1981), City Action Teams (1985), 16 Task Forces (operational by 1991), Simplified Planning Zones, City Challenge agencies, Technical and Enterprise Councils (TECs), and Estate Action programmes (Willmott and Hutchinson 1992).

Another important way in which the relationship has been shaped by central government is the orchestration of competition for funds at national and local levels (Department of the Environment, 1994). Local authorities are required to compete for additional central government funds. This is now conducted, not merely by showing disadvantage, as in the past, but by arguing positively the case for their localities in competition against other localities for limited additional resources set aside for regeneration. An important criterion to determine "winners" is the demonstration of the involvement of local business interests, the new agencies and community interests in these programmes. The clearest statement of this approach is contained in the *Single Regeneration Budget: Note on Principles* (Department of the Environment 1993).

At the local level, voluntary organizations and community groups, although no strangers to competition for funding have, in turn experienced curbs in grant aid available from local government as its funds were restricted (Hall 1989). For many voluntary organizations there has also been the new experience of competition for contracts with local authorities, and new conditions for financial support imposed by new funding agencies like City Challenge companies.

The third feature of the environment involves the promotion of the view that a common bond exists between local government, government-sponsored agencies, local business initiatives, the local voluntary and community sector and local individuals. The common bond is enshrined in the notion of "partnership", and the assumption that all parties are committed to the same extent to the development of the area or locality. This notion of the common bond of interest is enhanced by a plethora of consultative mechanisms. These embrace attempts to ensure representativeness in the composition of locally-based public sector agencies, advisory Neighbourhood and Community Fora in City Challenge and some local authority areas, and periodic market research exercises enquiring into perceptions of needs and attitudes in the area. Funds and other resources for these activities have been provided by local authorities and other public sector agencies.

These three elements – the dominant ideology, incentives created by funding, and the common bond – I describe as the climate in which the relationships between the actors in urban regeneration are worked out. In the past fifteen years these features have proved sufficient to establish the production of consent in areas of regeneration. That is, they enable government and its agencies, at both national and local levels, to exercise the role of leadership, of the direction of education and of tutelage with sufficient common interest among participants to give shape to current notions of urban regeneration.

### Black and ethnic minority communities and the climate of relationships

Black and minority communities comprise a significant challenge to the climate of relationships created by the three conditions identified above. The challenges they present take three forms.

First, their experience of urban regeneration challenges the assumption that an area focus will meet the specific requirements of diverse needs for economic development. The lack of specificity in addressing ethnic minority needs has been criticised as one of the major shortcomings of the Urban Programme in its application to the ethnic minority communities. Based on his study of urban regeneration in Birmingham, Ratcliffe has argued that policies of urban regeneration need to address the issue of racial inequality directly, rather than rely on the trickle-down effects of conventional economic regeneration models (Ratcliffe 1992). In a review of national policy, Hausner and Partners argue (1992: 25):

> The distinction between "need" and "benefit", between "specific" and "incidental" benefit, are not pedantic, but reach the heart of the policy issue. Doubtless certain types of project without a specific focus will benefit ethnic minorities through a colour-blind approach. ... Local authorities need to be aware, however, that adopting this approach by itself runs the risk that projects will not adequately address specific ethnic minority needs, and that recruitment techniques will not proactively target ethnic minority communities.

Secondly, the values and belief systems with which many black and ethnic minority organizations operate do not necessarily encourage the assumption of a commitment to a primary interest in *area* regeneration. A shared history of rejection and exclusion as well as past policy assumptions, based on notions of perceived fundamental racial and cultural differences, result in a higher priority being given to notions of race and difference than to area interests. It is the former which guides their approach to urban regeneration. Cook (1994: 7) has argued, for example, that

> The most significant drawback of the SRB for black people is that it does not require Training and Enterprise Councils (TECs) or local authorities (LAs) to finance the production of economic strategies specifically for black communities. It assumes that a generalist approach will meet the needs of black people, and that is not the case.

Thirdly, the organizational base of black and ethnic minority communities in localities is often too weak and fragmented to support the new terms and conditions of funding, particularly where contractual relations are being encouraged and grants are being withdrawn. Much of their influence and many of their activities at the level of community groups and voluntary organizations have developed out of small-scale, holistic initiatives, not geared to specific contract funding (Small 1994). During the 1980s many of these projects received reduced funding and many simply folded. Hinds (1992: 53) has documented this process of contraction in the case of the Afro-Caribbean community. He notes from a survey of 71 Afro-Caribbean organizations that "compared with the period 1986–91, by 1991–92 at least 35% of Caribbean organizations which were funded were worse off."

These processes of structural exclusion and marginalization have resulted in two strategies among black and ethnic minority groups to develop relationships around regeneration. One has been to negotiate ethnic minority representation in consultation with urban regeneration at national and local levels. Sia, a national development agency for the black voluntary sector, is one organization which has initiated this process. The agency has established a database of 2,500 B & ME organizations in the United Kingdom and lobbies the state and its agencies through publications, newsletters and nationally-organized seminars. Much of this activity is intended to encourage negotiation between the black and ethnic minority communities and government and other agencies at national and local levels.

The second strategy reinforces the perspective of assumed fundamental difference and offers a restricted understanding of "networking". Here "networking" or "network formation" is treated as a group-support process or a modern organizational tool, but with the important proviso that the priority for its operation is located within the black and ethnic minority communities rather than across these communities to the state and its agencies. The 1990 Trust, for example, describes this approach as follows: "everything we do is informed by the views and experiences of ordinary Black people living in different communities throughout the UK. This principle is called *networking*. Networks are communities of interest bound together by people responding to an issue or particular need" (Annual Report 1992/93: 13).

One major grouping with which The 1990 Trust is involved is the Black Liaison Group. This consists of around 50 national and London-based black organizations, including the Society for Black Lawyers, Association of Black Probation Officers, National Convention of Black Teachers, National Convention of Black Mental Health, SCORE UK, West Indian Standing Conference and the Association of Black Journalists. The purpose of bringing them together is "to work on specific issues and to provide a unified voice where appropriate" (Annual Report 1992/3: 14).

On a larger scale, the national "Agenda 2,000: The Black Perspective Conference", held in October 1993, identified as one of the key areas for action "to create opportunities for networking at a national level" (Sia 1993: 29).

Thus, two perspectives can be identified. The dominant official view is governed by the idea of a common bond which is to be implemented by partnerships for competition at the local level. These partnerships, in turn, can be effectively propelled with the aid of networking across a considerable range of actors, among whom are expected to be found representatives of black and ethnic minority groups. In contrast, among very many black and ethnic minority community associations, the experience of marginalization and the limited success which has grown out of developments based on notions of difference and distinctiveness suggest that these are the more profitable avenues through which to pursue regeneration. In this context of widely differing perspectives, what is the result when the notion of the common bond is implemented?

## Implementing the common bond[1]

The operation of networking at the local level can be represented from the perspective of black and ethnic minority groups as consisting of three focal areas. The first has already been identified as central government. I have argued above that central government operates the dominant influence in this relationship, setting the climate for regeneration relationships.

The second focal area comprises the interacting dominant partnerships of local government and public sector agencies of the centre in the locality. The latter include TECs and City Challenge initiatives and more recently the Single Regeneration Budget (SRB hereafter) programme operated through the Regional Government offices. This grouping, although at times involved in limited internal conflict, operates within the established framework. Their combined power through partnerships wields considerable influence in each locality, giving distinctive features to the way that relationships are worked out between these agencies and ethnic minority communities. These governmental and local public-sector agencies are together sufficiently influential to give particular shape to local strategies beyond intergovernmental relations.

Ethnic minority organizations and communities form the third focal area in the pattern of networking which operates at the local level. Due to their diversity and lack of influence to dictate either the form or structure of the partnership for urban regeneration, they remain for the most part the subject of attempts at incorporation. Each of the three features of the climate described above are used to this end. The common bond is particularly important, however, as it cements loyalty to the new methods of operation imposed during the 1980s. The way in which it operates appears to give each area its distinctive feature. At the same time, the attempt to impose a common bond is perhaps best described as a struggle, and is not a foregone conclusion as the examples below illustrate.

The City of Birmingham has been particularly active in the development of a programme of incorporation towards the creation of a common bond for ethnic minority groups. Described as "consultation and citizen engagement", this process has taken a variety of forms, ranging from networking to market research on black and ethnic minority needs and formal group consultation. As described by the City's Strategic Planning and Research Unit:

> the aim of networking is to establish contact with groups that are not traditionally involved in decision-making processes such as mother and toddlers groups or community social clubs. For instance Asian women are unlikely to respond to an approach from a white man but will "open the door" to another Asian woman. This approach is particularly effective when citizens feel alienated from decision makers or are suffering from consultation fatigue.
>
> (City of Birmingham, 1995)

Attempts at incorporation also operate at a city-wide level. The Race Relations Unit in the Strategic Management Department has the responsibility for establishing relationships with ethnic minority groups across the city. In 1992, a city-wide consultation participation framework was developed and agreed by the Community Affairs Committee of the City Council. The principles for consultation have been developed by the city's Race Relations Unit. The Unit itself consults on specific issues as well as through a number of umbrella forums which include: the African and Caribbean Peoples Movement; Bangladeshi Islamic Consultative Council; Birmingham Chinese Society; Council of Black Led Churches; Council of Sikh Gurdwaras in Birmingham; Hindu Council of Birmingham; Midlands Vietnamese Community Association; the Pakistan Forum; and the Irish Forum.

High levels of commitment to the establishment of the common bond were also apparent in other localities, particularly through the City Challenge programmes. In Wolverhampton, community involvement was depicted as one of the fundamental principles underlying the City Challenge initiative. The City Challenge programme saw the need to create an organization to develop and transmit the views of the community as a whole (Khamis 1992: 2). In Kirklees, the City Challenge project was stung to respond to generalized allegations of a lack of minority participation in urban regeneration made by Medas (1994).

There is evidence that at the national level, although previously earmarked funds were included in the resources opened to competition, this strategy has failed to benefit black and ethnic minority groups. A review of the first-round results of the SRB programme has demonstrated that the needs of the ethnic minority communities were given low priorities by key partners and that there was an absence of successful, ethnic minority-led bids. (Mawson et al. 1995).

Locally, disenchantment has been registered in a variety of ways. For example: a recent City Challenge Service User Needs Survey for black and ethnic minority groups in the Aston ward of Birmingham concluded:

> a picture emerged of a situation where respondents who might have been willing to accept the difficulties that the Council faced, were alienated by a lack of effective communication and became resentful. A culture of potential partnership had consequently become one of conflict.
>
> (Woodhill Barrett Associates, 1994: 8)

In Kirklees, the City Challenge project offered considerable evidence of black and ethnic minority group participation in City Challenge initiatives, as well as positive returns to these communities from participation in the major programmes of economic regeneration, housing, the social and community programme and education and training. The programme also chose to encourage participation by ensuring that one-quarter of funding in community development was devoted to black and ethnic minority groups in the area. This proportion roughly matched the proportion of the ethnic minority community in the City Challenge area.

Some ethnic minority community associations in Kirklees suggested an alternative picture which challenged the positive picture of a common bond in the making. One associate of an Asian organization suggested that there existed "a community misperception of City Challenge by black and Asian groups as a social welfare programme and less as an anti-poverty programme with economic imperatives" (Interview A 1995). Black and Asian community associations in this area have also complained of slow information provision and inadequate consultation on needs. The funding which had flowed to these groups in the locality through City Challenge community programme it was suggested appeared to "sharpen divisions between different elements of the community as each saw it could become self sufficient ... it also reinforced an inter-generation split between youth groups and the more established elders" (Interview B 1995).

The sense of exclusion was put more directly in Wolverhampton. At the institutional level, one Afro-Caribbean community association representative found that through formal processes of consultation with local government it was difficult to get proposals changed even when in draft form, "people who present a document want to go forward with it". The encouragement to join public-sector networks of the establishment also required "community representatives to offer reports like them. I feel that black representatives should give their point of view then it's up to the officers to include them" (Interview C 1995).

In Wolverhampton it was also alleged that funding networks effectively limited the opportunities for the funding of Black and Asian groups. One respondent noted,

> In the voluntary sector there are a clique of people who get access to funds ... I used to think it was my imagination, but now I know that other organizations find the same. There are people who have been around a long time. They are in the (Wolverhampton) Partnership Forum, but you're not encouraged to join. They have social relationships. Black organizations are on the outside – we are dubious about working with them.
>
> (Interview D 1995)

While the processes and observations described above are common experiences, there are important exceptions. Not all black and ethnic minority organizations are on the outside. Some of their leaders have become or are in the process of becoming effectively incorporated. For example, a number have established identifiable networks of influence with mainstream state agencies. In Birmingham, for example, earlier patterns of incorporation, which operated to the advantage of white voluntary bodies and to the exclusion of black voluntary organizations, can be demonstrated to be working to the advantage of a few minority organizations. In 1985, a review of the partnership funding process in Birmingham observed:

> White voluntary bodies were also more likely (than black and ethnic minority community organizations) to have and use informal contacts in relevant departments; so that proposals could be informally assessed before submission. This strategy ... worked against the interest of many black groups."
>
> (Inner Cities Research Programme 1985: 148)

While many black voluntary organizations faced funding cuts or closure through lack of funds during the 1980s, at least one Asian Resources Centre (ARC) thrived. From a staff of 1 in the late 1970s, the organization now employs 9 full time staff in its varied areas of work. The organization has had a high profile through media exposure and continued community support. The ARC has also had only two directors in its 15 years' existence. The present director's span of contact illustrates the potential for networking. He serves on the Black Carers Forum, the Mental Health Carers Forum, the Joint Care Planning

Team for the Elderly, North Birmingham Community Care Trust and the Heating and Weather Protection Group, among other mainstream activities. His longest term as a representative serving on an official committee he estimated to have been ten years, his shortest membership term he estimates to be three years. The participation at this level was acknowledged as creating opportunities to be informed and prepared for patterns of demand for care provision as they developed. As he acknowledged "we have regular contact with certain individuals and departments in the City, when developments are happening our friends keep us informed" (Interview E 1995).

In Kirklees, a similar pattern of widespread contacts is discernible for the present chair of the Pakistan and Kashmiri Welfare Association. He serves as a school governor to two schools, he has been co-opted on to four committees of the Kirklees Council, is an Executive Member of the Kirklees Racial Equalities Council, a Board member of North Kirklees Arts Council, Chair of the Asian Community Forum of Batley City Challenge and is a reporter for the *Daily Jang* in the Kirklees area. His Welfare Association is soon to develop a new Community Centre with City Challenge funding.

Inasmuch as a common bond exists, it needs to be activated. One method is through City Challenge funding, to the requirements and on the terms of City Challenge. The partnership in funding the development of a temple project in Wolverhampton illustrates this process. Wolverhampton City Challenge and a Sikh Temple Committee eventually agreed joint project-funding for a new community building, but from the outset there existed fundamentally different perspectives on the project. The temple applicants were expecting a grant to enable them to carry out changes in a form and manner with which they were familiar. This included voluntary work on the project when time would allow, piecemeal development, open building design and unspecified area usage. For their contribution to the funding of the project City Challenge required tendering procedures, various working groups for building purposes, a freestanding building on completion and indications that identified area needs would be met. Thus very different working conditions and patterns were the price of the common bond. This appeared to be a price that the community association was ultimately willing to pay.

## CONCLUSION

At both national and local levels there appears to exist an underlying tension between enhancing a notion of a common bond (area development) and the recognition of ethnically-based difference (incorporation through specific group recognition). The state is ambivalent about this tension. With a few exceptions, black and ethnic minority groups live less easily with this ambivalence than the state and increasingly demand an ethnic-specific focus to urban regeneration. The outcome of the first round of the SRB negotiations does indicate an overall process of discriminatory exclusion. The perception of many representatives of community associations in these local negotiations also supports this view.

However, to describe the process of community politics in urban regeneration as characterized entirely by exclusion would be too limited. In some localities there are indications that ethnic minority incorporation rather than exclusion is also a reality. In 1976 Newton identified how established groups from among the white voluntary sector could maximize their power and influence through the co-operation of and close involvement with the local state. We appear to be witnessing the beginning of a similar process as a part of the context of black and ethnic minority community politics.

The two examples of influential individuals in Birmingham and Kirklees suggest the early form of a pattern of community politics which is using ethnicity as a mechanism to shape and enforce claims on resources to a real, if limited, extent. There are signs, albeit at an early stage, of established leaders of community associations beginning to exercise a degree of authority which would have been unexpected even a few years ago. These groups are operating in a relatively quiet and unheralded way. They negotiate with government officials, attend meetings with them, send and receive policy documents and are regularly consulted by public officials. The leaderships of the Asian Resource Centre in Birmingham and of the Kirklees Pakistan Welfare Association indicate the operation of this process.

Both exclusion and incorporation exist side by side and operate as part of the community politics of urban regeneration as the process affects black and ethnic minority communities. As future rounds of winners and losers are decided by competition, it will be instructive to identify how many more black groups will become incorporated into the partnerships, and the extent to which ethnic-specific contributions to urban regeneration will be developed.

## ACKNOWLEDGEMENT

I am grateful to Chris Collinge of the Centre for Urban and Regional Studies for his help in the early formulation of key ideas around networking and urban regeneration which inform this chapter. Responsibility for their interpretation however rests with the author.

## NOTE

1. Quotations in this section are taken from interviews with representatives of community associations interviewed by the author. The interviews form part of a larger study of *Networks in Urban Regeneration* funded by the Joseph Rowntree Foundation.

## REFERENCES

Agenda 2,000 1994. *The Black perspective conference report*. London: Sia.

Ben-Tovim, G., J. Gabriel, I. Law & K. Stredder 1986. *The Local Politics of Race*. Basingstoke: Macmillan.

Brown, C. 1984. *Black and White Britain*. London: Policy Studies Institute.

City of Birmingham Strategic Planning and Research Unit 1995. Consultation and Citizen Engagement. Birmingham: Council House.

Champion, T. 1996. Internal Migration and Ethnicity in Britain. *Social geography and Ethnicity in Britain: Geographical Spread, Spatial Concentration and Internal Migration*, P. Ratcliffe. (ed.). London: HMSO.

Cook, J. 1994. Time For A Black Perspective On Urban Regeneration. *NCVO Urban Issues*, October 5–8.

Department of the Environment 1993. *Single Regeneration Budget: Note on Principles*. London: HMSO.

Department of the Environment 1994. *Annual Report*, London: HMSO.

Goldbourne, H. 1990. The contribution of West Indian Groups to British politics. In H. Goldbourne (ed.) *Black Politics in Britain*, Avebury: Aldershot.

Hall, S. 1989. *The Voluntary Sector Under Attack?* London: IVAC.

Hausner, V. & Associates 1992. *Economic Revitalization of Inner Cities; The Urban Programme and Ethnic Minorities*, Department of The Environment, London: HMSO.

Hinds, A. 1992. A Report On Organizations Serving The Afro-Caribbean Community, West Indian Standing Conference, London.

Inner Cities Research Programme 1985. Five Year Review of Birmingham's Inner-city Partnership Programme, University of Birmingham: Aston.

James, W. & C. Harris 1993 (eds). *Inside Babylon: the Caribbean Diaspora in Britain*. London: Verso.

Khamis, C. 1992. Community participation in Wolverhampton City Challenge – the Beginnings of a Case Study, Conference paper prepared for OECD/CDF Conference. *The Challenge of Urban Regeneration: Strategies for Community and Business Involvement*, 16–17 September, Birmingham.

Mawson, J., M. Beazley, A. Burfitt, C. Collinge, S. Hall, P. Loftman, B. Nevin, A. Srbljanin, & B. Tilson 1995. *The Single Regeneration Budget: The Stocktake*. Birmingham Centre for Urban and Regional Studies, University of Birmingham with the Faculty of Built Environment, University of Central Birmingham: England.

Medas, M. 1994. *From City Challenge To Single Regeneration Budget: A Black Perspective*. London: Sia.

Owen, D. 1994. Spatial variation in ethnic minority group populations in Great Britain. *Population Trends*, 78, 23–33.

Qaiyoom, R. 1993. *Empty Vessels, Hollow Sounds: Local Government and Ethnic Minority Consultation*. London: Sia.

Ratcliffe, P. 1992. Renewal, Regeneration And "Race"; Issues In Urban Policy. *New Community* 18: 3. 387–400.

Rex, J. & R. Moore 1967 *Race, Community and Conflict*. London: Oxford University Press.

Rex, J. and S. Tomlinson 1979. *Colonial Immigrants in a British City*. London: Routledge and Kegan Paul.

Small, S. V. 1994. *From Arts to Welfare: A Bibliography of the Black Voluntary Sector*. London: Sia.

Solomos, J. & L. Back 1995. *Race Politics and Social Change*. London: Routledge.

Werbner, P. 1991. Black and Ethnic Leadership in Britain: a theoretical overview. *Black and Ethnic Leaderships: The Cultural Dimension of Political Action* P. Werbner & M. Anwar (eds). London: Routledge.

Wenham, M. 1993. *Funded To Fail, Nuff Pain No Gain*. London: LVSC.

Willmott, P. & R. Hutchinson 1992 (eds). A Perspective On Britain's Deprived Urban Areas, *Urban Trends*. London: Policy Studies Institute.

Woodhill Barrett Associates 1994. *Service User Needs Survey – Black And Ethnic Minority Communities In The Aston Ward*. Birmingham.

# CHAPTER ELEVEN

# The public policy agenda: campaigning and politics for a multi-ethnic good society

## Kaushika Amin and Robin Richardson

"That was more or less it": with these words Tony Benn tersely concluded an account of a brief discussion amongst senior members of the Labour Party on Wednesday 16 January 1974 (Benn 1990: 91). The conversation had been about the Labour Party's electoral strategies and campaigning in the 1970 general election, and about priorities and emphases in the campaigns for the February 1974 election which were just beginning. Benn's account shows senior politicians obstinately and pedantically quibbling over factual accuracy in relation to voting, seats and electoral support but indifferent, apparently, to ethical issues relating to the building and maintenance of a good, or even good enough, society:

> Harold said, "Ignore Enoch Powell, because last time the attack on him lost five seats." I interrupted and said, "Look, Harold, I've heard you say this two or three times before and never contradicted you, but it just isn't true." "Well I've said it five times that you lost us five seats." "Let me deny it once," I said, "and then you can proceed." That was more or less it.

"More or less it": the words seem to summarize and to comment on an overall debate as well as one brief exchange. It is relevant, however, to recall also more idealistic words used by senior politicians over the years about issues of cultural pluralism and combating discrimination. The idealistic statements imply that it would be premature and unduly cynical to conclude that electoral considerations alone are "more or less it", and that grand utterances about the *multi-ethnic good society* are never more than elaborate smokescreen or empty rhetoric. For such statements may be used to construct criteria and codes of practice, according to which the actions of politicians, not only as policy-makers but also as candidates for election or re-election, may be studied, criticized and evaluated. We shall accordingly recall here briefly the policy discourse of the last 30 years which has consistently emphasized the twin goals of social inclusion and cultural pluralism. We shall then recall that politicians of all parties have frequently failed, by their own lights, to strike an acceptable balance between their commitment to the multi-ethnic good society on the one hand, and their legitimate pursuit of political advantage on the other. We shall conclude by suggesting that the way ahead might involve each party developing and publishing a code of practice or, so to speak, a Voter's Charter.

## DISCOURSE ABOUT INCLUSION AND PLURALISM

A few years before the exchange recorded by Tony Benn, there had been the much-quoted speech by Roy Jenkins (Jenkins 1966) in which the twin goals of public policy had been defined as "equal opportunity accompanied by cultural diversity, in an atmosphere of mutual tolerance". Only a few months after it, there was the White Paper on racial discrimination which paved the way for the Race Relations Act 1976, and which repeated and re-emphasised the sentiments in Jenkins' famous words. In the 1980s the Home Office accepted a formal recommendation from Sir David Lane, a former Home Office minister and the first chairman of the Commission for Racial Equality, that it should explicitly stress both social inclusion and cultural pluralism in a formal statement of aims and objectives for a high-profile educational project funded by Section 11 monies (Lane 1988: 38):

> [Black and ethnic minority] school-children are to be regarded first and foremost as British, with a commitment to this society and in a system designed to give them the best possible preparation for taking a full part in Britain's national life but without sacrificing their particular cultural identity.

This brief reference in Lane's report was then elaborated two years later into a formal statement for the use of all Section 11 funding, not just for those provided for education (Home Office 1990):

The Government's fundamental objective is that Britain should be a fair and just society where everyone, irrespective of ethnic origin, is able to participate freely and fully in the economic, social and public life of the nation while having the freedom to maintain their own religious and cultural identity. Members of ethnic minorities, a growing proportion of whom were born in the United Kingdom, are an integral part of British society.

For a report in April 1995 to the United Nations Committee on the Elimination of all Forms of Racism (CERD), the Government expanded slightly but significantly on this statement and applied it to all public policy (United Nations 1995):

It is a fundamental objective of the United Kingdom Government to enable members of ethnic minorities to participate freely and fully in the economic, social and public life of the nation, with all the benefits and responsibilities which that entails, while still being able to maintain their own culture, traditions, language and values. Government action is directed towards addressing problems of discrimination and disadvantage which prevent members of ethnic minorities from fulfilling their potential as full members of British society.

Both the Section 11 formulation and the later CERD statement refer to participating freely and fully in the economic, social and political life of the nation. But the phrase in the earlier statement about "their own religious and cultural identity" was interestingly changed five years later into "their own culture, traditions, language and values". The later phrase arguably reflects an understanding of identity as multi-faceted and open-ended, something which is developed and chosen rather than fixed and given. In its inclusion of language and values it implies considerable acceptance of, and commitment to, a fuller concept of pluralism. The reference to problems of discrimination and disadvantage appears to acknowledge, more explicitly than the earlier statement, the realities of racism. In due course researchers may be able to describe in detail the negotiations and deliberations which presumably took place within the Home Office in the early 1990s as the one formulation was transmuted into the other.

In the meanwhile, both formulations can be seen and used as succinct and non-partisan descriptions of – as the phrase might be – the multi-ethnic good society (Runnymede Trust 1994), and therefore of the overall goals of public policy to create and maintain such a society. Their twin emphases on social inclusion and cultural plural-ism permit specific areas of social policy to be analyzed and evaluated, for data can be collected to assess progress over time: to compare and contrast Britain with other countries; to compare different cities or regions of Britain with each other; to compare the situations, life-chances and trajectories of different communities; and to compare progress and trends in different fields of policy.

In slightly more detail, the features of the multi-ethnic good society can be summarized as follows:

### Politics and government

People with a range of ethnic identities ("minority" as well as "major-ity") can and do play a full part in party politics at local, national and European Parliament levels, as party activists, candidates and elected members, and as officers and civil servants in the planning and running of public services and bodies, at all levels of seniority and responsibility.

### Employment and occupations

People with a range of ethnic identities can and do participate fully in the economy, across a wide range of manufacturing and service industries, and at all levels of the occupational class system, including the professions and management. Members of ethnic minorities are not concentrated in particular sectors of the economy or at the lowest levels of responsibility and remuneration and are not affected dispro-portionately by unemployment.

### Crime, law and justice

Levels of inter-ethnic tension and violence are low. People with a range of ethnic identities can and do play a full part in running the justice system, in all its branches. No ethnic minority is dispro-portionately the victim of threats and violence or disproportionately involved in crime and deviance.

### Material conditions of life

People with a range of ethnic identities live in close proximity to each other and share the same public spaces such as shops, markets, schools and recreational areas. No community is disproportionately affected by poor material conditions of life, for example overcrowded and undesirable housing, inadequate access to transport and services, or a deprived physical environment.

247

## Education, arts and culture

People with a range of ethnic identities can and do participate in the creation of public mainstream culture, including the curriculum of schools and universities; the production of literature and of the performing and visual arts; journalism and the media; and recreation, sports and entertainment.

Each of these five areas of social life, to repeat, can be defined in sufficient detail for measurements and objective comparisons to be made. Baseline data, disaggregated to an extent by ethnic group, has been collated and published over the years (for example, Runnymede Trust 1994a.) There are major differences, as has been well documented, between the situations of different communities: some "participate freely and fully in the economic, social and public life of the nation" considerably more than others. The overall picture, however, continues to be unpromising. Figures published by the Department of the Environment in 1994 show that the 12 local authority districts with the greatest extent of material deprivation are all in London. In order of deprivation they are as follows – with percentages in parentheses showing the projected proportions of black and ethnic minority people in the year 2011 (London Research Centre 1995): Hackney (38), Tower Hamlets (46), Southwark (33), Islington (26), Newham (61), Lambeth (37), Haringey (36), Camden (24), Hammersmith and Fulham (19), Westminster (27), Brent (52) and Lewisham (33) (Department of the Environment 1994. See also Gordon and Forrest 1994). With regard to income, almost a third of black and ethnic minority people belong to the poorest quintile of the population (Hills 1995: 14).

## CAMPAIGNING AND POLITICS AND THE MULTI-ETHNIC GOOD SOCIETY

Progress in Britain towards the multi-ethnic good society, as figures show, has been patchy and unsteady. It remains unclear whether public policy should target resources directly at ethnic minority communities, or to anti-poverty and regeneration programmes in areas such as those listed above, in the expectation that they will benefit minority communities indirectly (Saggar, this volume. See also Modood 1994). Insofar as there has been progress, this has sometimes seemed to occur in spite of, rather than because of, the actions, policies and decisions of elected politicians. By the same token, however, lack of progress cannot be attributed solely to the failures and omissions of politicians, as distinct from those of other opinion-leaders, elites and interest groups, in relation to the overall public policy agenda. However, a recurring aspect of British electoral politics with regard to race over the last 40 years has been an unresolved tension between the exigencies of campaigning and the promotion of racial justice, and for this the leaders of political parties must take a large share of the blame. Commenting on the Queen's Speech in autumn 1995, *The Times* noted that a governing party has to manage a tension between "the turning of a political vision into reality" and "engaging in a high-stakes game of wits with the benches opposite". It bitterly regretted that the government was managing this tension so clumsily and uninspiringly (*The Times* 1995):

> The Government will dot and cross, clean and tidy, duck and weave: and do little else of legislative substance from now until the next election ... Gone are the early years when legislation was the end product of a philosophy, the turning of a political vision into reality. Now the Government is engaged in a high-stakes game of wits with the benches opposite. To judge by yesterday's legislative programme, the new session will be one attempt after another to trap Labour into opposing measures that might be expected to win populist support.

The strictures made here by *The Times* about one particular small episode in electoral politics can be broadened out to refer to a lengthy history of race-equality issues and the building of a multi-ethnic good society. All too often the public policy agenda on race equality has been shaped by "a high-stakes game of wits with the benches opposite" (a game in which, significantly, the most famous metaphor is about the playing of a card) rather than by a philosophy of the good society and by political vision. In this chapter we shall examine three main ways in which political parties have in consequence failed, both nationally and locally, to pursue the aims and objectives of the multi-ethnic good society. We consider in this connection: a) discourse about immigration and cultural homogeneity; b) discourse about so-called political correctness, the "loony left" and "do-gooders"; and c) the interweaving and overlapping of mainstream party politics with inter-ethnic and intra-ethnic tensions and agendas. The first two of these factors are associated in the first instance with the Conservative Party. Also, however, they are associated with the marked failure and reluctance of other parties to address them with adequate vigour and clarity. The third is associated mainly with the Labour Party.

In order to set the scene, it is relevant to recall two papers about political campaigning produced in 1994–95 from within the heart of the Conservative Party. The first one (Peston 1994) was intended to be strictly confidential and was accordingly franker and less idealistic than public statements by leading politicians usually are. The other was a newspaper article, but it too was more frank than is usual. Both provide salutary reminders that turning a political vision into reality is often a low priority compared with mobilizing and retaining electoral support, and that one of the visions obscured or damaged by this state of affairs is that of the multi-ethnic good society.

An article in the *Financial Times* observed that the first of these papers, a confidential strategy paper by John Maples, deputy chairman of the Conservative Party, "throws light on the usually obscured relationship between party machinery and government departments" and that, since it was intended for a tiny restricted readership within the party itself, the "language and tone are rather more frank and perhaps cynical than the normal ministerial soundbite" (Peston 1994). The Maples Memorandum, as it came to be called, was based on professional market research amongst potential Conservative supporters. It reported that such people believe that "the Conservatives have let voters down: they have been in government too long, are complacent and have lost a sense of direction. They fail to fulfil promises, are clumsy at implementing policy and shoot themselves in the foot", and that "there is a feeling of powerlessness and insecurity about jobs, housing, health service, business, family values, crime, etc, and no vision of where we are heading". However, these people are also "natural Conservatives", for they have "very right wing views on crime and immigration", "deep disapproval of scrounging on social security", "deep fear of loony lefties", and "distrust of politically-correct, liberal-minded do-gooders".

The electoral strategy, therefore, had three main components: a) to address people's feelings of powerlessness and insecurity – the "feel-bad" factor which has to a large extent been caused by global economic forces over which national governments may have only limited control (Hutton 1995); b) to support, therefore, or to appear to support, right-wing views on crime and immigration; and c) to attack "politically-correct, liberal-minded do-gooders", i.e. (presumably) people who do not appear to have major anxieties about their identity in a changing world, or who, anyway, do not express such anxiety through calls for repressive measures to control deviants and outsiders. The full list of issues in the Maples Memorandum is instructive, for it implies that discourse about any one of its items can act as a code for any one of the others: utterances about political correctness, scrounging and do-gooders, for example, can be understood as being about immigration (itself a code word for race, ethnicity and cultural pluralism), without the actual terms immigration and race being used. Similarly the term "crime" can be subliminally linked to the term "immigration", so that discourse of being tough on crime can become a proxy for discourse about the need for stronger immigration controls. "We cannot be tough enough for our audience", said the memorandum about crime, law and order, and it went on to recommend that there should be a critical focus on "those responsible for light sentences, safari trips, prosecution of people who 'have a go' at criminals, early release of criminals etc". In this context the memorandum recommended that legislation should be introduced which would split Mr Blair from the rest of his party: "A proposal on ID cards ... would force them to take a view. Either Blair will support our proposals and divide his party, or oppose us and show he does not really mean what he says about ... crime." When, in due course, the Government issued a consultation document on identity cards, the rationale was entirely explicit about tackling, simultaneously with the one measure, both crime and immigration.

In autumn 1995 a senior political correspondent for *The Times* elaborated on these points. The style and structure of his sentences suggested that even the term "parental choice" can be a proxy for "immigration", for the term "crime" in one sentence was varied into "law and order" in the next, whereas it was the term "parental choice" which was chosen to ring the changes on "immigration" (Riddell 1995):

> In a pre-election period, the Tories have always emphasised crime and immigration measures out of all proportion to their real significance in order to portray Labour as "soft". This is a sound electoral tactic. Labour is still vulnerable, particularly among some of its recent converts, on issues such as law and order and parental choice.

The Maples Memorandum recommended the use of vivid and concrete stories rather than abstract arguments:

> While ABC1s can conceptualise, C2s and Ds often cannot. They can relate only to things they can see and feel. They absorb their information and often views from television and the tabloids. We have to talk to them in a way they can understand.

"Talk to them in a way they can understand": the research director at Conservative Central Office in the period 1990–1995, Andrew Lansley, recalled in autumn 1994 the principal stories and strategies which he and his colleagues had employed in the general election in 1992 and which he strongly recommended for the next campaign also (Lansley 1995a). He referred in this connection to a private paper written in

summer 1995 for Labour's national executive committee by Jack
Straw, the Shadow Home Secretary, in which it had been argued that
Labour should travel light in its campaigning when it came to specific
policies, but should concentrate instead on Tory "negatives". It
should focus, in short, on reasons for not voting Tory rather than on
reasons for supporting itself. The Conservative Party research director
acknowledged that this is a legitimate and even conventional strategy
in political campaigning ("it is clear that negative campaigning does
deliver votes in the endgame"), but was confident that it could be used
to greater effect by his own party than by the opposition. Similarly the
Maples Memorandum had emphasized that the Conservative Party
will "need to scare the voters about Labour and the Liberals". Lansley
referred to public perceptions of the Labour Party as likely to increase
taxes and to be dominated by the influence of trades unions, and then
added:

> Immigration, an issue which we raised successfully in 1992 and
> again in the 1994 Euro-elections campaign, played particularly
> well in the tabloids and has more potential to hurt. So does
> the issue of identity cards. If Labour lines up with the civil
> liberties lobby, then Blair's efforts as Shadow Home Secretary
> to remove crime as a Labour negative will be reversed. Then
> there is the "loony left" and political correctness. Voters can't
> define it, but they don't like it and Labour councils are the
> arch exponents.

The article concluded with metaphors from both game-playing and
open warfare:

> On past form, Blair is going to demand more radical change
> from his party. He will have to navigate under fire of an inten-
> sity he has never known and can hardly guess at. He may even
> have to take friendly fire from his own side. Experience says
> that some of our attacks will strike home, however well-
> prepared he might be. It is clear that negative campaigning
> does deliver votes in the endgame. But no one in the Conserva-
> tive Party should suppose that Labour will self-destruct. Our
> campaign is going to have to defeat theirs. The Conservatives
> need to raise their own game and establish a renewed basis of
> trust with the electorate before they can mount a successful
> negative campaign. Once that is done, however, there is no
> shortage of themes with which to go on the attack.

In a later article Lansley denied that he had commended the playing of
the race card (Lansley 1995b). He quoted in this connection a remark

reported to have been made by Jack Straw to Members of the European Parliament earlier in the year: "We should not allow so much as a cigarette card to come between the Labour Party and the Tory Government over immigration." He saw this as "evidence that Labour had identified immigration as a negative issue for them", and said that "here is Jack Straw trying to close it down as a source of electoral disadvantage". He concluded his article by, in effect, suggesting that "the racism card" is Labour's way of responding to the so-called race card played by its opponents:

> Labour's desire to treat "immigration" and "race" as the same issue is misleading and dangerous. It is Labour who are "playing the race card. They are trying to smear the Conservatives as a party which panders to prejudice as a means of avoiding answering hard questions about their own immigration policy. I understand very well what Labour are doing. But dressing up electoral opportunism in the clothes of principle does not present an attractive picture.

Politicians and their research directors who claim to be speaking with principle when they accuse their opponents of electoral opportunism inevitably sound as if they too are merely positioning themselves for electoral advantage, or in order to minimize disadvantage. People outside the turbulence of day-to-day politicking, however, may perhaps apply the distinction between principle and electoral pragmatism with greater authority. In this connection it is relevant to observe that indeed there appears to be a "racism card" in the pack as well as a "race card", and that left-of-centre politicians do appear to play it. Partly, this card involves maintaining (though not at all unreasonably) that most certainly discourse about "immigration" is discourse also about "race", in effect if not in intention; more especially, it involves "trying to smear the Conservatives as a party which panders to prejudice as a means of avoiding hard questions about their own immigration policy".

In the light of the Maples Memorandum and Lansley's two articles, it is interesting and salutary to revisit the 1992 election campaigning and media coverage. For much of the campaign there was little public discussion of race and immigration. In the last few days before the election, however, considerable media coverage was given to a speech by a Tory candidate in Scotland, Sir Nicholas Fairbairn, who declared that under a Labour government Britain would be "swamped by immigrants of every colour and race and on any excuse of asylum or bogus marriage, or just plain deception, and with the abolition of the Prevention of Terrorism Bill, the terrorists of the IRA would come here as invited guests". The juxtaposition of immigrants "of every colour and race" with deception, bogus marriages and terrorism was crude but accurately reflected white racist prejudices. The same speech echoed crude racist fears about biological hybridity: if the Scottish National Party were successful in the forthcoming election, it was said, there would be citizenship rights for everyone born in Scotland "be he Greek, Tasmanian or the bastard child of an American service-man". The following day, five days before the election, the *Sun* ran a prominent story beginning as follows: "Tens of thousands of immigrants will be let into Britain if Labour win the election. Experts warn it will cost hundreds of millions in social security payments, put added strain on the Health Service and make it harder for our young people to find jobs." A speech by the Home Secretary, Kenneth Baker, about "floods of migrants and would-be asylum-seekers" and "this rising tide" in mainland Europe was given a twist in many papers to make it explicitly about Britain and about the Labour Party. The *Daily Express*, for example, filled almost the whole of its front page, two days before the election, with a huge headline: "BAKER'S MIGRANT FLOOD WARNING". It added as a prominent sub-heading "Labour set to open doors" as if this were a quotation from the Home Secretary's speech. The phrase had not, however, appeared in the official Conservative Party press release. The subsequent admission by the party's director of research that immigration was "an issue which we raised successfully in 1992 and ... played particularly well in the tabloids" (Lansley 1995) suggests that an additional spin was given to Mr Baker's speech by an off-the-record briefing to certain papers.

Examples of the race card, pandering to fears of immigration and loss of identity and purity, have been taken here so far from the campaigning strategies of the Conservative Party. However, a study of electioneering in Tower Hamlets in the early 1990s showed clearly with copious examples that the race card can entirely readily and shamelessly be played by the Liberal Democrats (Liberal Democrats 1993). The same study also mentioned that the worst piece of campaign material which it examined had in fact been produced by the local Labour Party. Labour and the Liberal Democrats, in short, are not in a strong moral position to complain. Even if they were, the fact remains that they often react with timidity and a certain querulousness when the race card is played by their political opponents. For example, they appear to complain that the playing of the race card has damaged their own electoral interests rather than progress towards a multi-ethnic good society. For example, again they make personalized attacks on individuals (as in 1994–95 on the Home Secretary, Michael Howard, for his alleged inconsistency as an individual in introducing asylum control measures which in an earlier age would have prevented

254

his own parents from entering Britain) rather than reaffirm their own commitment to racial equality and justice, and to the place within such a commitment of a rational, research-based, humane and positive immigration policy.

## Political correctness

Both Maples and Lansley mentioned the central importance, from their own point of view, of attacking so-called political correctness, as well as the loony left and do-gooders. Both implied that attacks on these amorphous subjects may function as coded attacks on cultural pluralism and on the rights of black and ethnic minority people to play a full part in the building and sustaining of political, social, economic and cultural life. People classified as ABC1, claimed Maples, are capable of seeing the links, without these being spelled out with perfect explicitness. People classified as C2 or D, however, he added, need concrete images, stories and pictures. One particularly vivid example of this approach to communication occurred in the run-up to the 1992 General Election. About three weeks before the election itself, on the morning after the Labour Party had outlined its alternative budget, the *Sun* carried a cartoon showing Neil Kinnock as a diminutive Robin Hood figure, and the other Labour leaders as medieval outlaws similarly clad in the stereotypical garments of medieval England. They had ambushed and captured a rich person travelling through Sherwood Forest, and were saying to him: "We rob from the rich and give to the Lesbian Rastafarian Community Centre".

The cartoon artfully synthesized a wide range of issues: crime, law and order (including so-called mugging), the implication being that opposition leaders are soft on this issue; fear of immigration and cultural pluralism, in the reference to Rastafari; fear of gender-equality issues and plurality of lifestyles and moralities, in the reference to lesbians; and fear of grassroots capacity-building measures, in the reference to a community centre. These fears were combined with the *Sun*'s traditional opposition to redistributive socialism. Further, by evoking a populist folk hero, Robin Hood, within the context of a lampoon of latter-day approaches to redistribution, the cartoon implied a discontinuity between traditional British (or English) narratives, legends and folklore on the one hand and the culture of the main modern opposition party on the other. Thus the race card (the reference to Rastafari) was played as part of a composite attack on the political correctness which is, allegedly in the demonology switched on by the cartoon, a distinctive feature of Labour-controlled local authorities. The cartoon was a fine case-study application of Lansley's observation, quoted above, about political correctness and the loony left. To recap: "Voters can't define it, but they don't like it and Labour councils are the arch exponents".

Labour-controlled local councils did, no doubt, make mistakes in the 1980s (see, for example, Cross et al. 1991 and Saggar, 1991) but they also made major contributions, through their race and gender equality programmes, to the development of the multi-ethnic good society. They received relatively little support for this work from national headquarters, however, and in the 1990s many of their achievements have been cut back. Here too there are examples of the Labour Party trying to minimize the damage caused by the "P.C.card" (as phrase might be) to their own electoral chances rather than to serious and well-intentioned efforts to promote and protect racial equality and justice. It would surely not be particularly hazardous for Labour leaders to make robust statements in support of equal opportunities policies in local government, particularly since such policies are pursued by Conservative-controlled councils as well as by others, and since they are to be found in the civil service, health services and police services as well as in local government.

## Labour Party and ethnic politics

The Labour Party also has to address the fact that at local levels it is frequently perceived to collude with, or actually to exploit, inter-ethnic and intra-ethnic tensions and agendas for the sake of electoral support (for example, Eade 1989; Solomos and Back, 1995). Individuals have been accepted as candidates in municipal elections, it has sometimes seemed, because they could attract and deliver substantial numbers of votes, not because they were committed to the aims and objectives of the party. The party's leadership at local levels has, therefore, sometimes appeared to collude with voting choices which belong more to the internal politics of specific communities, families and neighbourhoods, and perhaps also to diaspora politics, than to the management and leadership of an urban area in multi-ethnic Britain. Overlaps between mainstream politics and ethnic politics frequently work to the disadvantage of women, of the younger generation, and of the non-religious (Ali 1992). See also the breakdown by gender and ethnicity of local government councillors in Geddes, 1992, quoted in Runnymede Trust 1994a: 20.

The pattern of relationships between white political leaders (senior officers as well as elected members) and ethnic minority communities is reminiscent, it has been suggested (Ali 1992), of that which exists between a colonial administration and local elites. Both sides have a vested interest in the maintenance of essentialist stereotypes and fixed, impermeable boundaries: "all families are extended, children respect their elders, and women are veiled creatures living in the shadows". A similar relationship exists in many cities between senior police officers on the one hand and male community leaders on the other. In politics and administration across the whole range of social policy in a particular metropolitan area it may happen that (Ali 1992):

> each side, leader or governor, trades with the other at the margins, anticipating occasional gains but mostly content to recognise their relative power and the boundaries of jurisdiction in each sealed system.

On occasions, however, the entryism of community politics into mainstream politics and management has not remained at the margins but has severely threatened white power bases. When this has happened, the response of the Labour Party has been barely distinguishable, in the perceptions of its black and South Asian members, from crude cultural racism. A Birmingham Labour MP, for example, was reported in autumn 1994 as complaining that in British inner cities nowadays there are just two brands of politics: "There is traditional British politics where people tend to observe certain accepted rules, and there is the politics of the Indian subcontinent where anything goes" (Runnymede Trust 1994b). Researchers in Birmingham a few years earlier reported statements such as the following from white Labour activists, similarly appearing to reflect cultural racism (Solomos and Back 1995: 97–99):

> There are people from the subcontinent who have a very different view about politics from the way politics is in Britain. If you are in a political party in India you can get favours done for you. It's about having connections and money does change hands.

> ... the expectation of ethnic minority councillors is that it is all about power and the means justifies the ends.

> It is absolutely normal out there [Pakistan] which is to say the patronage system is just the norm. It is absolutely normal out there, they have a Godfather figure who comes along to meetings, who does all the dealings ... Now when I came in to this situation I thought this is really wrong ... we ought to be informing people and let them make up their own mind, well that is a very very naive theory. After a period of time you begin to live with things that are way below your principles.

> [Asians] are great believers in property ownership, in busi-

nesses. I would say that I've yet to meet the Asian who is a natural socialist, an ideological socialist, but even the Asians who support us really aren't any different from the Asians who support the Right.

A party official in Gorton, Manchester, was quoted in 1994 regarding the large number of new applications for membership of the constituency party: "They came out of the blue, computer printouts from Walworth Road with hundreds of applications, all Asian names. Alarm bells rang" (Runnymede Trust 1994b. See also the chapters by Geddes and by Adolino in this volume). The situation in Gorton was explained as follows by Muhammed Ajeeb, a long-serving councillor in Bradford who had on five separate occasions failed to gain a nomination for a seat at Westminster (Runnymede Trust 1994b):

Gorton is an expression of frustration among our people. Frustration either ends in apathy or doing something drastic. We have lived here for many years and supported Labour but we are never given a voice and have no outlet to express our frustration. What we are seeing now is a desperate move by desperate and angry people. This is our country now and we must have a voice at every level. It's nonsense to say that with a population as large as ours there are no worthy candidates. If the party does not give us a voice there can be no surprise if we try to get one for ourselves.

## CITIZENSHIP AND IDENTITY

It is appropriate, on that note, to stand back from specific debates and issues in order to map the overall concept of citizenship, and within this context to reflect on implications of the term "ethnic identity" which we used as a recurring key term here earlier, but without elucidation, in our summary of the multi-ethnic good society. It is helpful to distinguish between four main strands or dimensions. These are concerned respectively with a) status, rights and obligations b) social inclusion and active participation c) sentiment and sense of identity and d) political literacy, capacity and skill. The first two of these are largely structural or political: they are readily affected by social policy. The second two are largely personal and cultural: they provide the context in which politicians seek office and power, and the emotional and amorphous anxieties, concerns and ideals to which politicians appeal. The first and third are relatively passive and

258

minimal: necessary components of citizenship but not sufficient. The second and fourth are relatively active and maximal: they complete the concept of citizenship and show therefore its full scope and importance. The four can be represented as a simple matrix (see Figure 11.1).

The first component is to do with issues of formal status and rights – for example, rights of residence, rights to take part in elections and stand for office, and rights not to be discriminated against. The establishment of rights is, of course, an essential thread in all political endeavour to create the good society. The second component is to do with social inclusion: not just the absence of discrimination but, rather, the lively presence of many opportunities and spaces for citizens and residents to take part in the cultural, economic and political affairs of the community. The term "community" in such a formulation refers not only to the affairs of the national state, but also to those of a local neighbourhood; to the micro-politics of an organization or institution; and, in an age of increasing globalization, to a wide range of supranational and transnational networks, relationships and collectivities. "In the good society", John Kenneth Galbraith has maintained, "there cannot, must not, be a deprived and excluded underclass ... There must be full democratic participation by all, and from this alone can come the sense of community which accepts and even values diversity" (Galbraith, 1994: 3). In this respect, active use of the franchise is essential (ibid):

> There will be a much better, more civilized attitude towards minorities, recent migrants, the unfortunate in general, if it is known that they are politically active. We have seen a great improvement in political and social attitudes towards the black minority in the United States of America as its voting power has become evident. Politicians are often compelled to virtue by the thought of votes.

The third component of citizenship is to do with sentiments, loyalties and – as the term increasingly is – identity. Much emotional and cultural energy is likely to be expended on this topic in the coming years, particularly in the context of the millennium celebrations. The

Figure 11.1  Four components of citizenship

|         | Structural/Political | Cultural/Personal |
|---------|----------------------|-------------------|
| Minimal | Rights               | Identity          |
| Maximal | Inclusion            | Competence        |

essential questions have been addressed by academics throughout the social sciences (Roosens 1989, Hall 1991, Modood 1993, Said 1993, Pieterse 1995, Cohen 1995, Rex 1995). Notions of cultural, ethnic and national identity also exercise politicians of all parties, as they manoeuvre and bid for electoral support, and as they seek to diminish the attractions of their opponents and rivals. Turbulence around notions of identity provides the context in which significant political leadership is exercised and required (Dodd 1995: 49–50):

> This is going to become a more, not less, turbulent place, as Britain renegotiates its life with itself and others, in an increasingly globalised world. It won't be like a Grantchester tea-party but the majority of the British have never bought into that myth; they've simply not been offered anything else. What this Britain will need – among much else – is politicians who are willing to enter this turbulence and find ways of telling national stories that are inclusive and open-ended.

The fourth component of citizenship is to do with the control and deployment of political resources, and the exercise of political literacy and skill. At the individual level, it involves having knowledge about the political situations in which one is involved, and competence in advocacy and mobilization to defend and pursue one's interests. At the collective level, for example that of a community or neighbourhood organization, it involves capacity, contacts, communication and legitimacy.

The multi-ethnic good society is a community of communities. Each community has its own cultural markers, its own stories about the past, its own resources and power. But the boundaries between communities within the overall community of communities are frequently fuzzy, rather than hard and fast: there is frequently a no-person's-land, in-between space or grey area between them, for it is possible for one person to belong to two or more communities at one and the same time, as it is possible for a person to pass from one ethnic or national identity to another. Also there is much interchange, much give and take between different cultures and ethnicities. In any case, the boundaries between ethnic identities are not the only significant boundaries within the overall community of communities. Also there are boundaries which criss-cross national and ethnic categories, for example those which are to do with religion, occupation, gender, age, sexuality, ideology, single-issue campaigning, region and class.

With regard to the boundary between mainstream culture and minority identities, Bhikhu Parekh has written as follows (Parekh 1995):

The collective identity of a plural state ... is differently textured from that of the culturally homogenous nation state. It is complex and nuanced, and necessarily multi-stranded and multi-layered. One has to learn to be both Scottish or Welsh and British, both German or Italian and Swiss, both Basque and Spanish, both Punjabi or Gujarati and Indian. The larger identity is grounded in and energised by the particular, and the particular fulfils itself and finds a safe nest in the larger unit. The balance between the two is not easy to work out and sustain. If one of them were to be privileged or to become overbearing, the balance would be destroyed, leading either to secession or to intense repression, and involving massive violence.

Themes of dual identity were famously developed in the United States by William Du Bois in the early years of the twentieth century. In *The Souls of Black Folk*, Du Bois wrote in 1903 (quoted in, for example, Harris et al. 1995: 2):

The Negro is ... gifted with second-sight in this American world ... It is a peculiar sensation, this double consciousness, this sense of always looking at one's self through the eyes of others ... One ever feels this twoness – an American, a Negro; two souls, two thoughts, two unreconciled strivings; two warring ideals in one dark body, whose dogged strength alone keeps it from being torn asunder ... He would not Africanize America, for America has too much to teach the world and Africa. He would not bleach his Negro soul in a flood of White Americanism, for he knows that Negro blood has a message for the world. He simply wishes to make it possible for a man to be both a Negro and an American ...

At first sight, the sense of identity sketched by Parekh and Du Bois may appear rather more complex than that of most people. But actually all of us experience analogous tensions and opportunities, for we are all pulled by our heritages and belongings in a range of different and contrary directions, and cannot easily make choices amongst them. "I ... have ropes around my neck, I have them to this day", says a character in one of Salman Rushdie's short stories (Rushdie 1994: 211), "pulling me this way and that, East and West, the nooses tightening, commanding, choose, choose ... I choose neither of you, and both, Do you hear? I refuse to choose." The character is presented to the reader as a representative human being, not as a bizarre or mentally sick eccentric. All of us, as we go about our daily lives and as

261

we face the future, experience hybridity and have to make choices, and have to refuse to choose, amongst and within the heritages to which we have been born and in which we take part.

The Runnymede Trust handbook on the national curriculum, *Equality Assurance in Schools*, compiled through a lengthy process of public consultation in 1991–1992, put forward the proposition that all pupils and students in schools need a sense of personal, ethnic and cultural identity which has three separate but interacting components. An implication is that political leaders should commend these components in their speeches and statements. Identity needs to be (Runnymede Trust 1993: 13):

- confident, strong and self-affirming, as distinct from uncertain, ashamed or insecure;
- open to change, choice and development, as distinct from being dogmatic, rigid and opinionated;
- receptive and generous towards other identities, and prepared to learn from them, as distinct from feeling threatened and hostile, and wishing to exclude or to be separate.

In her 1994 Reith Lectures Marina Warner included a lengthy reflection on concepts of national and ethnic identity and referred in this context to the Caribbean poet Derek Walcott. The lesson taught by Walcott, she said (Warner 1994: 93), is that "no home is an island; no homegrown culture can thrive in permanent quarantine. We're all wayfarers and we make our destinations as we go." She cited a remark made by a character in Walcott's version of *The Odyssey*, "We earn home, like everything else", and commented (Warner 1994: 94):

> Walcott doesn't mean paying the rent or the mortgage. He means taking part in the journey, using memory, imagination, language to question, to remember and to repair, to wish things well without sentimentality, without rancour, always resisting the sweet seduction of despair.

In Marina Warner's terms, the building of the multi-ethnic good society is "taking part in the journey". The journey moves from a past which needs repairing as well as merely recalling, and which requires the exercise of the imagination as well as the memory. It stretches into a future, in preparation for which political campaigning needs to discard both sentimentality and bitterness, and to build hope rather than despair, sweetly seductive though the latter may often be. It is

262

within the context sketched here by quotations from the writings of Du Bois, Parekh, Rushdie, Walcott and Warner about identity that we turn now back to the turbulence of party-political campaigning in modern Britain, and propose a code of practice for the mainstream parties.

## THE NEED FOR A CODE OF PRACTICE

If politics and campaigning are to contribute constructively to a public policy agenda about racial equality and justice in a community of communities, it may be that each of the main parties needs to draw up a charter or quality-assurance document setting out what it stands for – and what it will not stand for. The items in such a document might be clustered under four main heading: 1) "rules of engagement" in relation to campaigning; 2) the responsibilities of elected politicians for educating, informing and leading public opinion, as distinct from pandering to prejudice; 3) aspects of internal party organization from an equal opportunities point of view; 4) and the public policy agenda generally.

Each political party has of course its own ethos, traditions and conventions, as well as its own ideology, roots and electoral strategies. Also each one is a coalition of separate, sometimes conflicting, interests. We believe, however, that the code of practice sketched below is applicable to all mainstream parties.

We are not pressing for some sort of political correctness. Nor do we suppose for one moment that election campaigns can happen without robust arguments or emotive appeals, and without parties seeking to outwit and embarrass their rivals and opponents. Nor are we suggesting that fundamental issues about the nature and directions of British society, including immigration and asylum policy, should not be debated: we are not, for example, urging a return to "the liberal hour" (Banton 1985) and all-party consensus of the 1970s. Rather, our emphasis is that securing electoral support is not the only duty of a mainstream party in a democracy. The essential point was well made by Lord Lester and his colleagues in their report of autumn 1993, in the wake of the British Nationalist Party's by-election victory in Tower Hamlets (Liberal Democrats 1993):

> The right to free and unfettered political speech and debate is fundamental to a liberal open society. It is a sinew of democracy, enabling, among other things, the effective expression of the popular will at elections ... But if the right to freedom of

263

political speech and public debate is essential, it is not an absolute right which has no limits. There are other fundamental democratic values ... Because of the vital importance of promoting equality of opportunity and respect for everyone, of respecting the human dignity of everyone, and of discouraging group prejudice and the scapegoating of minorities, political activity must not be allowed to be abused in the competition for the popular vote. The right to political expression cannot be abused by exploiting or encouraging racial, religious or cultural prejudices. Political activities must not only be honest and truthful and lawful; they must seek to avoid, whether blatantly or covertly, stirring up prejudice, or encouraging racial or religious discrimination.

Political parties have a duty, in short: a) to uphold standards of honest debate; b) to uphold the right not to be threatened by virtue of one's cultural, religious or ethnic identity; c) not to pander to racial, religious or inter-ethnic prejudice; d) not to fan or create fears of violence and conflict.

## TOWARDS A CODE OF PRACTICE FOR POLITICAL PARTIES

### A draft checklist[1]

*Discourse about immigration, identity and race*

1. Politicians are aware that anything they say about tightening up immigration and asylum controls may be construed as implying that they are not committed to tackling racial discrimination, harassment and violence in mainstream society.
2. Politicians are aware that speeches and statements about immigration controls may, regardless of what they actually intend: (a) pander and give comfort to racist views in the majority population and (b) increase anxiety and insecurity in minority communities.
3. Politicians make high-profile statements (a) confirming their commitment to a culturally pluralist society and (b) condemning all forms of racial discrimination, harassment and violence.
4. Politicians set out the principles of a rational, humane and positive immigration and asylum policy.
5. Politicians dissociate themselves from statements made within their own party which appear to express or pander to racial prejudice.

6. In discourse about national identity, politicians do not reflect assumptions that to be British is necessarily or customarily to be white.

*Race and racism cards*

7. When politicians believe that their opponents have pandered or are pandering to racist views, they go further than merely making personal attacks on specific individuals.
8. When criticizing the playing of the race card, politicians make clear their own commitment to a culturally pluralist society and their condemnation of all forms of racial discrimination, harassment and violence.

*Publicity material*

9. Party political broadcasts and advertising leaflets, posters and circulars reflect the multi-racial nature of British society.

*Selection of candidates*

10. The party takes steps to ensure that procedures reflecting equal opportunities principles are used in their selection processes for new candidates. Amongst other things this may mean:
    a) drawing up formal statements of selection criteria
    b) ensuring that shortlisting and questioning-schedules are based on these selection criteria
    c) ethnic record-keeping

*Supporting black and ethnic minority candidates*

11. The leadership is aware that there are likely to be expressions of strong hostility by white people, during the election campaign, towards their black and ethnic minority candidates.
12. Leaders are ready to make well-publicised statements or speeches condemning racist attacks or slurs on their black and ethnic minority candidates.

*Inclusion and participation*

13. The party uses positive action strategies, similar to those which are used in local government and the civil service, in order to increase the involvement of black and ethnic minority members in their decision-making and policy-making.
14. The party uses its influence to nominate black and ethnic minority people for membership of major public bodies and committees.

15. The party ensures that ethnic minority people actively involved in party politics do not have to specialize mainly in race-equality issues, but, on the contrary, are expected to contribute to the full range of mainstream decision-making and policy-making.
16. The party takes steps to minimize overlap between mainstream politics and politics within and between specific minority communities.
17. The party collects basic data on the number of their borough, district and county councillors belonging to ethnic minority groups; publishes this data; and keeps a record of changes over time.
18. The party knows the ethnic composition of its own staff, nationally and regionally, and monitors changes over time.
19. The party has appointed or designated staff to specialize in equality issues within the party's own structures and procedures.

*Policy reviews*

20. In all relevant policy-making, the party consciously considers the implications of its proposals and decisions for race equality: for example, in policies on tackling poverty and unemployment, and on education and training.

To repeat: we are not proposing a de-politicized or multi-partisan approach to the building of the multi-ethnic good society, nor are we suggesting that politicians should desist from vigorous argument, emotional appeals or robust mutual criticism. Our concern rather is that electioneering strategies should not actually damage the multi-ethnic good society. It would be naive to expect that the political parties themselves will take a high-profile initiative to create and bind themselves by the kind of code of practice which we have sketched here. They might well have no choice, however, but to review their practices if they were held to account by sections of the media, and by influential independent bodies and watchdog organizations, groups and projects.

"That was more or less it," said Tony Benn, quoted at the start of this chapter, appearing to suggest that for most politicians most of the time there is nothing more important than electoral calculation. Voters in a democracy, however, get the politicians and the politicking which they deserve. Through watchdog organizations and through the independent media it could happen that voters force politicians to observe, in relation to the multi-ethnic good society, a Voter's Charter. The existence of such a charter would not, of course, solve or prevent the full range, or anything like the full range, of the problems which we have recalled here. It might well, however, be an important step in the long journey, still in its earliest stages, towards the goals which the government says it wants, that all people should "participate freely and fully in the economic, social and public life of the nation ... while still being able to maintain their own culture, traditions, language and values". It is, in any case, surely well worth trying? Not even to try might be to submit, in the words of the 1994 Reith Lectures quoted here earlier, "to the sweet seduction of despair". The notion of a multi-ethnic good society requires not only politicians but also voters to maintain that electoral considerations alone are *not* "more or less it".

## NOTE

1. The draft code of practice quoted in this chapter was developed at the Runnymede Trust in the period 1992–1995, and parts of it were first published in *Politics for All: equality, culture and the general election 1992* (Amin and Richardson 1992: 60–62). A revised version of it was submitted to political parties in the run-up to the 1997 General Election.

## REFERENCES

Ali, Y. 1992. Muslim women and the politics of ethnicity and culture in Northern England. In G. Sahgal & N. Yuval-Davis (eds), London: Virago Press.

Amin, K. and R. Richardson. 1992. *Politics for All: equality, culture and the general election 1992*. London: The Runnymede Trust.

Banton, M. 1985. *Promoting Racial Harmony*. Cambridge: Cambridge University Press.

Benn, T. 1990. *Against the Tide: diaries 1973–76*. London: Arrow Books.

Cohen, R. 1995. Fuzzy Frontiers of Identity: the British case. *Social Identities* vol. 1, no. 1. Oxford: Carfax.

Cross, M. et al. 1991. *Racial Equality and the Local State: an evaluation of race policy in the London Brough of Brent*. University of Warwick: Centre for Research in Ethnic Relations. Department of the Environment 1994. *Index of Local Conditions: an analysis based on 1991 Census data*. London: Department of the Environment.

Dodd, P. 1995. *The Battle over Britain*. London: Demos.

Donald, J. and A. Rattansi (eds) 1992. *"Race", Culture and Difference*. London: Sage Publications for the Open University.

Eade, J. 1989. *The Politics of Community: the Bagladeshi community in East London*. Aldershot: Avebury.

Galbraith, J. 1994. *The Good Society Considered: the economic dimension*. University of Wales College of Cardiff.

Geddes, A. 1993. Asian and Afro-Caribbean representation in elected local government in England and Wales. *New Community* vol. 20, no. 1.

Gordon, D. and R. Forrest. 1994. *People and Places 2: social and economic distinctions in England*. University of Bristol: School for Advanced Urban Studies.

Hall, S. 1992. New Ethnicities. In J. Donald & A. Rattansi (eds), London: Sage for the Open University.

Harris, H. et al. (eds) 1995. *Racial and Ethnic Identity: psychological development and creative expression*. New York and London: Routledge.

Hills, J. 1995. *Inquiry into Income and Wealth: volume 2, a summary of the evidence*. York: Joseph Rowntree Foundation.

Home Office 1990. *Policy for the Administration of Section 11 Grant*. London: The Home Office.

Hutton, W. 1995. *The State We're In*. London: Jonathan Cape.

Jenkins, R. 1966. Speech to the National Committee for Commonwealth Immigrants (NCCI), 23 May. London: NCCI.

Lane, D. 1988. *Brent's Development Programme for Racial Equality in Schools*. London: The Home Office.

Lansley, A. 1995a. Accentuate the negative to win again. *Observer*, 3 September.

Lansley, A. 1995b. Race issue leaves Straw blowing in the wind. *Observer*, 10 December.

Liberal Democrats 1993. *Political Speech and Race Relations in a Liberal Democracy: report of an inquiry into the conduct of the Tower Hamlets Liberal democrats in publishing allegedly racist election literature between 1990 and 1993*. London: Liberal Democrats.

Martin, D-C. 1995. The Choices of Identity. *Social Identities* vol. 1, no. 1. Oxford: Carfax.

Modood, T. 1992. *Not Easy Being British*. Stoke-on-Trent: Trentham Books with the Runnymede Trust.

Modood, T. 1994. *Racial Equality: colour, culture and justice*. London: Institute for Public Policy Research.

Parekh, B. 1995. The concept of national identity. *New Community*, vol. 21 no. 2. Oxford: Carfax.

Peston, R. 1994. Tories need "killer facts" to stop electoral death. *Financial Times*, 21 November.

Pieterse, J. 1995. Unpacking the West: how European is Europe?. See Rattansi and Westwood (1995).

Rattansi, A. and S. Westwood (eds) 1995. *Racism, Modernity and Identity: on the western front*. Cambridge: Polity Press.

Rex, J. 1995. Ethnic Identity and the Nation State: the political sociology of multicultural societies. *Social Identities* vol. 1, no. 1. Oxford: Carfax.

Riddell, P. 1995. A speech to test Labour: the election starts here. London: *The Times*, 16 November.

Roosens, E. 1989. *Creating Ethnicity: the process of ethnogenesis.* London: Sage Publications.

Runnymede Trust 1993. *Equality Assurance in Schools: quality, identity, society.* Stoke-on-Trent: Trentham Books for the Runnymede Trust.

Runnymede Trust 1994a. *Multi-Ethnic Britain: facts and trends.* London: The Runnymede Trust.

Runnymede Trust 1994b. Party politics in multi-ethnic Britain: four current battles. *The Runnymede Bulletin,* No. 280, November. London: The Runnymede Trust.

Rushdie, S. 1994. *East, West,* London: Jonathan Cape.

Sahgal, G. and N. Yuval-Davis. 1992. *Refusing Holy Orders; women and fundamentalism in Britain.* London: Virago Press.

Saggar, S. 1991. *Race and Public Policy.* Aldershot: Avebury.

Said, E. 1993. *Culture and Imperialism.* London: Chatto and Windus.

Solomos, J. and L. Back. 1995. *Race, Politics and Social Change.* London and New York: Routledge.

*The Times* 1995. Duck and weave: new laws for an election campaign that is well under way. 16 November.

United Nations Committee on the Elimination of all Forms of Racial Discrimination (CERD). *Report from the United Kingdom,* April 1995.

Warner, M. 1994. *Managing Monsters: six myths of our time.* London: Vintage.

# CHAPTER TWELVE

# Piecing together the puzzle: ethnic and racial politics and the British electoral map

## Shamit Saggar

## INTRODUCTION

The theme of racial politics in Britain appears to operate at two, possibly three, reasonably distinct levels. First, there is the phenomenon of the electoral participation of Britain's ethnic minorities. This topic, as this volume has demonstrated, has been the focus of quite considerable academic, media and party interest over the years. Underlying much of this attraction has been the search for explanations for both mass and elite participation that are empirically well-informed, whilst consistent with a range of theoretical views of ethnic minorities' immigrant, class and geographic features. As different contributions to this volume have made clear, the interpretation put on *actual* patterns of ethnic minority electoral behaviour (EMEB) remains inconclusive and trapped in the quagmire of conceptual and methodological dispute. This somewhat blurred picture has, not surprisingly, allowed politicians almost unrivalled opportunities to put their own party-driven spin on the political attitudes and behaviour of ethnic minorities. The "ethnic vote", as it has been dubbed, has become more-or-less whatever politicians desire.

Secondly, there is the impact of race and immigration upon the country's political tradition generally and its electoral dynamics in particular. This sub-theme has very probably been the principal challenge faced by political scientists, political historians, psephologists and others, but it has not been met with anything like the same vigour or interest as the question of EMEB. To be sure, a number of significant academic studies have grappled with explanations for the "race/politics" narrative spanning much of the post-war period, but, in the end, few have addressed the fundamental question: in what ways, and to what lasting degree, has British electoral competition been affected by the arrival and settlement of non-white immigrant citizens? There is no doubt that the British political tradition has had to change in order to accommodate and perhaps reflect this new reality, although an overview of the academic and non-academic literature provides no satisfactory answer to the question. At best, much has been written and said about, and we can garner some insight from, the notorious "race card" – to cite one obvious example of the "impact-upon-politics-at-large" question. What is not so well understood are the underlying and related questions, such as those pertaining to how and why political parties make or avoid making policy commitments, and exploit or neglect specific issues.

At the outset of this final chapter it is worth adding that a third dimension of racial politics might be identified. This concerns the electoral meaning and implications of "race relations" in contemporary Britain, and, a little provocatively, asks whether some of our racial politics are driven by so-called vested interests and their critics. This approach is somewhat neglected in academic circles, although it is by no means hard to identify in the coverage given by press and politicians to a range of race-related themes. Furthermore, it is an unconventional and even unfashionable approach, since race-relations activists are frequently condemned by those who argue that racial politics are the unwanted products of an unloved industry. In other words, according to this viewpoint, British electoral politics is not necessarily concerned with race. The proposition is that it is "race relations" and its adherents that drives, and even defines, the racial theme on the British electoral map. This third interpretation is certainly worth flagging here, though it is not taken up in the discussion that follows.[1]

In this final chapter each of these aspects of British racial politics will be explored, and it will be suggested that the significance of race and ethnicity themes in the electoral process is heavily conditional upon which of the first two aspects is under examination. Further, it will be argued that British racial and electoral politics cannot be described and explained successfully without drawing this basic distinction.

271

# ETHNIC MINORITY PARTICIPATION

An ethnically-related theory or understanding of political thought and behaviour: this question appears to be at the heart of most empirical research on ethnic minority political participation. Having said that, the substance of such an understanding – or indeed understandings – is rather less clear.

At one end of the spectrum the argument has been put that the ethnicity of ethnic minorities lies at the very core of their political outlook, their patterns of participation and, quite possibly, their way of comprehending British society and politics. It is a claim that does not want for anything in the grand sweep of its perspective and that sees ethnic minorities as, in some ways, set apart from the political culture of contemporary Britain. Indeed, a sub-component of this approach in the academic literature has tended to emphasize the continuing importance of so-called "homeland" politics in the collective outlook of immigrant ethnic minorities. Such immigrant-driven orientations undoubtedly play a part in the ethnic politics of several South Asian and Caribbean groups, but it would be hard to portray its changing role in anything other than inter-generational terms.

The analytical difficulty in assessing the causal relationships at work here arises from the presence of complex co-relationships and influences that have a bearing on the political orientation of ethnic minorities. For instance, the heavy manual-occupation concentration of post-war non-white immigrants served to bring this otherwise ethnically heterogeneous group into contact – and even common cause – with one another. The political development of "black", and its juxtaposition with "white", had much to do with the emergence of a particularly strong form of ethnic minority political identity that was geared toward resisting both class and racial discrimination. Another illustration of this analytical complexity is the geographic clustering of ethnic minority settlement in Britain. This historical pattern – comparatively little changed after a half century of non-white immigration – often resulted in ethnic minority voting patterns being sharply skewed in favour of the Labour Party. Such strong and resilient Labour loyalties have in turn been accounted for in largely or exclusively ethnic-specific terms. As we have seen in the pages of this volume, this view may have been mistaken, since Labour's urban heartlands, where so many ethnic minorities are concentrated, have tended to continue to back the party for any one of a variety of non-ethnic reasons.

If this kind of "ethnicity counts" thesis is worth something, it is perhaps that it highlights the fact that the *process* of politics is different among most, if not all, ethnic minorities in Britain. That is to say, many of those involved in political socialization and participation by non-white voters commonly act on the basis that their group's ethnic identity matters and matters most of all. To the extent that this is a rough yet reasonably fair description of how non-white voters are courted – not least by many non-white political elites – then it is not hard to see that politics at a very general level is indeed very different and distinctive. Lines of ethnic brokerage, channels of indirect contact with leadership, and styles of political communication that rely on the ethnic press, are all simple though obvious illustrations of, first, how the process can be set apart from the mainstream, and, secondly, how it is engineered and perceived in such terms.

At the other end of the spectrum, there lies an opposite view which denies that there is anything terribly distinctive or lasting in the political behaviour of ethnic minorities. Aspects of this argument have been rehearsed previously in this volume, and have tended to focus on the seeming lack of widespread evidence for a distinctive "ethnic" or "race agenda" shared by non-whites. Certainly, non-whites do not share the same set of priorities in issue terms, but it has been noticeable that, all told, their priorities have not differed greatly from that of their white counterparts. Added to this is the fact that very little has been offered by the major parties – the Labour Party specifically and most controversially – by way of an explicit, racially-defined message aimed at catching and holding on to non-white voters.

The upshot has been that, through a combination of these two factors, it is reasonable to claim that race and ethnicity questions have *not* been the driving force behind the electoral outlook and behaviour of ethnic minorities. In blunt terms, "ethnicity does not count", and certainly not to the extent that it becomes a pivotal determinant of EMEB. This interpretation has received widespread support across academic circles. It is a perspective that has frequently focused in on survey-based research on issue identification and saliency. That said, there are some problems with this account, and the extent to which it is an accurate reflection of the conduct of electoral politics.

Two "spoilers" stand out in particular. First, the fact remains that the tactical approach of political parties to the possible existence of a "race agenda" has been to cover their bets and assume that it does. All the major parties have, over the course of the past twenty years, dipped their toes in the water trying to court ethnic minority votes (and money!) by some appeal to ethnicity. It is true that non-Labour efforts on these lines have been influenced by the largely-false belief that ethnic minorities constitute a key segment of the floating electorate. Nevertheless, in terms of party calculations, ethnicity has counted, and has enabled all the major parties to insist that, whatever the indirectness of their appeal, ethnic minority voters are not just like all other voters.

273

Secondly, if parties have tended to behave in this way, the practice of viewing all political participation through the prism of ethnicity has also been seen in the behaviour of a number of non-white political elites. Indeed, in numerous areas of high ethnic minority concentration, the term "community politics" has commonly become synonymous with "ethnic politics". These leaders have generally approached the task of non-white political mobilization as a question of appealing to existing ethnic identities. In its crudest form, this has amounted to, for example, Sylheti "community leaders" making attempts to rally, even deliver, the electoral support of Sylheti Bangladeshis in a particular electoral ward or constituency. Such a description has the effect of seeing these electors' votes solely in terms of an "ethnic vote", and one which is regimented and mobilized on the basis of common kinship or even ownership. The result is that the evidence for how and to what degree ethnicity counts is usually not found in survey research data which pits a bald and superficial notion of ethnicity against a long list of supposedly non-ethnic issues or concerns. Instead, the supporting evidence is more likely to be found by examining the nature and dynamics of political discourse and organization within a given ethnic minority group. The group's pertinence may be especially enhanced if it is one that is geographically clustered in its location, and thus can be said to have the potential to exert electoral leverage in relation to, say, multi-member local-government councillor elections. To be sure, this level of empirical evidence has usually come from more detailed qualitative examinations of local ethnic minority political participation. Such studies tend to endorse the argument that ethnicity is something more than an hollow appeal that characterizes traditional immigrant politics. At the very least it amounts to a mechanism that serves to organize and even partially-reinterpret a multitude of issues and concerns. But, more than this, it can be used to redefine politics as a whole for certain groups of ethnic minorities, by drawing out the differential impact of all issues and policies. Ethnicity must, therefore, count in this model, since politics generally has become a matter of racial and ethnic considerations underpinning all other issues.

The previous discussion has suggested that ethnicity cannot be so easily dismissed as an explanation for EMEB. Survey evidence certainly has its limitations in telling us how ethnicity is conceptualised by ethnic minorities themselves. However, the debate cannot be satisfactorily dealt with by looking at the evidence for non-white outlook and behaviour. This picture needs to be put in the context of how voter agendas are handled and mediated not just by parties but by election campaigns as well.[2] In particular, we need to be sensitive to the way in which agendas are actually constructed, not least because of the disproportionate attention given to certain issues over others under campaign conditions. The wider issues or priorities that make up an agenda are subject to what is sometimes termed the crowding effect, which takes place to reduce the debate within a particular election to a very small number of issues. Take the 1992 campaign which, despite the broad agendas that parties and specific groups of voters may have had going into the election, ended up as a debate over tax and shaped the behaviour of large numbers of undeclared voters. Similarly, in 1997 many roads in the campaign ended up at the "time for change" door. So, no matter what agendas may look like, elections and the business of voting has a lot to do with "menu choice". Voters generally do not get to write the menu, and even parties cannot be confident that they are able to write the whole of the final version. The significance of this is that, even if we suppose that ethnic minorities and major parties could arrive at a broadly-defined "race agenda", this would be subject to the menu-writing pressures of election campaigns. There is considerable reason to think that any one of a long list of issues would be likely to eclipse race and ethnic concerns under such circumstances. Therefore, for reasons to do with the way in which election campaigns are actually conducted, any specific agenda subscribed to ethnic minorities can be easily pushed to one side. Ethnic minorities at best can formulate an agenda of their own, but they cannot write the menu over which the real elections are fought.

### Labour's loyalists?

The more enduring puzzle within the broad picture of EMEB has been the longstanding electoral support for the Labour Party. Over all the elections for which we have reliable data (starting in 1974) the overwhelming bulk of non-whites who have voted have backed Labour, and the much-predicted desertion of these supporters has come to very little. But the affiliation with Labour is still a puzzle. Is it founded on the heavily working-class profile of original labour migrants (in which case, patterns of labour market participation would appear to hold the key to underlying political loyalties)? Social class-based approaches certainly highlight the fact that the ethnic minority electorate is heavily composed of voters of lower socio-economic status. However, they fall short in failing to account for the remarkably high levels of Labour support among the proportionately smaller middle-class, non-white electorate.

An alternative, argument attempts to characterize Labour's runaway "victory" as the consequence of its appeal as the more attractive – or least worst – option presented to ethnic minority voters. This account places a heavy premium on the party's self-

275

conscious record in promoting various specific rights and interests on behalf of the ethnic minorities, with successive anti-discrimination legislation in 1965, 1968 and 1976 being prime examples. The party has, at least to some extent, presented itself, and been perceived as, the ethnic minority-friendly party. As implied, the degree to which it has distinguished its appeal on these grounds, and whether it has only done so by targeting its message, are points open to lengthy debate. A variant of this school of thought has placed the emphasis on Labour's enduring strength in rather more negative, anti-Conservative terms. Labour, it is argued, not only finds it easy to project itself as the "least worst" option but, crucially, has been greatly assisted in this by the ghost of Powellism haunting the Conservative Party. Typically, episodes such as the intervention of rogue Tory backbenchers such as Sir Nicholas Fairbairn MP in the 1992 campaign, describing non-white immigration in apocalyptic and explosive terms, have not only have the effect of shoring up white, anti-ethnic minority sentiment, but also serve to stem any significant ethnic minority seepage from Labour to Conservative. A similar effect may have resulted from the Nicholas Budgen intervention in 1997. Labour continues to win non-white votes, so the argument goes, because the Conservatives are unwilling and/or unable to seize an opportunity that undoubtedly exists.

The conclusion from all this is that Labour's success is built on shaky foundations, and the party has continually to fan the embers of negative campaigning against the Tories. Equally, Labour is dependent upon the regular airing for voter consumption of Conservative splits on racial questions. Even taken together, it seems unlikely that these factors would fully account for Labour's track record of winning non-white votes with relatively modest effort. For one thing, Conservative attitudes may well be sharply divided on racial affairs, but remarkably few of these disagreements end up being public rows. Additionally, Labour has always had to be mindful that, after its notorious U-turns on immigration in the 1960s and 1970s, its claim to the "least worst" label may be perceived in "only just least worst" terms among the non-white electorate.

The Labour Party's attitude towards its ethnic minority constituency is perhaps ultimately determined by tactical priorities in fighting election campaigns. The party can, and indeed has, insisted that it best deserves the label of "most ethnic minority-friendly" without necessarily committing itself to a whole raft of explicitly racialized policies. That is, it is not bound or obliged, for example, to stand up for demands for US-style affirmative action involving racially-based quotas. Far from it, one might add, since the party has historically always included a strong element (especially amongst its leadership) that has been deeply sceptical about such moves. However, as a party it still perceives itself as representative of non-white interests, but only via a series of non-racial, indirect policy positions and commitments. The indirect appeal usually stems from its focus on a range of familiar left-centre concerns, such as employment, housing, and urban renewal, which protect or further ethnic minority interests *en passant*. Radical critics both inside and outside the Labour Party have always attacked this cautious approach for these very reasons, but it is worth spelling out the logic behind presenting policies in this generalized way. First, and most obviously, any policies that overtly court ethnic minority support and comprise racial preferences would be bound to invite strong criticism and a white backlash, which would be expected to have an electoral cost. Secondly, such policies would be likely to divide the party internally, and it could expect to pay a high price for any public display of disunity, especially if it were based on a core ideological rift. Thirdly, the party, in common with its rivals, is fully briefed on the danger and awkwardness of trying to implement policies that are anything other than colour-blind. If this type of policy were to be attempted, it would be likely to be accompanied by significant legal anomalies and unforeseen consequences. The party might then reasonably ask whether any major departure from the principle of "equality before the law" would be worth the effort.

Labour, therefore, is sufficiently well placed on a range of indirect ethnic minority concerns to recognize that going any further may lead (at best) to the prospect of diminishing electoral returns or (at worst) the codification of putatively unpopular and divisive racial policies. In these circumstances, a party strategist might ponder what lay behind the failure of Labour's opponents to secure any breakthroughs in the past twenty years. It might be that the party was already doing more than enough to keep its ethnic minority supporters in line. More might be foolish and unwarranted, and a little less might not be out of the question.

## IMPACTING ON THE BRITISH POLITICAL TRADITION

The presence of an ethnic minority population of a little over three million in contemporary Britain has had a confusing impact upon the electoral calculations of the major parties. As we have already noted, they have all toyed with, and sometimes embraced, ethnicity as a means of securing competitive advantage. But, more significant perhaps, has been the parallel strategies that the parties have generally deployed in relation to a) harnessing non-white electoral support, and

b) addressing the putative interests of ethnic minorities. One element of this "twin track" approach has been to try to carve out a distinctive strategy, whilst the other, more dominant, one has sought to lose both "ethnic votes" and "ethnic interests" in the colour-blind world of mainstream party competition. Whether this "twin track" can be characterized as coherent, or whether it suggests split thinking taken to the point of self-contradiction, is the subject-matter of this section.

It is commonplace to hear the criticism from a variety of ethnic minority political elites that the major parties selfishly exploit both strategies. The parties' presence is only too evident when harvesting votes and money, but they are strangely reticent when it comes to giving open commitments to introducing racially-defined public policies. The reasons behind this reluctance have been highlighted above. However, these do not deflect from the criticism made by many of the non-white elites. Their central point remains that the parties – of which many are paid-up members and committed foot soldiers – are guilty of a crude calculation in which the fear of a white backlash is given precedence over concern for non-whites interests. This charge does have some truth in it. The evidence, even if it is thought to be ambiguous with regard to the contemporary picture, is all too easy to point to when examining the record of previous governments. Time and time again, major figures in British politics from the 1950s onwards have either led or endorsed moves against immigrant, ethnic minority interests. The evidence litters *both* Labour *and* Conservative records over this long period, and the politicians who were exceptions to the general rule – and there were *some* – were still very few in number. British political parties in office have shown no great willingness to champion ethnic minority interests. Non-white elites, as a consequence, have noted the importance of major concessions such as anti-discrimination legislation, and have concluded that such breakthroughs have been the exception rather than the rule. From this comes the common characterization of political parties as exploitative at the interface between elite and mass ethnic minority politics.

Such a charge of exploitation ultimately needs to be addressed. To dismiss it as the whinging of a disaffected minority elite may be tempting, but this would be to underestimate the depth of feeling that this allegation can arouse. One important question would be whether there is a distinction between the political parties' perceptions of mass non-white voters and elite non-white leaders. If there is such a distinction, the parties would need to handle the elite in a different manner from the mass. This in turn would explain the criticism of elites by politicians. As the parties move to making policy commitments specifically aimed at courting ethnic minorities on racial or ethnic grounds, these commitments usually have a mass-oriented appeal. The target – and by extension the cause of – such an initiative is thought to be ethnic minority voters at large, although this may not always be true. In fact, the relevant commitments (which invariably constitute only a tiny aspect of their manifestos) can just as easily be accounted for as largely symbolic concessions to gain the support – but not the votes – of non-white activists within party ranks. The case of Labour and its commitments-as-concessions immediately comes to mind, since in this case the efforts of the relevant activists can easily be identified and followed. A similar picture can be drawn of Conservative thinking and commitments, although the scale and throughput of efforts by non-white activists has been of a much lower order.

The point is that these kinds of policy commitments are both few in number and likely to have everything to do with internal party lobbies. The black-activist lobby in Labour's ranks clearly cannot be dismissed out of hand and has in recent times developed a heightened sense of focus and self-confidence. In any case, activists, unlike voters at large, are known to take such commitments very seriously.[3] They also ensure the safeguarding of Labour's survival in numerous "hopeless" constituencies, and elsewhere supply a small army of party workers in marginal seats which the party aims to capture or hold. Intra-party politics explain policy commitments, and the same applies to commitments in the field of race. Therefore, the criticism of neglect and exploitation takes on a rather different aspect, since it is chiefly about the neglect and exploitation of party activists rather than ordinary voters. Parties recognise that, in terms of mass appeal, they cannot get away with being all things to all men; so, where policy commitments have to be given, they will be. Non-white activists' role in securing commitments is very different indeed from – and not to be confused with – that of non-white voters. The original allegation somehow looks a little less damning, once this factor is taken into account.

## SENSITIVITY VERSUS TARGETING

British electoral politics are geared to a dominant two-way struggle for elective office. The two major parties, according to this scenario, have an incentive to ensure that all voters are courted and that no stone is left unturned to do so. This imperative is of course driven by a clear rational, profit-maximising logic. It sees ethnic minority voters as potential recruits but, crucially, on equally rational grounds does not deceive itself into believing that all such voters are equally good prospects. In fact, they are not, and most are not only regular supporters of the Labour Party but also remain stubbornly loyal despite the party's preference for indirect appeals. At the same time, both parties recognize that the sort of overt policy commitments which can be embraced with universal or general popularity are rare. Most policy commitments represent a trade-off in the sense that attracting one group of voters carries the penalty of repelling another by whom the commitment is disliked or even resented. Labour commitments on lifting National Insurance employee ceilings or Conservative undertakings on minimum wage abolition are familiar illustrations of this trade-off. A similar process would appear to be at work in the case of the parties' attempts to address ethnic minority interests and concerns.

Faced with this problem, the choice for parties has centred on the degree to which they have been prepared to target ethnic minorities. In electoral terms this choice has amounted to making commitments, followed by appeals which are aimed either wholly or overwhelmingly at non-white voters. A brief scan of party competition in this field over more than two decades reveals that, in general, parties have avoided targeting on any significant scale. As mentioned above, party leaderships have viewed the targeting option with unease and embarrassment. Few have been prepared to argue that there was an electoral dividend in choosing up such an option; most, indeed, have stressed the opposite. Looming large in both parties' strategies has been the spectre of a white backlash – that is, an electoral penalty, the likely scale of which has tended to be measured with a Smethwick-inspired nervousness. Targeting ethnic minorities amounts *de facto* to a commitment to embracing this group, and the unwritten iron law of modern British racial politics is one which advises the greatest caution, to say the least.

Bearing this in mind, it is still possible to show how the parties have managed to avoid exploiting populist white support by taking up naked anti-ethnic minority positions. Some major party politicians have of course done just that, but the general picture spanning much of the 1960s and 1970s is one in which both party leaderships have resisted the temptation to exploit racist sentiment. Even in the late 1990s, the unmistakable triumph of cautious pragmatism is discernable, although of course a great deal of coded anti-ethnic minority and anti-immigrant propaganda lies just below the surface. Again, a trade-off is at work but one which is theoretical rather than real. Most inter-party competition is devoid of racial considerations but, given a shrewd nudge in the right spot, a change would not be hard to orchestrate. Political parties in general, and the Conservatives in particular, are aware of the possibilities, but remain for the most part content merely to depoliticize ethnic minority interests and concerns.

This trade-off not surprisingly can lead to a tension developing between parties' vote-maximizing instincts and internal pressures to keep the lid on race as a political issue. Moreover, all major parties have developed infrastructures that bring in ethnic minority funds, if not votes. Ethnic minority activists are found in all parties and leaderships in turn have been willing to grant some concessions to activists. This presents a picture in which the parties accept that *sensitivity* on ethnic minority issues and concerns is both valuable and rather more than an option.[4] In fact, it is virtually indispensable. The extent to which this is true may be a moot point, but in practice it acts as a real constraint upon unfettered party competition.

Crucially, the need for sensitivity does not necessarily entail a concomitant need for specific policy targeting. It is this vital distinction which perhaps best explains the broad thrust of party strategy in the area of race. This strategy, characteristic of both leading parties, has tended towards removing the race question from competitive party politics. But, where the race question has been unavoidable, or where the option to work a trade-off against ethnic minorities has been too attractive to resist, the result has been confused to say the least. Apocalyptic meltdown has singularly failed to come about, despite the dire predictions of influential observers. Tendencies in this direction have occurred and can be measured, as in the "profit" that was taken from "following the crowd" in general elections inspired by Powellite (1970) and Thatcherite (1979) rhetoric. But through this emerges a continuous, though sometimes shakey, line of guarded sensitivity without overt targeting. This characterization, in conclusion, seems to go to the heart of the British experience of racial politics impacting upon electoral politics.

## NOTES

1. Readers may wish to know that this point is the subject of further work in progress by the author.
2. I am grateful to John Crowley for bringing this distinction to my attention.
3. Ibid.
4. This argument was put to me by David Sanders to whom I am indebted.

# Index

283